INDIAN STREAM REPUBLIC

Library of New England

Indian Stream
Republic

Settling a New England Frontier,
1785–1842

Daniel Doan

With an Introduction and Afterword by Jere R. Daniell
Edited by Ruth Doan MacDougall

University Press of New England / Hanover and London

University Press of New England, Hanover, NH 03755
© 1997 by Donald Keith MacDougall; Introduction, Chronology, Afterword,
and Supplementary Bibliography © 1997 by Jere R. Daniell
All rights reserved
Printed in the United States of America   5 4 3 2 1
CIP data appear at the end of the book

To

PHILIP N. CRONENWETT

Curator of Manuscripts

Chief of Special Collections

Dartmouth College Library

"Falling in love with a locality can be as powerful an emotion as falling in love with a person. In some form it lasts a lifetime."

DANIEL DOAN, "Fifty Thoughts from Fifty Years"

CONTENTS

Introduction, Jere R. Daniell — xi
Chronology, Jere R. Daniell — xvii

1	Fair Free Land Nearby, 1785	1
2	The Moose, 1789	6
3	King Philip, Indian Chief, 1796	8
4	Two Land Companies, 1798	12
5	Proprietors of Philip's Grant: The Eastman Company, 1799	15
6	The Face of the Land, 1797–1803	19
7	The Shape of Things to Come, 1804–1811	25
8	Enter John Haynes, 1811	30
9	Ebenezer Fletcher Finds a Mill Privilege, 1811	37
10	Captain Bedel Goes to War, 1812	42
11	Postwar Pursuits and Events, 1815–1819	49
12	Boundary Confusion, 1783–1817	58
13	The Eastman Company Comes to Life, 1819	66
14	Rum and Tea at Fletcher's Mills, 1819	74
15	Colonel Bedel Looks North, 1820	79
16	Jonathan Eastman's Serious Task, 1820	84
17	Moody Bedel in the Lake Settlement, 1820	91
18	New Hampshire Jurisdiction at Indian Stream, 1820	95
19	Moody Bedel, 1820–1823	101
20	Enter Luther Parker, 1819–1828	110

21	The Committee of Safety Petitions the Legislature, 1829	123
22	The Claims of 1829	131
23	Jonathan Eastman Learns about the Committee of Safety, 1829	135
24	The Legislature Hesitates, 1829–1830	140
25	John Haynes: Register of Deeds, 1831	148
26	Luther Parker Writes to the Secretary of the Treasury, 1832	154
27	A Constitution for Indian Stream, 1832	163
28	A Brief Golden Age, 1832–1834	172
29	New Hampshire Moves on Indian Stream, 1834–1835	185
30	New Hampshire Defines Its Claim, 1835	194
31	Luther Parker Arrested, June 1835	197
32	Invasion Threatens Indian Stream, July 1835	203
33	Canadian Jurisdiction? August through October 1835	208
34	Canadians Arrest a New Hampshire Sheriff, October 1835	215
35	Bloodshed in Hereford, October 1835	222
36	Canadian Magistrate a Prisoner in Vermont, October 1835	230
37	The Occupation of Indian Stream, November 1835	234
38	Solutions, May 1836 through June 1850	248
	Afterword, Jere R. Daniell	257
	Bibliography	261
	Supplementary Bibliography, Jere R. Daniell	267

INTRODUCTION

Jere R. Daniell

❧ The Indian Stream Republic was a short-lived but successful experiment in self-government that took place during the 1830s in what is now the town of Pittsburg, New Hampshire. The experiment had its origins in an international boundary dispute—both Canada and the United States claimed the territory defined by the republic—and in overlapping claims of two land-development companies. Frontiersmen, who began moving to the contested region as early as the 1790s, wanted the authority to manage local affairs and were especially interested in giving legal standing to individual land claims. They wrote a constitution, lived under it for several years, decided their future lay with the United States, applied successfully for incorporation as Pittsburg, and in 1842 gained final confirmation of their governmental standing through the Webster-Ashburton Treaty.

Daniel Doan decided to write about Indian Stream in the early 1960s. The decision had multiple origins. Although employed full time at a Laconia, New Hampshire, machinery manufacturing company, he had always hoped to earn his living as a writer. He had published a few magazine articles and during the 1950s two novels: one, *Amos Jackman* (1957), became a Doubleday Dollar Book Club selection. Doan, in addition, knew New Hampshire's north country intimately. He grew up hiking in the nearby White Mountains, hunted with a friend near the Canadian border in Clarksville, filled dozens of notebooks with sketches of the region's flora and fauna, and honed his writing skills, using the north country as a literary laboratory. *Amos Jackman* was the story of depopulating a hill village in Orford, New Hampshire, where Doan's family owned property and where he himself farmed for a brief period after graduating from Dartmouth College in

1936. Now, a quarter century later, Doan felt prepared to produce a major work about northern New Hampshire.

The Indian Stream story had interested him for some time. He probably first heard about the self-created republic while at Dartmouth. Curious about everything having to do with the north country, he dug into whatever he encountered that had a regional focus. In 1955, Roger Brown published a small volume entitled *The Struggle for the Indian Stream Territory.* Doan found it and several older historical articles on events at Indian Stream interesting but fundamentally flawed. "In all the existing literature," he wrote in 1964, "there is something lacking. Who were these people? Where did they come from, how did they live, where did they go . . . ? What did they eat, what did they wear, what were their houses like? And the face of the land? . . . What did this frontier . . . do to its people? Toughen them? Break them?" Doan ended with the simple assertion that "In the accounts of the Republic of Indian Stream people are needed—their emotions and drives and personalities."

As Doan's enthusiasm grew he faced a set of difficult decisions. He was diagnosed as diabetic, a condition that certainly would curtail the outdoor part of his life and might drain him of the energy to continue a full-time job while writing in the evenings and on weekends. About the same time he learned of the diabetes, he attended a writers' conference at Bread Loaf. There he met George Griffen, a Rutgers University Press senior editor, who urged him to proceed with the Indian Stream project. Doan had been uncertain whether to write a historical novel—he was a big Kenneth Roberts fan and had read Ben Ames Williams's *Come Spring*, a novel about community building along the Maine coast—or a straight historical narrative. Despite his lack of training and experience, Doan was tempted to take the nonfiction route. Griffen agreed and got the enthusiastic support of William Sloane, his press director. In July 1964, Doan had moved with his wife to Sanbornton, New Hampshire. Then, in June 1965, Daniel Doan left his work in Laconia and committed himself totally to his career in writing.

The research on Indian Stream progressed rapidly. That April and again in July he visited Pittsburg. He filled the April notebooks with the kind of environmental detail that enriches his story. "Robins and sparrows here," an entry for April 25 reads. "Ice on Lake Francis and here at 1st [First Connecticut Lake]. Snow on north side of motel." That same year he traveled abroad to do research at the British Museum. Back in New Hampshire he combed both local and state archives.

The writing progressed also. In April 1966, Doan wrote to Sloane that he had all but completed a first draft; the following January he mailed his finished manuscript to Rutgers under the title *Forgotten Democracy: The Indian Stream Republic*. Nine days after the mailing Sloane wrote back to report his "terrifically favorable first impression," concluding, "I think you have found a publisher." There must have been a serious celebration in Sanbornton after Doan read Sloane's letter.

Rutgers, however, never published *Forgotten Democracy*. Sloane and Griffen ran into trouble with academic reviewers who criticized as unprofessional Doan's imagined scenes, attribution of undocumented emotion and thought to his protagonists, and lengthy passages about landscape. Sloane, trapped between his personal enthusiasm and an unfavorable review process, began dragging his feet. When Doan complained about Rutgers's lack of decision Sloane explained the problem. Doan, the novelist-turned-historian, defended his manuscript as best he could. He had "based the details on general natural reference known to be unchanged in Northern New Hampshire. The birds, animals, plants, and topography had to be in existence according to direct reference . . ." He had taken "a number of jeep trips on both sides of the border investigating old roads, streams and settlements. For instance," Doan explained, "I took pictures of the Fletcher Mill site, the Applebee farm location, the road on which or near which Blanchard was rescued, and so on." To no avail. Rutgers stopped answering the mail. In January 1968, Doan asked to have his manuscript returned.

Rutgers was as close as Doan came to finding a publisher. Sloane had once suggested commercial presses might be interested: Prentice Hall, Norton, Little, Brown, McGraw Hill, Macmillan, Harper & Row, Beacon, and Stephen Greene all either rejected the manuscript or discouraged him from submitting it. In 1969, Doan switched back to the academy but fared no better. Harvard, Yale, Wesleyan, Iowa, Cornell, and Dartmouth publications all said no. Doan persisted. When in 1971 what is now University Press of New England (UPNE) got started as the University Press of Northern New England, he sent *Forgotten Democracy* off once more. The response must have hurt. The rejection letter ended, "It is also our opinion, for what it is worth, that if the manuscript is brought to publication you will probably have to cut it down at least 50%, and even then we can't think of a publisher to whom it might be sent advantageously." Doan's only subsequent submission was of a few sample pages to UPNE in 1981. In response to the now-familiar rejection Doan wrote back, "I realize it deals with a subject of limited interest, which, however, fascinated me and was a very rewarding research project personally."

Daniel Doan suffered a stroke in 1987. He died on September 24, 1993.

* * *

UPNE now is proud to publish Daniel Doan's story of community building at Indian Stream. The manuscript hasn't changed, but many other circumstances have.

First, the story. Doan did succeed as a writer. He swallowed his disappointment and went back to other projects. In 1973 he published *50 Hikes in New Hampshire's White Mountains; 50 More Hikes in New Hampshire* came out in 1978. Together the two sold over a hundred thousand copies, are still in print, and have become classics. Philip Cronenwett, Special Collections librarian at Dartmouth College, is an avid outdoorsman and fan of Doan's hiking books. Dartmouth has a huge White Mountain collection in its archives. In the mid-1980s Cronenwett convinced Doan to leave his papers to the college and, when cataloging the first batch, discovered *Forgotten Democracy*. Later, Doan's daughter, Ruth Doan MacDougall—a writer who has published nine novels and edits new editions of the hiking books—decided to seek posthumous publication of the manuscript. In 1994, UPNE hired Philip Pochoda as editorial director. MacDougall, Cronenwett, and several others recommended Doan's oft-rejected narrative to Pochoda. He read it, and like William Sloane at Rutgers, became excited about publication. Unlike Sloane, however, Pochoda found reviewers who shared his enthusiasm. UPNE's editorial advisory committee gave its approval, and the project went forward.

Once, back in 1968, Doan had pointed out the personal and unpredictable nature of editorial responses to his work. The enthusiasm of Cronenwett, Pochoda, and the reviewers reflects more than their personal taste. It stems, in part, from the growing accessibility of and public interest in New England's north country. Vermont's Northeast Kingdom, New Hampshire's White Mountains, and Maine's vast and virtually uninhabited interior fascinate increasing numbers of outdoor enthusiasts, vacationers, and back-to-the-land neo-frontiersmen. The term "Mooselandia" is sometimes used to describe these regions collectively. Locals label as "Moose Alley" the several miles of Route 3 north of the Lake Settlement where many of Doan's protagonists pitched in the 1820s and routinely wander to the area to observe the huge, majestic animals. In short, there is much greater potential interest in good literature set in the Indian Stream region than there was a quarter century ago.

Growing public interest has been paralleled by increased writing about northern New England. Howard Mosher has put the Northeast Kingdom on the literary map with a series of superb short stories, novellas, and novels; three of his works have been made into movies. Settlement of New England's interior has been chronicled in Michael Bellesiles's *Revolutionary Outlaws*, Alan Taylor's *Liberty Men and Great Proprietors*, and Laurel Thatcher Ulrich's Pulitzer Prize–winning *Midwife's Tale*. Numerous books about New England's great northern forests have appeared. Publication of Doan's book adds a fresh historical dimension to this body of literature.

Finally, the world of academic publishing has undergone change. Many university presses no longer limit themselves to publication of formal academic works. UPNE, for example, has a New England list that includes works from numerous disciplines, written by both academics and nonacademics. UPNE also has just founded an imprint entirely devoted to the publication and republication of regional novels. In 1973, Erwin Griswold told Doan that he wasn't surprised about the rejections because the manuscript was "neither history nor fiction." In today's world plenty of editors and readers feel free to ask, "Who cares?" A good read is a good read.

Daniel Doan, of course, had no opportunity to fine-tune his manuscript. UPNE asked Ruth Doan MacDougall and me to help in that process. We made few changes in the text. The only significant ones involved shortening chapter 6 and collapsing two original chapters into what is now chapter 27. Ruth, exercising what she calls the "family voice," did all the rewriting. My main contribution has been to make the text more reader friendly. I've written this introduction and the afterword and am responsible for the headnote, chronology, maps, and tables. The staff at UPNE, Ruth, and I all agreed that the text should be published without footnotes. Doan left citations for only two chapters. We also found Doan's proposed title, *Forgotten Democracy: The Indian Stream Republic*, redundant and changed it.

October 1995

CHRONOLOGY

Jere R. Daniell

1789	Jeremiah Eames surveys New Hampshire's northern boundary
1796	Philip's Grant—basis of Eastman Company claim
1798	St. Francis Grant—basis of Bedel Company claim
1799	Jeremiah and Thomas Eames survey for Eastman
1811	John Haynes pitches on Gage Brook
1815	Ebenezer Fletcher completes mill
1820	Eastman Company bridge at Fletcher's Mills
1820	Moody Bedel moves to Indian Stream; Luther Parker moves to Indian Stream
1822	Districts for schools and highways established
1823	Moody Bedel returns south
1824	New Hampshire legislature asserts jurisdiction over Indian Stream, making it part of Coos County
1828	David Robbins terrorizes Indian Stream
1829	Bedel and Eastman agree to negotiate; Committee of Safety formed
1830	Bedel and Eastman companies merge
1831	King of Netherlands awards Indian Stream Territory to Canada
1832	(*June*) United States Congress rejects king of Netherlands's recommendations; (*July*) Indian Stream constitution adopted
1834	New Hampshire starts enforcing laws in territory
1835	(*March*) Clark Haynes and Reuben Sawyer successfully resist arrest by New Hampshire sheriffs; (*June*) New Hampshire reasserts jurisdictional claim, and Indian

Stream joined with Clarksville and Stewartstown for purposes of representation in the New Hampshire legislature;
(*June*) Luther Parker arrested on Canadian warrant;
(*September*) Canadian magistrate Alexander Rea offers Canadian administration in Indian Stream;
(*October*) John H. Tyler arrested by New Hampshire deputy sheriffs and rescued by friends;
(*October*) American mob rescues Richard Blanchard, arrested by Canadian supporters, and abducts Alexander Rea;
(*November*) New Hampshire militia troops stationed in Indian Stream territory

1836 (*February*) Militia forces leave;
Luther Parker moves from Indian Stream to Wisconsin

1840 Indian Stream incorporated as the Town of Pittsburg

1842 Webster-Ashburton Treaty
Indian Stream territory officially becomes part of both United States of America and New Hampshire

INDIAN STREAM REPUBLIC

CHAPTER 1

FAIR FREE LAND NEARBY, 1785

Two years after the American Revolution, a woodsman named Luther Fuller hunted the upper valley of the Connecticut River in northern New Hampshire. Legends relate earlier explorations, but Fuller's was the first to be recorded, because he later testified for the New Hampshire claim to the border territory at a time when the United States and Great Britain were warning each other from the beautiful valley. An independent democracy had caused a confrontation.

But in 1785 the valley was wilderness. Luther Fuller looked for moose, marten, beaver, timber, farmland. Nobody knew where the international boundary lay; it had not been surveyed, and its location was as theoretical as certain other bounds specified in the Treaty of Paris that ended the Revolution. Nor had the line been blazed between Massachusetts's district of Maine and the state of New Hampshire, "north two degrees west," above Lake Umbagog.

Without a permanent cabin or clearing of a white man, traversed by only a few Indian hunters from the St. Francis tribe in Canada, the valley's forest of maple, birch, spruce, cedar, and fir stretched for twenty-five miles unbroken toward the vast swamps and ridges of Maine.

Three main tributaries drained into the Connecticut River from the northern highlands. Beyond these ridges water flowed into the St. Lawrence River. Hall's Stream joined near the critical east bend of the Connecticut River above the settlement of Stewartstown. Indian Stream entered at the flat land of the valley floor, and Perry Stream poured off a plateau not far below the long pitch from Lake Connecticut. This lake was the first reached by an upstream traveler. The chain of three lakes linked by the dwindling river led to the source in a spring-fed rivulet above the third lake.

The eastward swing of the river, its source, and its northern branches appeared incorrectly on a map used by Benjamin Franklin in negotiating the Treaty of Paris. A controversy over the boundary ensued and lasted for fifty-nine years. It began quietly enough, for the valley was a remote wilderness. When New Hampshire sent a survey party north, including Luther Fuller, six years after the signing of the treaty, hardly anyone took notice that the men established the two northern corners of the state on land claimed by Great Britain.

Although no settlement followed Luther Fuller's earlier exploration in 1785, stories of the northern territory circulated in the downriver towns. Trappers and hunters as well as scouts and rangers had long traversed the northern wilderness separating Canada and New England.

Such a hunter and trapper was Andrew Gilman, well acquainted with the north country of New Hampshire through his friend, an Indian chief known as King Philip. In 1762 and 1763, Gilman spent several months with the Indians in the valley of the Upper Ammonoosuc River and farther east along the Androscoggin River. Caribou and moose roamed the flat country of the tributary Magalloway. Marten, the American sable, leaped boldly to death in the trapper's deadfalls. Beaver, venturing ashore after fresh poplar bark, stepped into a steel trap or fell to a lead ball from a musket. Andrew Gilman stayed with the Indians from March to June in 1763. He returned as he had come, by way of the Upper Ammonoosuc, perhaps floating his furs down by dugout canoe to the junction with the Connecticut at the present town of Northumberland, and on down the big river to the trading post at Newbury, Vermont.

In later years, hunters like Andrew Gilman could spin a yarn or two for the men gathered in country stores, for the young men free of the revolutionary army, uneasy, land-hungry, poor.

The woods had beckoned to five generations of New England men. Away from the coast lay the wild, free, dangerous, Indian-haunted forest of the hunter. As far back as the 1620s, Thomas Morton lived an adventurous life with the Indians, and became a thorn in the side of both Plymouth Colony and the Massachusetts Bay Colony. He showed the Indians how to use firearms, and he traded guns, powder, and lead for furs. The authorities of Massachusetts Bay arrested him as a renegade, disturber of the frontier, and corrupter of the Indians. He had been born too soon; he belonged with the Rocky Mountain trappers two hundred years later, with Jim Bridger, Kit Carson, and Jedediah Smith.

The western mountain men were preceded by the forgotten trappers of New England, New York, Pennsylvania, Virginia—the first of the breed in

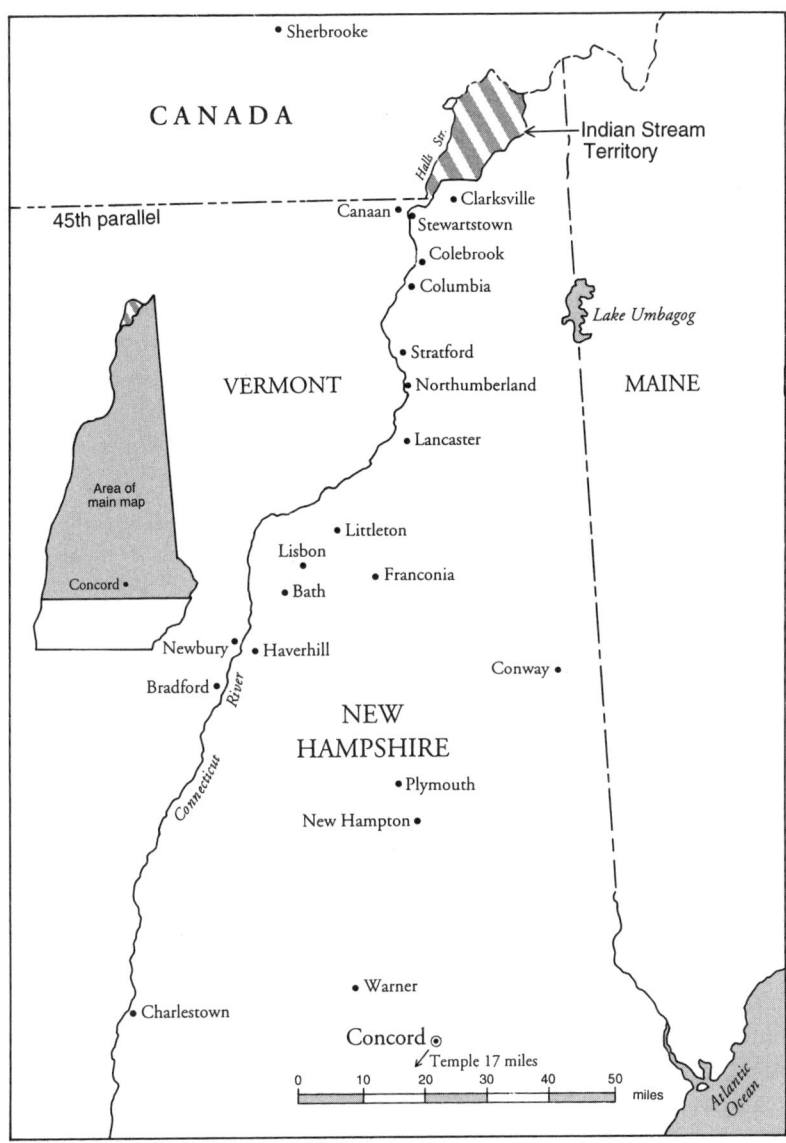

1. Vermont and New Hampshire.

America. The New England trapper had not the freedom (nor the limitation) created by the weeks of trekking across the plains six hundred miles from the last white settlement. In the East, civilization lay relatively close in mid-eighteenth century. Regulation and law of a kind, the security of a fort, even the social conventions, existed only a week or two away, on foot or by

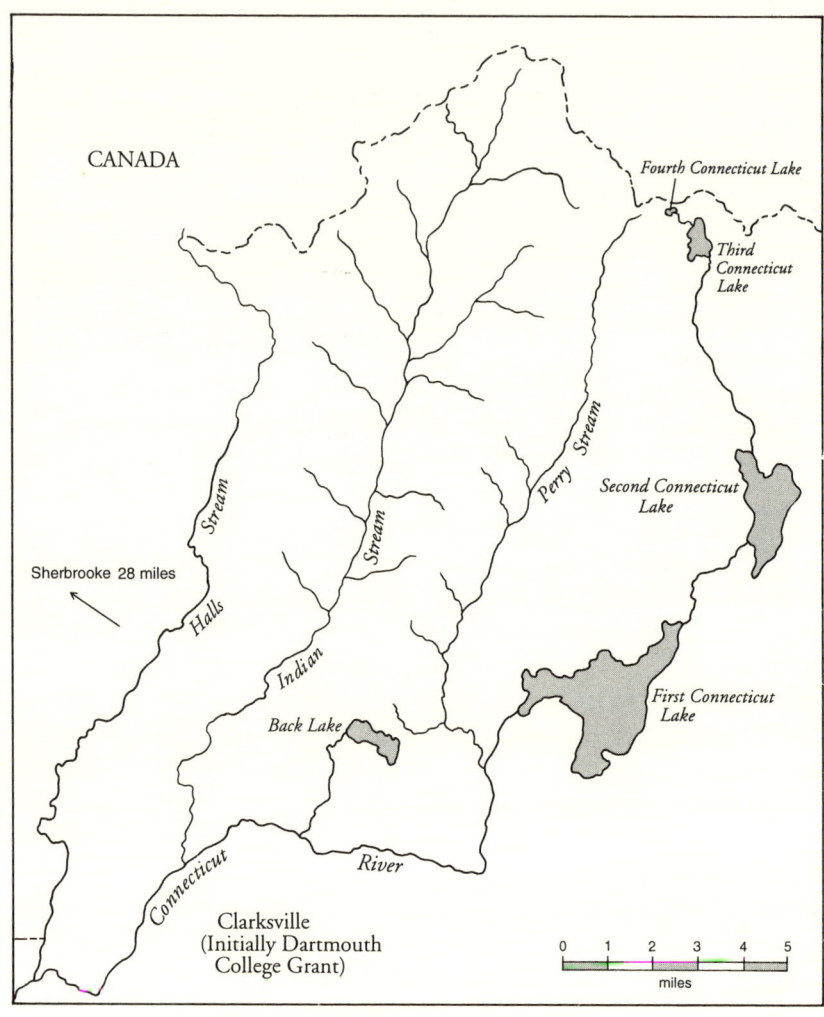

2. Indian Stream Territory.

canoe. But the men were the same rovers, the same seekers after the far ridge, the river source, as much as they were trappers of beaver and marten. In New Hampshire a few names remain: Darby Field, who climbed Mount Washington for the reasons that always move explorers; Nash, first white man to see Crawford Notch offering a pass to the coast; Willard, hunter of the Kilkenny Mountains; John and Israel Glines, trappers of the flat wilderness north of the White Mountains in Jefferson; Eleazer Rosebrook, frontiersman of Colebrook before he built his mills and tavern near Crawford Notch; Captain Thomas Baker, destroyer of the Indian village at the junction of the Pemigewasset and the river he named; Captain John Lovewell, slain with Paugus near Conway, 1725; John Stark, captured by Indians, 1752, on the Baker River, a companion killed in the ambush, furs lost to the value of £560 sterling.

The wanderers and the rovers, the explorers, the footloose, the men seeking quick wealth through fur, the men defending their log huts, the men taking to the woods-life as to a drug (pounding heart of the chase and the ultimate freedom, which they could never give up)—all went their ways, passed into history. French Canada became English Canada. The Royal Province of New Hampshire became the State of New Hampshire.

Although Luther Fuller's exploration of New Hampshire's remotest valley brought no settlers, in time other men became interested. Six years after the northern boundary was made to hinge on the ambiguous "northwesternmost head of the Connecticut River"—a wording in the Treaty of Paris that would plague both the United States and Great Britain for fifty-nine years—Nathaniel Wales and David Gibbs came north from Lisbon and Haverhill, up the Connecticut, past the settlements of Lancaster, Northumberland, Colebrook, through the valley lands of new towns where the river meandered in numberless oxbow curves, up past the rapids at Stewartstown, where across the river in Vermont the town of Canaan had scarcely become enough of a settlement to hold town meetings yet was still ahead of Stewartstown, on past the cedar post of surveyors Vallentine and Collins marking the old New York Province, now Vermont, with Canada north, to the last free land in the valley. Their arrival at Indian Stream began the completion of settlement along the Connecticut—three hundred miles of wilderness made over in a hundred and fifty years, from the sea to Canada. Men needed land; it was life and wealth and security.

But land had to be developed. A community would form at Indian Stream, and in forty-five years the members of this community would establish their own government, the outgrowth of their cooperation as settlers. They would attempt an impossible independence from both the United States and Great Britain, and in doing so would come dangerously close to precipitating war between the two nations.

CHAPTER 2

THE MOOSE, 1789
(Wales and Gibbs as they perhaps arrived on Indian Stream.)

At the slow confluence of the stream from the north and the river from the lake, a young moose with trowel horns and prongs stood knee-deep on a sandbar and sniffed the air that blew down the larger, faster water. The river curved and slowed at the junction. A canoe and two men appeared below. One man poled from the stern, one waded ahead with the tow line. The man on the line paused for breath at a ledge against which the water swirled. He tipped the battered cocked hat against the sunlight on the water. Wet to the top of his linsey-woolsey breeches, gray woolen stockings soaked, he rested one moose-hide moccasin on the ledge. He stepped ashore and hitched the line to a tree and went back to his companion in the canoe, pointing upstream. He took the flintlock, looked at the priming, took the powder horn and bullet pouch. He vanished into the bushes.

The moose continued to stand on the sandbar. No scent of wolf or bear came downstream; he did not know the scent of man. The motion of the men did not alarm him. His routine crossing was here, toward the hardwood ridge to the south where his long, swinging strides would bring him to the beaver pond on the brook that flowed out of the southern hills. Lily pads spread over the water there, anchored by succulent roots that would make him the easiest, tastiest meal in the valley.

Behind the moose stretched the tall swale grass of the meadows where the stream came out of the highlands and wound in tortuous curves through alders and willows and tamarack, past a few pines and elms in the intervals, past the bleached poles of an abandoned beaver dam. September frosts had colored the grass a pale brown. The feathery seed clusters waved in the cool breeze.

The moose, aware of the motion downstream and at last doubtful of its meaning for him, turned slowly, for he was hunger-minded toward the far shore. He stepped dripping from the river to a clump of alders. There the first ball from the flintlock struck him. He crashed away from the river and stood again, bewildered by the strange roar of the gun and by the shock in his side and failing of breath. Cut by an invisible force, a willow branch fell before his eyes. Another shock twisted his neck and he plunged forward.

A cocked hat and musket barrel and keen face emerged from the bushes across the river. An arm, after a time, waved; a voice sang out toward the man in the canoe.

Moose hide made first-class leather. Moose quarters and loin provided all the meat two men could want, and the carcass was bait for wolf, bobcat, marten, bear, fisher . . . their fur not yet prime but in a month or more it would be; meanwhile a camp of logs and bark, wood to chop against the cold nights, more moose to hunt, hides to clean and peg out.

When freeze-up approached, and the first early snow sifted down upon them one night, the men loaded hides, fur, and meat into the canoe. They were reluctant to leave. They talked of a cabin for another year, and thought of land and families. The open meadow would grow wheat, rye, maybe corn if the frosts held off. They agreed to return. It was a good place, but for this year they headed the canoe downstream.

CHAPTER 3

KING PHILIP, INDIAN CHIEF, 1796

He remains a shadowy figure, playing a conflicting role between the white men and his own people. He signed away his tribal lands for food, clothing, shelter, and—some said—for rum. As the chief, thirty years before, of the tribe with which Andrew Gilman hunted, he became in his old age an outcast wanderer, camping with two squaws on the edges of the growing settlements, making solitary hunts, when he was able, in the lands between Lancaster and the Canadian townships. There he found a white man who would look after him in return for a deed to his land. His land? So it was thought of by the white man, but to him the conception of property was no clearer than to any Indian of the Algonquian group, comparable to the property sense of a timber wolf sharing hunting rights with other members of his clan. Landowning by means of a piece of paper lay beyond the reach of his mind.

But Thomas Eames was Philip's trusty friend. A son of Northumberland's old Colonel Jeremiah Eames, he could slip through the woods like an Indian. The red men themselves admitted his prowess in hunting moose and deer. He had been on the survey party headed by his brother, Jeremiah Eames, Jr., when they ran the eastern and northern boundary of New Hampshire in 1789—the same year Wales and Gibbs camped at the mouth of Indian Stream. Thomas Eames knew the country. He knew the Indians. His word was good; Philip trusted him.

Philip was close to eighty in 1796 when he made his mark on the deed to Thomas Eames and other "peculiar friends." He had lived through almost all the border warfare of the eighteenth century. He was a mature warrior and chief, forty years old, when Major Robert Rogers led his Rangers against the St. Francis Indians in October 1759. He seems to have favored the English, and later the Americans, and maintained his dwindling tribe in northern New Hampshire without ever permanently joining the St. Francis Indians.

The St. Francis tribe did not constitute a tribe at all, in the ethnological sense. Comprised of remnants from the various Algonquian tribes of the New England valleys, who had been harried by their traditional enemies, the Iroquois, and by disease, more recently driven north by the English, it included any Indians gathered under French protection near the mouth of the St. Francis River, where it flows into the St. Lawrence. It included people of the Anasagunticooks from the Androscoggin valley, Pennacooks from the Merrimack, Pequawkets from the Saco, and Abenakis from the Kennebec. At the same time, remnants of the tribes lingered on in their old hunting grounds and planting grounds. Unlike most of these, Philip seems never to have lived for any considerable time in Canada. New Hampshire men called his group of families the Coos Indians, or Co-wass Indians, after their camping ground in the meadows of the Connecticut known as Upper Coos near Lancaster.

Philip saw many changes: the English triumph over the French, the struggle of the Colonies with England. He saw the new nation united under General Washington. Now, this year, 1796, General Washington would not be president again. As Philip's white "friends" knew, or later came to know, Washington would speak (three months after Philip marked the deed) against entangling "our peace and prosperity in the toils of European ambition . . ." The Federalists would put up John Adams for president. Perhaps the "friends" did not share the feeling against Adams as a representative of wealth and power; they were important and powerful men in New Hampshire themselves, down at Concord: John Bradley, Jonathan Eastman, and from Moultonborough in Strafford County, Nathan Hoit.

Philip could not comprehend or care. An old man, once powerful enough to be known to the whites as King Philip, he was poor and tired, too dependent on the white men's firewater. He was no longer the judge to whom the white men appealed, as they did when John Jordan of Maidstone fired his musket at three Indians and wounded one dangerously, and Philip acted as arbiter in arranging justice and restitution. He was still a friend of the whites, but without the importance he had when he favored their cause during the Revolution. With his wife, Molly, and another squaw "which camped with him," he needed shelter, food, and clothing. The Eames family, prospering on the farm in the rich valley interval of Northumberland, would look after them in Philip's weakness and old age. Thomas was his trusted friend. Seeing the end of his days, Philip wanted to put the two crossed lines on the paper, as Thomas and the others asked. He had made provision for his rights to continue in the land, so what was he selling? The white men had agreed that he could hunt and fish there—this was on the paper. He could plant four bushels of corn and beans. Perhaps they would not allow him to burn the meadows or girdle trees, but there was plenty of land ready for Molly and Mooselock to plant. And after him these same rights would continue to his heirs and "sucksessors and all Indian tribes forever." These were the rights that mattered.

He made his mark. His wife, Molly Mussell, made hers. Then the other squaw, Molly's helper, Mooselock Sullsop, stepped to the table and made her crossed lines. Philip did not know whether he would see another June roll around, with green on the hills again. Now, June 28, 1796, the blackflies and midges ruled the woods. He was glad to be in the settlement, relieved in his mind about the meat which he could no longer kill himself, for Thomas would provide it.

Jeremiah Eames as witness, along with Ely Bruel, explained to Philip that he would have to appear before Colonel Eames, the justice of the peace, and swear that he had signed of his own free will, that nobody had made him. And he must bring Molly and Mooselock.

Two days later they did this. The deed was ready for recording down at Haverhill, the shire town (with Plymouth) of Grafton County: Northumberland was in Grafton County then, for Coos County did not exist. Much of the land had never been surveyed, including most of that which Philip conveyed to Thomas Eames, John Bradley, Jonathan Eastman, and Nathan Hoit.

Nevertheless, the Eames brothers knew the territory, and Jeremiah undertook to draw a map for the new "owners." They had made sure that the deed described the territory carefully. They knew it included granted land as far north as Canaan, Vermont, and Stewartstown, New Hampshire. Beyond these towns to the east lay the land they wanted, north of the Fortyfifth Parallel, along the upper Connecticut, stretching to the highlands of Canada. This valley would show on Jeremiah's map, included within Philip's bounds, which disregarded town lines, and state and national boundaries.

Jeremiah had been over much of the country. He had a knack for drawing. As he talked to Thomas, who had seen some streams and carries he had not, Jeremiah drew a tree and a horse on the edge of the big sheet of paper.

He trimmed another quill. The starting bound was easy: over beyond Fort Wentworth where their father had commanded during the Revolution, on the bluff above the junction of the Upper Ammonoosuc with the Connecticut. Draw in the south bound: the Upper Ammonoosuc to the pond, over the carrying place that led to the river flowing into the Androscoggin. A big swing up through Lake Umbagog and Mooselookmegantic, on into Canada and the St. Francis River, and back to Northumberland by way of Lake Memphremagog and the Nulhegan River and the Connecticut. It was a big swatch of land.

Jeremiah, all the same, had his doubts about the title. Being a young man of careful thought, he wrote a note to enclose with the map when he sent it to John Bradley in Concord. There had been an Indian village on Lake Mollychumgamogg seventy years before. The tribe was almost extinct now. Old Pacsmagenogg was their chief. Could go to Canada and get conveyance from the tribe to Philip . . . also needed four pounds of powder, eight pounds of lead, a dozen flints, and two or three blankets . . .

Philip did not live long after he had provided against his failing powers. Thomas Eames cared for him scarcely a year before he died. Then Thomas arranged the funeral, and continued to feed and house Molly and Mooselock. He estimated the cost at thirty-five dollars annually. Molly, in time, became restless and concerned for her soul. Molly was a good Catholic. She had no confessor in the Protestant village of Northumberland—or to the south for that matter. Thomas hired two Indians to take her to Montreal to have her sins pardoned. He gave her two crowns to pay the priest, whom Thomas called a friar. Mooselock went along, inseparable still, presumably. Neither returned.

CHAPTER 4

TWO LAND COMPANIES, 1798

King Philip's deed formed the uncertain foundation for the earliest land company to speculate in the territory at the source of the Connecticut. Uncertain it was for two reasons: Philip's title itself was dubious; and federal legislation of 1790 and 1793 forbade individuals buying land from Indians. Despite these handicaps, on June 17, 1797, the men named in Philip's deed met in Concord and organized themselves as the Proprietors of Philip's Grant. The original four, Thomas Eames, John Bradley, Jonathan Eastman, and Nathan Hoit, sold to Thomas Cogswell and others 9/13s of Philip's land for $5,000. This brought into the group both the money and the political and legal prestige of the Cogswells of Gilmanton. At the first meeting, Thomas Cogswell was chosen moderator, John Bradley, clerk and treasurer. The Proprietors of Philip's Grant arranged future meetings, company rules, and organization.

The following year, Jonathan Eastman, Jr., bought into the company. With Pearson Cogswell, he was to be a most active member, and would give his name—and that of his father—to the group, which came to be known as the Eastman Company. The original four investors had increased to sixteen men interested in profits from the northern land. The company had as its operating base Concord, in contrast with the second company that evolved and held its meetings near Indian Stream in the disputed territory itself.

This second company originated in 1798 with another Indian deed for the basis of its claim to the same territory deeded by Philip. The validity of each title was argued over many years without regard to the essential illegality of both. In October of 1798, seven Indians journeyed south from St.

Francis to Concord, and protested to the legislature the action of Philip two years before in selling tribal land. They claimed the right to speak and act for the tribe. Their leader, Captain Cegar, bore the title of Orator to St. Francis. He declared that Philip had no tribal rights; Philip was an impostor. Captain Cegar, the other sachems, the tribe, disavowed all Philip's acts. In their turn, they would sell the true title to tribal land, including far more than Philip pretended to convey. They would deed all of northern New Hampshire from Haverhill on the Connecticut to the Ossipee River on the border of Maine—then Massachusetts territory—north to the line between the United States and the government of Great Britain, except one town they had already sold.

The members of the New Hampshire legislature viewed this proposal as absurd, for the state already had most of the territory offered. But three individuals thought that such a piece of paper might be valuable. Moody Bedel of Haverhill had heard of the valley of the upper Connecticut through his townsman David Gibbs. He may have known it earlier during his travels with his father in the campaigns against Canada during the Revolution —he a boy of twelve then. Or he may have visited it more recently, for Gibbs and Nathaniel Wales had settled there in 1790—pitched, as it was called—on the land where they camped the year before. They had put up cabins and had cleared farms, moved up their families. Gibbs had later moved to St. Simoneau in nearby Canada. Together, the three men, Moody Bedel, Nathaniel Wales, and David Gibbs, paid the seven Indians $3,100 for the deed to northern New Hampshire. Eventually they called themselves the Proprietors of Bedel's and Associates' (or "Others'") Grant, and became known as the Bedel Company. In contrast with the Eastman Company, they were oriented toward the north, sold land to men of northern New Hampshire, Vermont, and Canada, had no pretensions to legal and political power, and were entirely responsible for the early settlement.

The companies, however, operated from the foundation of the Indian deeds in much the same manner. Each company regarded its deed as establishing its right to the land north of the Forty-fifth Parallel, and particularly to that north of the Connecticut River in the area. Neither company had any illusions that they owned the granted lands of New Hampshire, which were included in the deeds, nor did they pretend to lay claim to those areas extending into Canada and Vermont; they had no intention of developing nearby granted towns such as Colebrook or Stewartstown. They used the deeds to claim the upper Connecticut valley from Stewartstown to Maine and Canada.

The deeds formed the basis of the right to make land sales and to encourage settlers. Both companies sold land in large amounts to speculators, and they offered to settlers acreage in return for clearing land and building roads. In these enterprises—profit and development—which overlapped, the Bedel Company had more immediate success, for Wales and Gibbs were on the land. As early as 1799, their competitors, the men of the Eastman Company, realized they must make surveys and organize a settlement or lose the chance to profit if the land increased in value.

In their disregard of the federal statutes, the companies reflected the independence of the states from federal jurisdiction, the almost unbelievable (in today's world) looseness of the ties between the states and the federal government. Indeed, the men who organized the companies may have had at first no inkling that they were breaking federal law. They probably would not have cared—did not care. Enforcement never *did* catch up with them, or try. In later years as the Eastman Company attempted again and again to secure its claim by New Hampshire legislative grant of the lands, when Levi Woodbury and the Webster brothers were associated with it, the lawyers took note of the federal statute and prepared a possible way around, but the route was never needed.

All this came later; the immediate need was to explore and survey that remote country. The Eastman Company held its third annual meeting in June 1799.

CHAPTER 5

PROPRIETORS OF PHILIP'S GRANT: THE EASTMAN COMPANY, 1799

At Concord, that thriving town of two thousand souls, where the Merrimack River curved through a thousand acres of interval, the "peculiar friends" of Philip, Indian chief, met with other men of the land company. This was June; the last year of the eighteenth century approached the halfway mark. The fields along the slow river, coming green and lush, held grass knee-high. The trees spread leaves scarely a month old, still vivid green, bordering the river, bordering the bluff that sloped up to the eastern plain, and contrasting with the pines that remained dark under the clear sky. Cattle grazed and calves blatted and colts romped.

Down the long, wide, main street, under the green trees, horses trotted fast in single rigs past ox-drawn carts, work teams, carriages. Riders with saddlebags, horses muddy from north settlement roads, merchants from Portsmouth in the latest coats, woodsmen in linsey-woolsey and moosehide moccasins, militia officers, and soldiers—all moved along the street among farmers and teamsters in cowhide boots and tow-cloth frocks.

Before the inn of Benjamin Hanaford, saddle horses stood in the shade at the hitching rail. A two-wheeled chaise driven by a man in an elegant plum-colored coat, cocked hat, and knee breeches, pulled up as the man hauled back on the horse's reins and jumped out. A boy stepped forward and led the horse toward the stable. The man joined others going into the inn, men dressed for riding in short coats, breeches, and boots, men in homespun with broad hats. The Proprietors of Philip's Grant had gathered.

Inside beyond the public bar, the door of a private room closed. Thomas Cogswell brought the meeting to order. He welcomed the new members of the company, reviewed its progress since the first meeting two years before, and discussed prospects. More objective and definite, the clerk and treasurer, John Bradley, talked of costs for the survey of the northern lands. To raise money, assessments would be required against shares. Of various current expenses, one account to settle should be that of Thomas Eames for taking care of the Indians. The committee appointed the previous December, to lay out lands, could be authorized to settle with Thomas Eames. And so it was voted. Both the company and Thomas Eames had completed their obligations to Philip, Molly, and Mooselock.

The intrusion of the northern man's account brought the wilderness to the inn, pointed up the difference between a good board house with paneled walls and the log huts that provided shelter where Philip had roamed. Here were also, outside the glass window panes, cultivated fields of waving grass and wheat; north there were black stumps between hills of dwarf Canada corn pushing through the exposed forest mold. Here rail-and-stump fences and stone walls kept in fat cows; there cattle ranged in forest clearings made by windstorms and in abandoned beaver ponds turned to meadow, while the crops were fenced, leaving the cattle at night to the prowling wolves. Here women lived secure; there women feared losing themselves as prey to the forest and wild animals when they went in search of the cows to milk.

In other ways, the meeting took notice of activity in the north: Jeremiah Eames and Thomas Eames had begun the survey of the company lands. Jonathan Eastman would visit the territory as representative of the company. He was not a woodsman comparable to the Eames brothers, but he stood for the organization, and there might be news to bring back about Bedel, Wales, Gibbs, and their settlers.

For five days, from June 11 to 15, the proprietors met at Ben Hanaford's inn, laid plans, and discussed the allotment of land, sales arrangements, incentives to settlers, and the validity of the title from Philip. This went on in a spirit of enterprise and hope of wealth, which had little touch with the hard reality of cutting farms from a forest, building roads through swamps and bridging streams, constructing milldams and setting up saws and millstones—all necessary in creating valuable land from the wilderness. Some proprietors regarded the enterprise as pure speculation: thus might they buy a chance in a lottery, or gamble on a western land boom. Some proprietors believed that the land, unaided, would grow in value, like sound money out at interest. Others wanted their money in land rather than in pieces of paper. Others were anxious to make large, quick sales of their shares and get out before the bubble burst. But live up there? No, indeed. Most of the older men were well off, and regarded the Eames brothers as born to the border life, such as their own fathers had undertaken around Concord. They were too well off to consider settling themselves into a forest and becoming "planters" on the edge of civilization, for to them a "new plantation" offered nothing in fortune, as it did to poorer men. Some of them had large properties and businesses and political or professional commitments. The younger men looked upon a trip to the headwater country as an adventure. Having little but their energy and their fathers' names, they were willing to make surveys and explorations—with seasoned woodsmen. They were willing to run the errands of the company, because to their efforts in the long run might accrue the returns on this investment. But move up there and cut down trees? No, sir, thank you.

Of the more constrictive matter of title, of the legality of Philip's deed, no mention was made officially in the minutes of the meetings. Perhaps the question of Great Britain was discussed: might not the land north of the Forty-fifth Parallel belong to Great Britain? Nonsense; it was New Hampshire. Jeremiah Eames had surveyed it to the terms of the Treaty of Paris—Great Britain says he didn't. Who knows where the northwesternmost head of the Connecticut is? He says he marked it up on Hall's Stream—Britain claims the eastern source of the Connecticut. Damn them! That can't be the northwesternmost head, any fool can see! It's all there in the report of the boundary commission ten years ago. Then how dare Canada lay out a town within our boundary—rumor says they did, six–seven years ago. Wait until our survey's in. Possession is the important thing—that and records. Keep the records of the meetings clear; note the expenses, the names of the shareholders, the oaths of the officers. When the survey plan is in, draw lots for the division of land, sell to the first interested investors; they can worry about the title. The state committee on public lands? Tenuous problems. Gentlemen, the survey . . .

By November 1799, Jeremiah and Thomas Eames had completed cutting their measured compass lines through the woods, had blazed witness trees, had noted the bearings in a journal, and had drawn up a plan. The survey map, or plan, represented a town of sixty-four thousand acres lying between the Forty-fifth Parallel and Canada, not interfering with grants previously made by the states of New Hampshire or Vermont or by the Commonwealth of Massachusetts in its district of Maine.

Jonathan Eastman presented to the fall meeting a bill for £57 sterling, and the accounts of the Eames brothers. Eastman had ridden north through the prosperous towns of the Connecticut valley, past the peaks to the east known as the White Hills or the White Mountains, into the execrable roads through the blasted, girdled, burned forests of the settlements, to the new town of Stuart—Stewartstown—where Jeremiah lived. The items of his bill, listed in pounds sterling, shillings, and pence, included eighteen pounds of pork, also ham, cheese, sugar, butter, bread, beans, lodging, victualing, and horsekeeping. He had hired two men—probably as chainman and packman, for Jonathan Eastman could run a survey line himself—to "carry the compass," and these men required food, also tea, chocolate, and ginger. He had been on the road fifteen days, encamped twelve days. To the Eames brothers the proprietors owed £30 8s. 8d. To Jeremiah alone for thirteen days spent surveying, they owed £6 10s.—or ten shillings a day, good wages for the time, but Jeremiah was an expert.

The treasurer and the meeting approved the accounts, paid them from the assessments that had been made against shares, and approved the plan of their lands. In January, the seventh day of the new century, these lands, divided into thirty-two lots of two thousand acres each, fell to the various shareholders by the luck of a drawing.

For the next five years, however, the Proprietors of Philip's Grant, the Eastman Company, made little progress in developing their northern lands. By 1804 the settlement of their competitors, Bedel and his associates, dominated the territory. Meanwhile, the face of the land was changing.

CHAPTER 6

THE FACE OF THE LAND, 1797–1803

When Andrew Gilman made his deposition about the Indian chief, Philip, and about Philip's tribe and the lands they frequented, he was careful to point out—prompted doubtless by the Eames brothers, with a view to bolstering the title—that Philip and his people made improvements above the Ammonoosuc, and at the carrying place to the Androscoggin, and at Umbagog Lake. These were certainly only a few wigwams, fireplaces of stones laid in a circle, cornfields in meadows scarcely distinguishable from the wild land; yet they were evidence of title. Thus also did white men, who were often legally squatters, pitch on their claims to give evidence and support to their right to the land: a lean-to of logs with a hole in the roof for smoke to go out, girdled trees dead and bare above a few hills of corn, evidence of possession and of intention to improve the land, evidence of standing as a citizen. The very struggle to wrest a living from the wilderness by young men, usually poor and without other opportunity, could become the means of establishing themselves in security and comfort.

This was the impelling prospect that brought men into the northern forests—this and a buoyancy of spirit that belittled obstacles. The challenge of the land, and the promise of the times—a certain confident optimism—found a voice in the language of the settlers themselves. They called their clearings in the forest "improvements" or "betterments." Concrete evidence of work on the land—fields in the forest, fences, cabins, milldams—reinforced a title not always clear, even in granted towns. The law respected the effects and products of labor, should ownership be questioned, and the inclination of town proprietors was to acknowledge—or "quiet" or "secure" —a virtual squatter on the land if he had made improvements. Such was the usual arrangement to encourage poor but industrious settlers, or only a nominal sum was charged for the early lots.

In 1797 and in 1803, northern New Hampshire had a scholarly visitor, president of Yale College and inveterate traveler, the Reverend Doctor Timothy Dwight. On his second trip, as he journeyed north through the towns of Lyme, Orford, Piermont, Haverhill, and Bath, he found neat, new houses, fewer log cabins, fewer stumps in the fields, fewer girdled trees, although some of the roads were as muddy and root-trapped as before. His party left Lancaster on October 3, 1803, in the beginning color of the changing leaves—yellow, red, orange—and rode through Northumberland, past the Upper Ammonoosuc, where Philip once camped and where Thomas Eames lived. Dr. Dwight noticed the mills at Judd Falls near the village of Northumberland and remarked about the twenty-foot ledges that interrupted navigation.

Navigation of the Connecticut was interrupted farther downstream for all large boats. Fifteen Mile Falls at Barnet, Vermont, effectively stopped boats of all kinds. Wells River was the practical terminus for freight-loaded flatboats. Wagons carried goods beyond this point, although smaller boats and canoes were used to some extent on the upper river. The hard ice of late winter provided a favorite highway. But below Wells River the flatboats of twenty-five-ton burden transformed the Connecticut into an artery of commerce once locks and canals were built around the lower falls. In return for salt, iron, molasses, rum (and more rum), plows, crockery, kettles, and ropes at a charge of six dollars a ton from Hartford, Connecticut, to Wells River, Vermont, the farmers of the valley sent downstream shingles, potash, pork, grain, cheese, butter, and wool, and lumber in rafts sixty feet long and twelve wide. A river life sprang up comparable to that of the Mississippi: stout men and stout boats, men singing and roistering while their boat moved under sail, men poling the clumsy craft from the walkways along the sides when the wind was unfavorable, or rowing with long sweeps. On the lower river the boats, seventy feet long, housed their crew; upriver the men on boats with shallower draft stopped at farmhouses along the banks. Bill Cummins was the most notorious for strength: he could lift a barrel of salt with two fingers in the bung and set it on the mast-board. Twenty days up from Hartford to Wells River, ten days back down to tidewater—two hundred and twenty miles—the river floated the commerce of the valley for thirty years or more, till the railroads took over heavy transportation.

Dr. Dwight continued on to Colebrook, where he admired the activity and enterprise of Colebrook's one hundred and fifty inhabitants. Their roads, plantations, barns, and schoolhouses surprised him, for the barns were large and good, the schoolhouses well built, and although the dwelling houses were principally of logs, some of them were being built from logs sawed by the mills on the Mohawk River.

He and his companions stayed at an inn in Colebrook run by a man named Loomis, a member of a prominent family active in the law enforcement and the militia: Joseph Loomis, who became justice of common pleas for Coos County two years later; Horace Loomis, a sheriff, who later troubled the people of the Indian Stream territory with writs of attachment, which they thought illegal, for they didn't belong to New Hampshire; Lewis Loomis, in 1803 only ten years old, who became the champion wrestler of the north country, a collector of customs who maintained in 1832 that the Indian Stream territory, having been awarded to Great Britain, should pay duties. Dr. Dwight had no notion of all this, but he admired the lofty mountain two miles below the Loomis inn, across the Connecticut in Lymington, Vermont. It was of noble appearance, rising steep and isolated above the valley. The name Grand Monadnoc had been given it for its resemblance to the mountain in southern New Hampshire.

On Tuesday, October 4, 1803, wrote Dr. Dwight, "We left Loomis's and rode to the Line; crossing the Connecticut at a ford, two miles below, and passing through a part of the township of Canaan, in Vermont; or rather what was originally a location called Norfolk, lately annexed to that township. The river here was about fifty yards in breadth; and in this region is usually of a breadth between that and twenty-five yards. In almost all places it was much too deep to be forded; although the season was dry. The part of the road, which lies in Canaan, is chiefly by the side of a mill stream, called Leet's Brook [Leach's Stream]. Monadnoc was the last mountain, which we saw in Vermont; and Preston Hills, in New Hampshire. Northward of these mountains, the country consists of hills and vallies; the soil is fertile."

Beyond Canaan, Dr. Dwight rode to the international boundary surveyed in 1772 between the (then) Province of New York and the Province of Quebec. The surveyors, Vallentine and Collins, for whom the line came to be named, thought that it followed the Forty-fifth Parallel, but later calculation showed they were about a mile north. They ended its eastern progress at a cedar post on the west bank of the Connecticut. From there, the British said the boundary ran up the river to Third Lake. The New Hampshire men said whoa, back up to Hall's Stream; that's the boundary, up to its source in the highlands—or said so when they got around to surveying their north line in 1789.

Riding north of Canaan, Dr. Dwight did not see the wilderness, which existed toward the source of the Connecticut, but noticed that he had come again into settled country, in Canada. "When we came to the Line, we found the settlements begun, and extended to a considerable distance within sight; and, by their appearance, of some standing. By Mr. J. Ames [Jeremiah Eames], a respectable surveyor in Stuart [Stewartstown], I was informed, that beyond Hereford mountain, which ascends about five miles from the Line, there are no hills, of any considerable height, in Lower Canada, for a great distance. The whole country, he observed, consists of moderate elevations, beautifully sloped, and interjacent vallies, open and handsome. The soil, he further observed, is generally excellent; and the winters are by no means so severe, as to prevent the country from becoming a desirable residence."

By speaking so favorably of the country to his famous visitor, Jeremiah may have been indirectly promoting the Eastman Company land lying up the Connecticut. Jeremiah had been appointed on-the-spot agent by the Eastman Company in 1801, with authority "to put on settlers and give our Quitclaim deeds of conveyance" for one hundred acres after the settler had cleared five acres and built a house within two years. On the other hand, Jeremiah genuinely liked the country himself. He had moved to Stewartstown from the family farm in Northumberland in 1797. With his wife, Anna, and three children, he settled on lot number thirteen in the present West Stewartstown. He planned an inn and a mill. Also he planned to raise a family; three young ones were hardly a family. Eventually he had the inn, a store, mills—both a sawmill built in 1803 and a gristmill the following year—on the Connecticut, and the family. He and Anna had six more children. He became a selectman, a captain in the militia, and a prosperous farmer on the interval land along the Connecticut. Across the ford in Canaan, his wife's father, William Williams, had taken up land. Of course Jeremiah told Dr. Dwight about the country.

You had to make the land feed you, or you starved: its fertility became more than an academic problem, and before you started cutting down trees, you considered the known signs indicating fertility in a forest. Climate, too, might affect the fullness of your belly. A man looked hard at the land under the trees; he had to know the signs. River bottom land, or interval, would grow any crop in abundance. The deep, stone-free soil contained the fertility of ages of glacier and river waters. But land of this kind was limited. Plains above the interval might be fertile, or they might not be. Yellow-pine plains were sandy and barren. But a plain on which white pine grew was usually fertile. If white pines and butternuts grew together the land could be counted on to produce a crop right among the stumps without plowing: wheat, corn, grass. In the north country this combination failed the exploring settler, for pines became rare on the upper Connecticut and the butternut uncommon.

Judging land in the north meant new rules. A beaver meadow would be fertile. When the beavers ate all the nearby poplars and moved on, the dam rotted, the water drained off, and left a meadow. Its grass, when it was scythed and well dried by many turnings in the sun, would feed a cow for a winter. Interval land along the streams sometimes appeared in unexpected little pockets of alluvial soil. A man had to watch for these in the north country where the miles of wide interval no longer existed as they did downstream. Away from the valleys the problem became more difficult; stones invariably filled the soil to a greater or lesser extent—the greater being entirely uncultivable, good only for pasturage of pointed-nosed sheep. Land where white oaks grew was usually hard and stony. An undergrowth of brakes and fern meant that the land would not raise grass until plowed and hoed but was good for Indian corn before that. Spruce and hemlock often denoted a thin, cold soil; if growing with birch, the soil was usually good for grass.

All these things men such as Jeremiah Eames, moving north, had considered. Of course, at Stewartstown the interval was still extensive and the problem simpler. Farther upstream, the intervals were gradually closed in by the hills. At the mouth of Indian Stream where Nathaniel Wales and David Gibbs had settled, they farmed the last of the extensive rich interval land. Beyond this, between the rapids known as Great Falls (only one perpendicular drop, of twelve feet) and Perry Stream, there was more interval land along the Connecticut, but shallower, hemmed in. Above this, the river dropped rapidly from the lake—at one place, fifty feet in three hundred.

Dr. Dwight noted down this and other information about the land. Salmon no longer came up the river. Several dams below had stopped them. Colebrook settlers had "heretofore" caught great numbers of salmon, which returned to the ocean late in the summer. Stewartstown and Colebrook produced abundant crops of wheat, rye, barley, oats, flax, maize, and grass, also garden vegetables common in New England. Wheat yield was twenty to thirty bushels to the acre. Spring wheat was esteemed a surer crop than autumnal, for "the latter it is said being covered with snow before the ground is frozen becomes too warm and moulds and decays." The maize yield was forty bushels to the acre, but it had to be Canada corn, originally brought from that country, which produced abundantly with a quality not materially different from the flint corn raised in Massachusetts and Connecticut. Yellow in color, with eight to twelve rows of kernels, it was the earliest, next to chicken corn, and thus suited to the short summer of the north country.

Snow arrived in Stewartstown and Colebrook about the middle of November and was gone about the middle of April. Winters, however, varied. In 1798 a man crossed the Connecticut on the ice south of Colebrook on May 2.

Plowing was commonly begun the first of May. Maize could be planted near the end of May.

There were three kinds of currants in the woods, also gooseberries and a few blackberries, while raspberries filled the country, springing up in infinite numbers wherever the forest was cut down. There were wild cherries, cranberries, and fine strawberries. Apples did not do well on new forest land, but thrived after plowing to mix earth with the vegetable mold.

Beavers were still found on the Connecticut in 1803. Bears abounded. Raccoons and deer were scarce. There were no elks. Dr. Dwight noted, "Moose were diminished in their numbers, until since the year 1800; when the winters having been very mild, and very little snow having fallen, they have escaped the ravages of the hunters, and have become considerably numerous." (The hunters used snowshoes, a hard crust giving them a more definite advantage.) Wolverine, the size of a small dog, fierce and voracious, frequently destroyed sheep. There were foxes, squirrels, chipmunks, and hedgehogs. Dr. Dwight didn't mention the wolves, marten, ravens, mink, muskrat, bobcats, and lynx.

It was not so hospitable a country as the valley from Stewartstown to the sea, and it would never quite yield the wilderness; much of it has gone back to woods, with thousands of other New Hampshire farms.

But in 1803, men *knew* they could subdue the wilderness.

CHAPTER 7

THE SHAPE OF THINGS TO COME, 1804–1811

The year of 1803 brought Ohio into the Union. From negotiations with Napoleon came the purchase of the huge Louisiana Territory. Despite the objections of the Federalists, and difficulty in raising the $15 million, President Jefferson secured plains and mountains more than double the existing area of the United States. (An Englishman, Lord Ashburton, helped with the financing. Almost forty years later he and Daniel Webster would settle the long-disputed northern boundary.) The year after the Mississippi and Missouri watersheds became American, Meriwether Lewis and William Clark set out across the plains on their exploration to the Pacific.

While this western expansion took place, the attraction of wild land continued to lure New Hampshire men north and Canadian men south, to the upper Connecticut. Nathaniel Wales and David Gibbs were soon joined by others who followed the muddy woods track leading from Canaan along the north side of the river to its junction with Indian Stream. Men laid up log cabins and cleared land. The Eastman Company might hold meetings at Concord and might hire Jeremiah Eames to survey a town in the wilderness, but Bedel, Wales, and Gibbs were getting settlers into the area and were selling land.

Without men actually in the forest cutting down trees, building homes, and raising rye, wheat, and corn, the "development" sponsored by the Eastman Company had no reality. The surveyed lots had no meaning; the corner trees, although they displayed Jeremiah's axe blazes with the scribed bearings, had about as much significance as claw-scratched notices on a bear's range.

This pattern of competition between the two companies took shape for the first ten years of the nineteenth century. The Eastman Company established the formal land company with an annual meeting, sworn officers, records, shares, notification of meetings in newspapers, and a town survey plan. Their efforts with settlers were not successful, and none of the members of the company themselves took up northern land at this time. Jeremiah Eames "moved on" a few settlers but was unable to encourage them to stay and face the hardships. The Bedel Company, on the other hand, represented more nearly a loose affiliation of men who proposed to secure the land and then worry about an organization of proprietors, records, and officers. Settlers were to them of prime importance, as were roads and bridges, log houses, crops. And of course, these things would help turn a fast dollar by attracting speculators with money.

In the first fifteen years of the settlement, from 1790 to 1805, Nathaniel Wales continued to work his rough farm on the meadows along the west bank of Indian Stream. He also traveled in search of other areas for land speculation, and he undertook the development of Wales Location. David Gibbs cleared land on the east bank, nearer the junction with the Connecticut. Upstream from Wales on Indian Stream, a settler named Nathan Smith began cutting trees where the valley closed in toward the north ridge. In 1802, Wales sold 16,000 acres to Hobart Spencer for $3,000. Spencer listed himself as "of Indian Stream," but seems not to have stayed long. Two years later, Wales sold 30,000 acres to Thomas Cutts of York County, Massachusetts's District of Maine. He sold several thousand acres to a James Treadway.

In April of 1804, Wales wrote from Stewartstown to Moody Bedel in Haverhill: "Sence I saw you I have taken possession of pert of our Indian Lands . . . I think sum Business can be done. I can't write all." He was going on a trip north and west. Possibly lands could be exchanged. He would go to see Bedel if he thought best and had "dun all in my Power to incourage Setlars to cum on and I think I have got Business in a good way—if Attended too, Sumthing Can be made." Wales folded the letter, sealed it with wax, and addressed it to Captain Moody Bedel, Haverhill, New Hampshire, and wrote on the margin, "Favor of Mr. Tillsun."

Mr. John Tillotson, of Northumberland, often traveled down the river on business, for he was the first register of probate for Coos County, an office he held for thirteen years. He was also interested in the "Indian Lands," and eventually bought from Wales a large share of his holdings, 1/12 and 1/24 of the total. Wales also sold to Captain James Ladd, of Hereford, Canada, 1/12 share. Ladd moved to his land, made surveys, and soon, in

1804 and 1805, sold 185 acres to Samuel Orsborn, who brought his family. There were four families settled then, and various men making pitches for future use or to establish claims.

Of this oddly matched association of men, brought together by the land deed of seven St. Francis Indians, the militia captain in Haverhill was the most colorful. Captain Moody Bedel, forty years old in 1804, occupied himself with developing another town now called Benton, east of Haverhill, with politics, with his land in Bath, and with the militia. He was a personable man, fond of cigars and toddy. He aroused loyalty in his friends that lasted over the years. His fortune throughout his life continued to elude him. Despite his shrewdness in certain deals and lawsuits, he lacked sound business sense and perseverance. He was careless of details, for enthusiasm and emotion motivated him more than reason. Commissioned by President James Madison, colonel of the 11th Regiment of Infantry in 1814, he served through the Niagara River campaigns, notably at Fort Erie. Thus in maturity he renewed war experiences to which he had first been exposed at the age of twelve with his father in the terrible 1776 campaign against the British in Canada. And yet the army, perhaps from these experiences, never appealed to him as a way of life. He returned to New Hampshire in 1814. In 1804, however, this was years in the future, and he had business to tend to, a family to support, town affairs to oversee. In 1802 he had represented both Haverhill and Coventry (Benton) in Concord. During this period, he may have visited the upper Connecticut, but he did not undertake personally to work there for another six years. Taking up his own land and living on it with his family would be a last resort of the hard times following the War of 1812.

The Eastman Company, in 1804, had little interest in the activities of the Bedel Company—particularly, it did not concern itself with the settlers in the northern wilderness. The men of Concord and Gilmanton were not alarmed by squatters who built four or five log houses on farmland from which the stumps had not yet been pulled. Such settlers were only increasing the value of land, which the Eastman Company (thought the proprietors) would eventually own, when the legislature acknowledged Philip's title. Moody Bedel and his partners did not worry the officers of the Eastman Company nearly so much as the legislature's interest in possible state land along the border.

Hurriedly, Samuel Bradley wrote to John Bradley about completing all surveys of the area and laying out other townships before the state got ahead of them and took possession. He proposed to spend a week at the "grant" in September. This he did, for he was worried about the validity of the title from Philip. A court of law and the legislative committee might not regard Philip as capable of conveying lands but rather view him as a vagabond Indian. Visiting Conway and Fryeburg in the latter part of September, Samuel Bradley arranged for the depositions of five men who had known Philip as chief of the Coos Indians. The fees to the justices of the peace and to the deponents came to more than two dollars per document. Samuel Bradley was willing to pay for these buttresses to the title of Philip.

In a year or two the state legislature lost interest in northern lands. Settlement continued quietly at Indian Stream under Bedel and his associates; the Eastman Company continued quietly to hold meetings in Concord and to make plans for taking over the northern lands, without actually going beyond planning. Moody Bedel's active participation in the settlement began in 1810 and 1811, when he went to the territory and worked with a gang of men cutting roads and felling trees. He had married for a second time in March 1810. Mary Hunt did not favor frontier life. She probably stayed in Haverhill to look after the nine stepchildren. Moody planned to clear his own land near Lake Connecticut, and may have built a log house at this time. He was not having the success at land sales that Wales did, although he sold a thousand acres to Mathew Greeley.

Sales of lands by the Bedel associates had a confused, free-for-all quality. The proceeds of the deals that Wales made appear to have remained with him; he was selling his 1/3 share piecemeal. Bedel and Gibbs might also be characterized as rugged individualists in their business transactions. The three men had been brought together by the opportunity of pooling their resources to meet the Indian price of $3,100. They later, however, treated their 1/3 shares as being under their personal control, with no obligations to the others, selling land as they found customers. There is a deed dated 1807 by Moody Bedel to Amos Brewster of Hanover, conveying 312,000 acres (more or less) between Maine, Canada, and the northwesternmost branch of the Connecticut River. This number of acres is more than 50,000 acres greater than existed in the triangle. The sale must have fallen through, perhaps because Amos Brewster took a ride north himself, but it indicates the hoped-for quick return of the gambling land-speculator who combined the attributes of poker player and horse trader with those of frontiersman.

There were valid reasons for the sell-and-get-out philosophy. The land had four claimants: Canada, the United States (represented by New Hampshire), the Eastman Company, and the Bedel Company. The chances of keeping title to any land in the area were not good. Had a man regarded his claim, or pitch, or share, in the light of clear reason, unbiased by a gambling urge, by land-hunger, or by necessity, he must decide he'd best sell out and try elsewhere. Nathaniel Wales disposed of most of his 1/3 by 1811, no doubt with all these things in mind. He then in some unrecorded way ran afoul of the law. Sheriff Levi Willard of Coos County took him into custody. That year, in September 1811, he did not attend a meeting of the Bedel Company.

The meeting was held at David Tyler's house "at Bedel's and others' Grant." Moody Bedel was moderator. Of the eleven men present and considered to be proprietors, eight held their land "under Wales." The proprietors voted to confirm twenty settlers in the land they had pitched, including John Haynes, a most important future settler, to the amount of 100 acres, for clearing 5 acres and working on the roads. This followed quite naturally the presence in the company of the principal settlers, as well as non-resident proprietors. The shares were listed and a record of the meeting made. Moody Bedel held 1/3 share, except for 1,400 acres he had sold; David Gibbs, 1/3, though he seems to have been a resident of Canada at this time; James Ladd, 1/12, except for 3,000 acres he had sold; John N. Tillotson, 1/12 and 1/24; John Rowe, 1/12, and as attorney for Wales, 1/24, except for 1,500 acres; Nathaniel Perkins, claims for 200 acres; William Morrison, 250 acres; John Haynes, the largest claim of the settlers, 2,000 acres; William Quimby, 600 acres; Mathew Greeley, 1,000 acres; and Samuel Orsborn, 185 acres. They voted to assess 5/1000 of a dollar on each acre to raise money for surveys and roads.

No mention was made in the record that most of these claims and shares lay on land the Eastman Company considered its property.

This was the last meeting of the Bedel Company before the war. It put on the records the name of the man who would become the patriarch of the settlement, the Nestor of Indian Stream Territory: John Haynes.

CHAPTER 8

ENTER JOHN HAYNES, 1811

A man in his middle years, two years beyond forty, came north soon after serving a jail sentence in Haverhill. He had been convicted of passing counterfeit money. Nothing in the previous life of John Haynes, or in his later years at Indian Stream, where he lived to be eighty-five, provides a clue to this turning point. Nothing suggests a bitterness that unjust conviction might have caused him to feel or to express. His life otherwise was one of continuous probity. The conviction appears not to have affected the attitudes toward him of those who knew him.

The only indication of his feelings is in his seeking a new start. The northern territory was beyond the easy reach of law, but this seems not to have attracted him. He was prosperous enough to become a member of the Bedel Company in September 1811, the year he traveled north from his home in Lisbon. He claimed two thousand acres under the Wales title at the meeting held that year in David Tyler's house. In contrast, he had himself cleared land enough to be included with the twenty settlers to whom the proprietors awarded one hundred acres for labor on their pitches. The claim of two thousand acres seems to have represented intention rather than actual land speculation, or some deal with the proprietor, Nathaniel Wales, which disintegrated, for in 1813 he acquired land opposite the mouth of Indian Stream from John Rowe for moving Rowe to Indian Stream from Lisbon (assuming that Rowe's "Concord" residence was the town later known as Lisbon). He bought sixty acres that year from John Plumeley. It cost him $162, a high price, but the lot had deep rich soil and lay along the east bank of Indian Stream. In 1817 he made his first big purchase of land, one thousand acres for $1,000, from David Gibbs. In the meantime he had been clearing five acres on the Connecticut, for which the proprietors deeded him in 1818, or confirmed his possession of, one hundred acres at about the middle of the "dadewater," a slow section of the river several miles above the falls, and wilderness when he arrived seven years before. This was most likely his original pitch, upstream from Gage Brook's junction with the Connecticut. It became his home farm for many years.

John Haynes was born in 1769, son of Joseph Haynes, of Sudbury, Massachusetts, an early settler of Lisbon sometime before the Revolution. John's father enlisted in Colonel Timothy Bedel's regiment in 1777 and was commissioned a lieutenant. After the Revolution, John acquired lot number six in range seven, married Dolly Noyes, and built a log cabin. In time, the section became populated and known as Georgetown, with farms along Salmon Hole Brook, where a road led from the Connecticut valley to Sugar Hill and Franconia. It was a good place for a tavern. John opened one in his log cabin and thereby increased the scanty revenue from his fifty acres. Town meetings were held in alternate years at his tavern. John sometimes acted as moderator. He held the office of justice of the peace and of representative to the legislature. Seven sons and daughters were born to him and Dolly while they lived in Lisbon, their lives marred only by the death of David in 1801 at the age of three years and seven months. The youngest, Ross, was born in February of the year John went north to look for new land. Sarah, the oldest, was seventeen. Clark was twelve..

The roads had improved, but as John Haynes rode farther he encountered muddy cart tracks. After eighty miles he reached the end of even these, up the river from Canaan, at Indian Stream.

Beyond the meadows and clearings he found Captain Moody Bedel and others felling trees and cutting roads. It was the beginning of a long association with the older man, whose father had been his father's regimental commander. The friendly manner, the energy, the outgoing character of Captain Bedel were known to John Haynes, for Bedel was a prominent citizen of Haverhill, a landowner in the town of Bath (just south of Lisbon), and an active member of the militia. The two men may have shared an established friendship before John Haynes moved north. However this might be, Captain Bedel by 1815 relied on Haynes to keep the records of his company; as proprietors' clerk, John Haynes recorded deeds and made notes of the meetings.

That summer of 1811, John Haynes learned that Captain Bedel had more than road-cutting on his mind. He was negotiating with a man named Ebenezer Fletcher, of Charlestown, old Fort Number Four on the Connecticut, to build a sawmill and a gristmill. Fletcher was reputed to be well-to-do, an expert millwright and builder, a hard worker. The falls on the Connecticut beyond Indian Stream would be a good mill privilege. The water, controlled by a dam and guided over a wheel, would turn stones to grind corn; it would raise and lower the vertical saw to divide slowly the settlers' logs into boards.

Captain Bedel thought this the most important project after roads; both roads and mills would bring settlers. Already another good man might move in: Nathaniel Perkins of New Hampton liked the broad interval land of the Wales farm on the west side of Indian Stream. John Rowe owned it now. He was one of the proprietors of the grant, a "tenant in common," with Bedel, Gibbs, a man named Cutts of York County in Maine, and various others. John Rowe liked to call the settlement "Prospect"; in his land deeds he specified that it was "supposed to be in the United States of America," forecasting without realizing it the long controversy over the boundary. Rowe had arranged for a sale of land to Nathan Judd—probably one hundred acres. Judd was from Piermont, just south of Haverhill on the Connecticut. A man named John H. Perry was making a pitch up near Lake Connecticut; his name would come to designate the stream that flowed into the Connecticut River below the lake. Captain Bedel himself planned to clear land in that area and make a farm. There would be more settlers. The country was opening up.

In coming north, John Haynes turned from the western trend of the country. Although he had a younger brother, David, who settled and cleared land at Van Buren, New York, John found no appeal in western lands. As a young man, he faced enough trees to chop, right at home in Lisbon, and had no money for migration. The poverty of the town during and after the Revolution derived from the draining of manpower into the army, and from the heavy expense, £500 sterling, of a fort. The citizens appealed for relief from taxes in 1786. They were too poor to consider moving away, although opportunity beckoned the next year, when the old Congress adopted the Northwest Ordinance.

Land north of the Ohio River was to be surveyed into sections and townships six miles square, and provision made for territorial government and eventual statehood. The appeal to a young man of eighteen (which was the age then of John Haynes) came clear when his plow jarred on a New Hampshire ledge. But who could pay two dollars an acre? John Haynes stayed in Lisbon, as did most of the men.

Ohio became a state in 1803, and President Jefferson bought territory west of the Mississippi from France. New land opened up. Still John Haynes and Dolly stayed on the hill farm and served travelers rum, along with the meat and porridge and bread produced by the farm. Dolly had been born the year President Washington laid siege to the British in Boston, the year of Thomas Paine's *Common Sense*. John had been seven then. The years were passing. Lisbon at last began to thrive. The land changed to farms, not only in the valleys, but to the tops of the eastern hills. Men built mills on the streams that poured into the Connecticut. Wheat grew in the fields; cattle fattened on the upland pastures. In 1810, the New Hampshire Iron Factory Company began mining ore in town, with smelting and casting in nearby Franconia. And John Haynes became a solid citizen, until he found himself charged and convicted of passing counterfeit money.

He went north early enough in the summer of 1811 to establish a pitch that the proprietors recognized in September. He stayed at least until November, when he witnessed a land deed. The following March, he moved his family north. The normal procedure of the time was to use an ox sled to carry a family to a log cabin. There seems no reason to doubt that John Haynes did this, for in his deposition of 1830 he speaks of his pitch in 1811. A pitch meant a hole in the wilderness with a log house in it. March was the month of good travel, when the frozen river crusted hard over thick ice, and a yoke of oxen could haul a sled upstream if roads were impassable or nonexistent. Swamps, streams, and ponds were also frozen. At times a man could walk through the forest on the crust without snowshoes. If John Haynes did not settle that year on his pitch near the bow of the river at the middle of the "dadewater," a few rods above Gage Brook, his judgment was less acute than his later life indicated, for the pitch was in the dwindling supply of meadowland upriver from the wide interval bordering Indian Stream. (It is now under the water of Lake Francis.) John Haynes was sagacious enough to explore for the best remaining land, and he was a good woodsman.

A man of forty-two could still feel adventure ahead as he walked up the bank of a river unknown to him in its remote stretches beyond roads. Its dark evergreens, past the final clearing, the sound of the river rushing down from the lakes and streams, the expectancy aroused by the light that comes through the trees ahead (would it be a meadow, a beaver pond, or a windflattened tangle of trees?), and the sense of freedom because of the bread and pork and the blanket in the pack on his back—it all brought to mind the contrast between the forest and the settled order of the downriver country.

What did John Haynes think about as he first walked up the Connecticut beyond the last clearing? Of the jail term, undoubtedly. How sweet the breeze down the river, how soft the forest floor under his boots! He almost certainly thought of freedom and independence, thoughts that made him consider the conditions of his hometown and his own prospects there. For a man of independence, Lisbon was getting crowded: 1,126 people, neighbors in your pockets, watchers from the road keeping track of the furrow you plowed, loafers at the inn eyeing Dolly and plaguing the young ones, churchly citizens who were sometimes more noted for minding other men's affairs than for tending to their own, spying on the least violation of the Sabbath or on even more private actions.

And the town, yes, the town: its history had involved poverty and conflicting claims of rival proprietors, which ruined settlers who held title under the losing group. Since then the town had indeed prospered, and had come to be controlled more and more by rich men, men of politics and law and industry. Well enough was it for a yeoman to get up in town meeting and say his say, but so many men had fallen into debt to merchants and bankers and mortgage holders, till they were no longer freemen at all, that the opinion of an independent yeoman was a voice in the wilderness of avarice, fear, stupidity, envy, and deviousness. Somewhere there must be a place where a man could draw his breath clear of the stinks of little people, could stand alone on his own great piece of land—and there was plenty, more than this beginning of one hundred acres—with no taxes, no obligations, nothing needed but the strength of his own arms and back, the strength of his sons, on his own land, for his own family, with no neighbors so close their dogs' barking woke him at night.

John Haynes, leaving his troubles behind, walked up the Connecticut sometime in the summer of 1811 searching for his new land. His quiet mind worked over the observations of his senses, cogitating, classifying, storing away. The sound of the river stopped after the cascades that some men called Great Falls. Extending almost a mile from the initial drop of twelve feet, the rocky gorge might have held a different river from the smoothly flowing current back near Indian Stream's junction. As the sound of the river stopped, he found himself on a level plain or plateau covered by evergreens, where the river cut through the deep soil and wound in a tight bow toward the east, the water slow, the bank high on the north side. A small brook came in at the north of the bow. Old beaver meadows and interval land grown to swale grass and bushes gave him a view toward the series of northern ridges, beyond which must lie Canada. Doubtless the uncertain nationality of the territory crossed his mind but did not concern him. He was looking for land, not for a particular nation; his later actions were based on a devotion to law and order, either British or American, and for a time he stood for independent government. But that was twenty years in the future.

In the summer of 1811 he saw the clear green of maple leaves on the slopes, the paler green of beech, and the towering green crowns of yellow birch blending into the darker spruce and fir on the summits. East, beyond the cedars and tamaracks of the lowlands, lay another ridge—more of a mountain. To the south lay a mountain buttressed by ridges, long and arched, its end hidden by the nearby hill forming the southern side of the valley. That would be wild land granted to Dartmouth College.

The blackflies, active in the quiet, warm air of the old beaver meadows, swarmed like bees, while the dragonflies pursued each other in zooming circles, or chased the countless mosquitoes. August and September would bring relief from the flies, which then vanished from the woods. The meadows were studded by dead stubs of trees killed by the pond waters back when the beavers had maintained their dam and lodge, before they were trapped for the new style of beaver hats. The dead spruces caught on clothing like wire. The white birch stubs were soft and punky, drilled for nests by woodpeckers. On the brittle spruces, cedar birds perched or darted out after insects, fluttering their waxy wings in the sun.

For John Haynes, the sun may have faded that day. Across the valley sometimes came the roaring, rolling thunder from the south, as passenger pigeons flew over toward the northern ridges, where they nested in the thousands. They could eat up a grainfield in the time it took to load a flintlock, but they were delicious food.

Ahead, upstream, the river continued to wind in tortuous twists, almost cutting back into itself through the interval land, the banks not high, but steep, the current almost imperceptible. The abandoned pond bottom was treacherous underfoot: gnawed stumps stood hidden in the grass, and bushes covered the muddy canals that the beavers had dug back to the spruces and used for floating poplar sticks into the pond. The brook, no longer held back by the dam, ran tea-colored in a narrow channel over sand and clay and shards of flat stones like pieces of slate. There would be another beaver dam above to tint the water brown from the rotting vegetation and leaves and forest mold, and there was the lake that came to be known as Rogers Pond or Back Lake.

Moving along the river, pushing through the underbrush, John Haynes observed the types of trees. The big spruce trunks were sometimes too great for a man to lay up into a cabin. He would need a smaller, younger stand.

A big spruce tree was useless in a cornfield, but in time could be hewed into house timbers, sawed into boards. A pity there wasn't more pine—only a colony here and there on the knolls. But cedars, yes: shingles and clapboards there. Maples on the uplands: sugar there. Beech, birch: plenty of firewood there. He could see that this was deep soil all along the still, dark water in which sometimes a trout rolled. He could test the soil with a dead spruce sapling, trimmed with his hand axe, for a crowbar. Driven with both hands into the soil, it would tell him, as he leaned on it and worked it around and down, that there were no rocks to catch a plow, and the soil, clinging to knots on the pole as he withdrew it, showed good black earth below the ferns and spruce roots.

Another brook came down out of a hollow, two or three miles farther on. Its tinkling, dripping sound up in the woods came clear, and an opening there suggested a bog or beaver pond. It ran into a small pond before it drained into the Connecticut. Across the river another stream meandered through a marsh dotted with cedars, tamaracks, and spruces. He could see the lift of the hill north and east. With the flat meadows, it formed a combination of lowland and upland that would give a farm a variety of soils, for a variety of crops: flax, hay, corn, wheat, rye, potatoes, grazing for cattle on the hill, and a sunny exposure with protection from northern winds.

Eventually it was here that John Haynes cleared his land and built his log house. During his first days in the territory his thoughtful pondering must have led him to further exploration up to the big lake. He did not have a hair-trigger mind. He was looking for the best land he could find, with enough country around it, in which to buy more than the hundred acres he could earn from Captain Bedel's company, for he was thinking in terms of thousands of acres.

CHAPTER 9

EBENEZER FLETCHER FINDS A MILL PRIVILEGE, 1811

As did John Haynes, Ebenezer Fletcher followed a trail beyond the meadows and clearings and log houses at Indian Stream, with the sound of the Connecticut flowing over the rocks on his right, south of the trail. His ears, trained to the sound of falling water, as his hands were trained to the skills of a millwright, told him he had not reached the falls described by Captain Bedel. There would be a steady, liquid hum as he neared them; this sound was the purling ripple of rapid water coursing over a shallow bed of rocks.

Ebenezer Fletcher had ridden up from Charlestown, New Hampshire, a hundred and fifty miles south on this same river. There he had worked at Captain John Willard's sawmill, and had built a house and shop at the north end of Main Street. Forty-one years old, with less reason than John Haynes to want change, yet he was on the move to wild land.

The reasons for his interest are obscure. They did not have a source in debts, poverty, or failure. His position in Charlestown was that of a mature, capable, respected artisan, married, with a growing family of two boys and a girl. His ambition appears to have been modest but powerful. It turned him to look beyond working for Captain Willard; it carried him through years of hardship and toil. His dream must have been to be his own master in his own mill. He saw a way to this through the plans of Moody Bedel for the northern lands.

Captain Bedel wanted a mill in his new settlement, and Bedel and his associates were willing to offer land to a competent millwright who would move north and build the mill. The settlement was unorganized, so there would be no taxes. Water power was plentiful and steady. Miles of forest provided the best in raw lumber. Settlers were already raising grain to be ground. Ebenezer Fletcher rode north to see for himself.

He probably left his horse at one of the farms near Indian Stream. He may have been accompanied by Moody Bedel, and they may have stopped at the log house and barn and the fenced barnyard of Sam Orsborn. Orsborn had bought 85 acres from James Ladd, one of Bedel's associates, on July 1, 1804, twenty-six rods along the Connecticut east of Indian Stream. He was an old settler of seven years and now owned 185 acres, a good place to leave horses for men going upstream on foot over the rough trail, through the stump fields and the last tangles of felled trees, into the forest.

Ebenezer Fletcher looked for opportunity, which no longer existed in Charlestown.

The country appeared to be well watered. No drought seemed likely to dry the pond behind the dam he might build. Three reservoirs upstream, the three lakes, ensured an unfailing supply of water to the river. The forest growth showed the luxuriance that only plentiful rain could create. Ferns and grass were a succulent green in the openings, and the leaves of the great hardwood trees looked both fresh and lush, as though they received every few days a soaking rain.

Ebenezer took note of the straight trunks of the hardwoods. He believed in hardwood timbers for building; they were slow to work and heavy to handle, but everlastingly strong. He studied the ledges that appeared as the trail rose from the flat valley. The slab rock showed definite seams along which to split off building stones, square, flat-sided, easy to lay up into a foundation.

The nearest mills were in Stewartstown. Jeremiah Eames had built a sawmill and a gristmill in 1803 and 1804 on the Connecticut opposite Canaan, Vermont. These mills were nine rough miles from Indian Stream. To settlers who took up land farther upstream, toward Lake Connecticut, the distance might be almost twenty miles. Although the area here was too remote for a mill owner to sell lumber downriver in the great sixty-foot rafts that floated past Charlestown, and miles of rapids broke the navigable water, the country offered both a present need and a future growth of business to the first mill owner. And on the land that Captain Bedel offered, a farm could be cleared.

Nobody lived in a log house any longer than he had to. The men at Indian Stream would buy or trade for boards now, if they could get their logs sawed. And corn, rye, or wheat: a farmer had to have his grain ground before he could turn it over to his wife for porridge and bread.

Down-country, a millwright could help fill the pockets of someone else, no doubt of that, and he could work steady all his life, if he had a mind to security and to saying "Yes, sir" to the owners, and if he didn't object to moving to a different mill every time an owner decided to shut down for a time, or the water failed, or business fell off. Most of the streams in the towns down there had no more real good mill sites. Charlestown included little enough water power in its area from the beginning. In other towns, most of the good mill privileges had been taken up long ago, and now even locations with doubtful water flow and with danger of freshet damage brought outrageous prices. Every little brook seemed to have its mill, down there nowadays. Up here there was opportunity for a young man to build his mill for pay—for land.

He would not build a mill for the usual terms of settler's duty, one hundred acres for five acres cleared and a log house. A mill would be worth at least five hundred acres, figuring a dollar an acre. He'd hold out for that. Captain Bedel would see the worth and convince the other proprietors, if they held back.

But there might be difficulties over the location. Maybe the place Bedel had described wouldn't do. A good man in the militia might not know what constituted a good mill privilege, might not know the exact specifications sought, for which there could be no substitute. Ebenezer noticed that the trail showed considerable use. It had been cleared of fallen logs and brush, and a way hacked through the worst thickets of cedar and spruce. Still, he'd have trouble carting in the irons for the mill, unless Captain Bedel opened the trail for oxen. Maybe in the winter, a hand sled could be dragged through the woods, and he'd make as many trips as the machinery required. He probably could get the crank forged down to Lancaster. He could pick up a good used saw blade, which would work up and down through those logs of pine and spruce and cedar, steady and slow, but true as the frame he'd build. Then there'd be iron hoops to forge for the wooden hubs of the waterwheel, an iron shaft, bevel gear, and ring gear, as well as wooden pulleys to form from logs.

But that was getting ahead of himself. First he would make his pitch near the waterfall—if it suited him—and clear his land for crops of rye and corn and wheat, enough for his family, though he'd have to buy meal till he raised a crop. He'd start laying up the mill foundation, start cutting and hauling timbers. There'd be work enough for two yoke of oxen at least, with an extra man part of the time. But mostly he'd do the work himself and save the money he'd earned down at Charlestown, maybe keep his house there if he couldn't sell it at a profit. Probably four or five years would go by before he had the mills built for both logs and grain. But he was unhurried. That was the only way to build right.

And he would be getting away from the talk of war that had reached Charlestown. He liked to read newspapers, and knew about the ravings of Calhoun and Clay. Such men made people in New Hampshire wonder about the wisdom of a central government. President Madison had no control over the young fire-eaters. For New Hampshire, Mr. Madison was no use at all. If the young men down at Washington talked their elders into the idea that conquering Canada was an easy promenade over the border—and war came—nobody would bother this out-of-the-way corner, even though Canada might be the enemy up there beyond the ridges somewhere. Days of Indian raids were long gone, and besides, Lake Champlain had always been the important war route. Let the York Staters worry about it.

War *might* affect him through the boundary. If he located on the north side of the river, and Great Britain made good her claim to the river as the southern boundary of Canada, he'd wake up some morning a citizen of that country. Probably no danger—could beat the Britishers again, probably, if it came to that, and then the whole continent would be American.

War seemed a remote echo of the down-country problems, here in the wilderness. He was more interested in the river.

Not far from the trail, the water ran steady over rocks broken from the slate-like ledges of the region. Ages of water flow had worn their corners smooth. There were some boulders, but they looked of different stone. The rocks were slippery underfoot, shaded and mossy near shore, out in midstream cool gray and burnished by the water, but treacherous when wet. Plenty of water ran here for the salmon that no longer came upriver because of the dams; salmon would have made good winter victuals, salted down in kegs. Still, there probably were no cooper-split staves and made-kegs within a day's journey.

Now the land rose steeper. When he stopped walking and listened, he could hear the water falling on rocks. He turned down to the river again. The steep bank was grown with cedars and spruces whose tops he looked into as he climbed down, whose trunks beside him he couldn't reach around. He came out on a ledge where the river poured over in a steady fall to another ledge and into a pool by the south bank, not a stone's throw from him. Here was the place for a dam that would increase the natural drop of ten or twelve feet to sixteen or more, and hold back between the banks all the water he could use. The ledges would cradle the stone walls he'd lay up to support the timbers for the waterwheel, for the millstones, for the carriage to the saw. The ledges would fracture easily along the seams exposed on the banks and give him stone to lay up as true as bricks. He need not perform the tedious drilling and splitting of the heavy granite he knew in the southern part of the state, and the wall would last through his time and his sons' time, and longer.

Exploring above the falls, he found almost a mile of fast water and pools between the close banks. Then the ravine opened into an expanse of flat, forested land and interval—future farmland. But he was a millwright first, a farmer second. He had found his place at the falls.

CHAPTER 10

CAPTAIN BEDEL GOES TO WAR, 1812

Moody Bedel put limitations on his commitment to the northern territory. He would work there with woodchoppers and settlers, on the roads; he would even swing an axe himself on his own land up near Lake Connecticut, though there was no road to it yet; he would promote settlement, keep in touch with the other proprietors, arrange for the mills with Ebenezer Fletcher, check land claims and performance of settler's duty before approving deeds (there were sixteen families in 1811). But he did not want to live there permanently himself with his young second wife, Mary. He liked the town of Haverhill, the activity, the men of his militia company, the business transactions, and the deals and the politics in the surrounding towns of Piermont, Benton, and Bath. Besides, Mary did not like the prospect of border life.

In Haverhill, the green fields and valley stretching across to Newbury in Vermont, the houses around the common, the stores, the taverns, the schools, the churches, the good roads in all directions, the thriving crops and herds—everything made him feel this was his place, for he had watched most of its growth from a frontier settlement.

Northern lands were for the future; they represented an investment to be promoted and cherished—and exploited when possible. Perhaps in a few years, with the road improved to Fletcher's pitch, and his mills built, the settlement would grow enough to clear a road through to Lake Connecticut. Already John Haynes had decided to make his pitch on the west side of the Connecticut, halfway to the lake from Fletcher's, where the river flowed so quiet men called it "the dadewater." John Perry had his little clearing up on the stream near the lake. Royal Gage of St. Johnsbury was interested in a place at the brook that ran into the deadwater, adjoining Haynes. So in time they'd cut a road to the lake, through the claim Moody Bedel had started work on. But it might be years, and meantime there was the trouble with the British. When he left Indian Stream in the fall of 1811, Moody Bedel did not know when he would return.

The handiest tavern on the way south would be that of Jeremiah Eames in Stewartstown, across the river from Canaan. Jeremiah had become a solid citizen now, mill owner, tavern keeper, dealer in West India goods, selectman, and father of six more children, making a total of nine: Jeremiah, Anna, William, Lois, Persis, Cyrus, Hiram, Emily, and Susan. Adeline would not arrive till 1812. He had prospered as a farmer, also, and raised the best English hay on his meadows, as well as wheat and corn. The upland pastures supported his cattle and sheep. In the common and unfenced land, he identified his stock by cropping square their left ears. (Every man had his mark, recorded in the town books.) And he was agent for the Eastman Company. This last did not prevent him from being friendly with Moody Bedel. Jeremiah had a declining opinion of the Eastman Company, for it seemed almost defunct; nobody down there at Concord cared about northern land.

Both Jeremiah and Moody Bedel knew very well that the title of the Eastman Company conflicted with that of Bedel's group. This didn't interfere with their taking a tot of West Indian rum together. For Moody, possession was the ultimate ownership of the territory; he and his associates and their settlers actually held the land, and many lived on it. He wasn't worried. Everyone knew that Philip, the Indian, had been a tosspot—or so they said—no more able to give title than the village idiot. If Eastman, Bradley, and Cogswell had less power down around Concord, Bedel would not give their claim another thought. Besides, they didn't seem to care a tinker's damn about the land; nobody had been on the land from their company this summer and fall. Perhaps Jeremiah might know their intentions. Perhaps they weren't going to use their title at all. Perhaps they could be bought out cheap.

And Moody was interested in the militia arrangements on the border. Jeremiah would know many men could be called if trouble with Britain aroused Canada.

Actually the War of 1812 came to Stewartstown and Canaan as only a few border incidents, and as a garrison of fifty-two men in the blockhouse on Fort Hill, commanded by Captain Ephraim H. Mahurin of Colebrook, later a company commanded by Captain Freeman of Lebanon.

At Indian Stream, the war halted the settlement's growth. Some of the sixteen families moved away, fearing the proximity to Canada. A few new men arrived. Various persons, not interested in law so much as in smuggling, passed through, lingered in remote camps, maybe wintered beyond reach of all authority. No work on roads or bridges improved the communications of the settlement. Moody Bedel, the moving personality, had gone to war. If the people sold a few cattle over the border in Canada, driving them across the ridge into Hall's Stream valley, nobody bothered them, for they were practically beyond legal process, and the war not really their business.

Unpopular though "Mr. Madison's war" might be in New England, Stewartstown lay at the mercy of invasion from Canada, and regardless of what happened across the river in Vermont, the State of New Hampshire would defend itself. The fort was garrisoned until 1814, and the town became the state's northern outpost. There were only twenty-five legal voters, scarcely more than a hundred and seventy-five inhabitants. They had twenty-six horses, forty-two oxen, ninety-two cows, and ninety-seven head of young stock.

At the fort, news came of the border smuggling, mostly as incidents of customs violations between Vermont and Canada. Lieutenant John Dennett seized oxen that Sam Beach of Canaan claimed he was taking to Canada only to work at lumbering near his mill there. Dennett thought he had been taking across more oxen than he brought back. Oxen were meat as well as power, and in short supply on the Canadian side. In the altercation, Dennett shot Beach. He was charged with murder and jailed in Guildhall, but escaped and lived in the woods until the next summer, when friends of Beach found him and shot him.

A customs officer, Samuel Hugh, swore to stop the traitorous smuggling of cattle into Canada. He soon learned of another attempt and took men in pursuit over the border into Canada, where he halted the smugglers. One of them, a man named Merrill, defied Hugh and overpowered him with a pistol, until Hugh's men shot Merrill and wounded his brother. Victorious this time, Hugh continued his efforts to control illegal traffic over the border, until he was abducted from his house and jailed in Canada for several months.

These border incidents of 1812 and of the two years following had no great effect on the relations between Americans and Canadians after the war. They certainly did not lead to the so-called Indian Stream War of 1835. Both Americans and Canadians were involved in the smuggling; if anything, it established a certain bond between various men. The border area had a geography that made division by an arbitrary line almost impossible. For years, before the war and after it, travel between the two countries was easy and informal. Americans and Canadians held property on either side of the border, and Canadians designated the Indian Stream settlement as part of their township of Drayton. Friendships, intermarriage, and in the area of Indian Stream, even mutual participation in local government, created between Canadian territory and American territory an area in which social and commercial bonds suited the geography rather than the line north of Canaan.

The real cause of later trouble lay in the inconclusive Treaty of Ghent signed in December 1814. It left in dispute between the United States and Great Britain the old problem of the location of the northwesternmost head of the Connecticut River, hence also the territory of Indian Stream.

But during the war, to the settlers there, the cold summer of 1812 brought greater hardship than the conflict. Crops of corn and wheat failed to mature in the frosts of August and September. By the first week of October, the ground froze hard, and snow fell. Not only the people of Indian Stream suffered; all the inhabitants of northern New Hampshire and Vermont shivered as they tried to salvage kernels of corn from shrunken ears, and as they tried to thresh grains of wheat from stalks killed by frost in the middle of August.

By this time, Moody Bedel had taken up in earnest his military career. In May 1812, he set up a recruiting office in Concord. That September he sent almost four hundred new men to the regiment in which he held the rank of lieutenant colonel, the 11th United States Infantry. The regiment was largely composed of New Hampshire men, although stationed at Burlington, Vermont. Moody Bedel moved there with his family and took a house.

Among the New Hampshire men under his command was John W. Weeks, of Lancaster, who became a representative to Congress from Coos County. Lieutenant Jonathan Eastman, of the Eastman Company, served under Bedel when his regiment, the 21st, was joined to the 11th. Eastman and Bedel faced each other six years later as active competitors for the northern land. Two members of Bedel's immediate family enlisted for five years in his regiment: Hazen Bedel, his brother, and Timothy Bedel, his son by his first wife, Ruth Hutchins Bedel. Timothy died that December. After the war Hazen continued in the army for a time, then settled in Illinois.

The number of men that Moody Bedel recruited suggests his powerful, and apparently winning, personality. The war was unpopular in the northeast; Federalists denounced it, Connecticut refused troops. New Hampshire more closely aligned itself, during the first year of the war, with Madison's policies than did Massachusetts and Connecticut. The Federalists in the state, powerful but a minority, did not block the organization of the militia for defense, although they opposed control by the central government. The next year, 1813, they managed to elect a governor largely because the average citizen was opposed to the war on a national level but determined to defend his state, particularly against threats to Portsmouth by the British Fleet.

Moody Bedel was not average, and he had personal reasons for taking up arms against the British. He knew well enough the horrors of warfare, Indian attacks, and the deadly smallpox, but he again undertook a military role that fitted not his age or his inner inclinations, and certainly ran contrary to the lessons of 1776. Perhaps he thought in patriotic terms, perhaps he thought Canada could be easily overrun, perhaps he wanted another chance there, perhaps he was driven by the thought of his father's conduct at the Cedars. In the eventual crisis of his own military role, he acted in a way that his father's commander, General Arnold, would have found more than adequate had he known about the courage under fire displayed by this son of the man he arrested for cowardice.

Moody Bedel later regarded the surrender of his father's troops, under Major Butterfield at the Cedars in 1776, as a justifiable capitulation of starving and smallpox-ridden men to the "merciless and inhuman savages." He regarded the arrest of his father by "the traitor Benedict Arnold, the then Commanding Genr'l.," as completely unjust.

General Arnold took a different view, namely, that Colonel Timothy Bedel's place had been with his troops in the fort at the Cedars; his duty had been to oppose, with those four hundred men and two twelve-pound cannon, the British and Indians who approached. To General Arnold, forty British and three hundred Indians seemed good odds, hardly cause for Colonel Timothy Bedel to hurry back to Montreal for reinforcements, when the news of the attackers arrived. Major Butterfield had surrendered without firing a shot. General Arnold arrested Colonel Timothy Bedel and sent him to Philadelphia. There Congress acquitted him and recommissioned him, with the endorsement of General Gates—to the disgust of Arnold, who had a low opinion of both.

The charge of cowardice must have haunted Colonel Timothy Bedel's son: Moody went to war again after thirty-six years.

He moved his family to Burlington in the early months of the war, but later, as he prepared to leave for Buffalo in 1814, his wife and children returned to Haverhill. He disliked letter-writing, even to his wife. His brother, Hazen, wrote to Mary offering excuses: "You are well acquainted with my brother's antipathy to pen, ink, and paper." While Hazen wrote, Moody slept, for he had been on duty the previous night.

Moody also took lightly some of the army regulations. The march from Plattsburg to Buffalo with the troops seemed an unnecessary hardship, and Moody was fifty years old. He paid for transportation of himself and baggage by stage. This caused no difficulty at the time, for the money—$55.22—came from a Major Barton in the name of the paymaster, Hogan. But the War Department eventually rejected the claim made by Hogan for Bedel's transportation. It held that Colonel Bedel of the 11th Regiment of Infantry had been ordered to march with his men, and was allowed no transportation other than furnished them. Three years after the war, this refusal resulted in Moody's owing J. B. Hogan the amount of $55.22. An irate Hogan, who with difficulty traced Moody to Haverhill, wrote demanding the money or an explanation that would induce the War Department to pay the claim.

Regardless of his attention to his traveling comfort, and regardless whether he paid or explained the transportation charges (explanation seems more likely, both in character and in relation to the hard times of 1817), regardless of Moody's cavalier ways, he conducted himself with valor and distinction at the Sortie of Fort Erie, September 17, 1814.

The fort was in the hands of Americans. It guarded the entrance to the Niagara River opposite Buffalo. The British had been laying siege to the fort for over a month when the American commander ordered a sortie against their batteries and trenches. With General Miller of Temple, who had been promoted after his heroism at the battle of Lundy's Lane in July, Colonel Bedel led his men from the fort. Another column undertook a flanking attack. Under cover of rain, fog, and a barrage from the fort, Bedel and his men crossed a plain and wooded swamp toward the British batteries three hundred yards away. This was no mere raid; sixteen hundred Americans attacked under various commanders, seized two British positions, spiked cannon, and held the trenches during a bloody fight before returning to the fort. More than five hundred Americans and British fell. The British commander, having lost nine hundred men in his earlier assault on the fort, withdrew down the river to Chippewa. The American success was temporary. As the invasion of Canada stalled and failed in November, orders came to pull back to New York's side of the river, and to blow up the fort.

Moody Bedel's part in this war gained him nothing but poverty, debts, and a reputation for bravery. He may have been satisfied with the last, with vindicating the name of Bedel, while he hoped to recoup his fortunes at Indian Stream. In contrast with his father, his war record was untarnished, yet property, money, and security eluded him. His father's estate at the time of his death in 1787 was valued at £10,970. Moody's estate in 1841 came to $155.54. Material success escaped him, but descended to his son John, born at the Indian Stream settlement near Lake Connecticut. John became a lawyer and military man, a veteran of the Mexican War, brigadier general of United States Volunteers in the Civil War (by brevet for gallant and meritorious conduct), an able businessman, and nominee for governor of New Hampshire in 1869.

But John was unborn in 1814 when the Treaty of Ghent ended the war. His father and mother had not moved to the clearing and log house near Lake Connecticut. They would continue to live at Haverhill for another six years.

The terms of the treaty left to arbitration the international situation of the land Bedel and his associates claimed. It provided in article five that two commissioners be appointed to meet at St. Andrews in New Brunswick and ascertain the boundary points designated by the Treaty of Paris in 1783, after the Revolution. The government of Great Britain, advised by the Duke of Wellington that it could not demand American territory because it had not conquered any, yet continued to press its old claim of the Connecticut as the southern boundary of Canada from the Forty-fifth Parallel near Stewartstown to the last trickle of water running into Third Connecticut Lake. The land that Moody Bedel regarded as his own, along the north side of the river as it poured from Lake Connecticut (First Lake), might in the end become British. His service in the war had not secured his land there. In a little irony, years later, the United States government, through the signature of President Buchanan, granted to his widow, Mary, 165 acres in Minnesota for his service in the Revolution.

CHAPTER 11

POSTWAR PURSUITS AND EVENTS, 1815–1819

The settlers of Indian Stream led the strenuous lives of people in a new land. They were too busy subduing the forests and raising crops to be concerned over the factions beginning to split their settlement. Unaware of difficulties other than cold, hunger, exhaustion, and sickness, they merely noted new people moving in and taking up land farther back in the wilderness. These people held varied sympathies toward Great Britain and the United States and were from varied backgrounds, some Canadian, some New Hampshire. Yet others sought a middle way and personal security based on a careful calculation of all odds, as did Ebenezer Fletcher. Some men valued independence while favoring Bedel, as did John Haynes. He and nineteen men traced their titles to those confirmed by the Bedel Company in 1811.

Stirring times, when the Eastman Company would bid for the support of the settlers, lay five years away. That company was inactive between 1812 and 1819. The Bedel Company, however, held a meeting the year after the war, again at David Tyler's house located in "Bedel's and others' Grant." (Most folks called the area just "Indian Stream," as they might say "Colebrook" or "Lancaster.") The proprietors voted to allow another year for completion of settler's duty interrupted by the war. Nathaniel Perkins would make the certification that a settler had cleared five acres and so was entitled to a deed for one hundred acres. John Haynes continued in the office of proprietors' clerk.

This same year—one in which a hurricane devastated Concord and much of New England on September 23, 1815—Ebenezer Fletcher completed his mill. The settlers dragged in their logs by ox team. Ebenezer sawed the logs into boards on his up-and-down saw. A log house was no longer a necessity unless a settler was a newcomer and poor. They also brought bags of corn, wheat, and rye to Ebenezer for grinding between the rough, grooved stones.

Land, more and more of it chopped out of the woods and brought under the plow, produced this grain, and English hay for the oxen that worked it and for the cows that gave the milk to pour over cornmeal porridge. In the summer, upland pastures produced green forage for the young cattle, cows, steers, and a few horses. They fed in the tangled slash of felled, unburned trees. They wandered sniffing across the heaps of wood ashes dirty in the sun, recoiled from those heaps that hid live coals, and browsed to windward of the choking smoke from flaming piles of tree trunks.

The settlers preferred oxen to horses for working in the rough stump land. Oxen were cheap to raise and feed, and they provided steaks when necessary. They did not leap against a yoke if the plow caught on roots or stones. Horses—plunging into the collars or thrashing frantically in mud or bogs—broke harness, plows, and tempers. The oxen were easy, slow, and tremendous in their power. The great roan Durhams towered higher than a man. The livelier, mahogany-red Devons with the spreading horns could walk fast enough to make their driver step quickly to keep up. More common were the mixed-breed, small, tough, frontier cattle.

The oxen dragged logs, pulled stumps, and hauled stone. They hauled sleds of logs to Fletcher's mill, or bags of grain. They lurched slowly through rough meadows pulling sleds loaded with hay in the heat of July. Wagons bogged down or jammed between stumps. Sleds and the more primitive drags made of hewed logs, each with a long tongue and chain to the yoke ring, slithered through summer mud and squeaked over winter snow. The wagons with the two high wheels were used for hauling produce to Canaan, Stewartstown, or north into Canada. The settlers loaded their wagons with the products beyond what they needed to feed and clothe their families. During hard times or in the early years of their pitches they did not have this source of cash and credit.

Dr. Dwight had pointed out that almost anyone could earn $125 to $250 a year from a settlement farm, and be well off. The Reverend Doctor was incurably optimistic. Sometimes the land did not yield that much. But in good years, oxen hauled from the established farms at Indian Stream grain, hides, salt meat, ham and bacon, wool, maple sugar, flax, and potatoes, with a fat steer or two hitched to the tailgate. From the more remote clearings came shingles, clapboards, barrel staves, potash, furs, and moose hides, sometimes in conveyances drawn by two oxen yoked tandem in traces, picking their way single file along narrow trails in the woods. Ebenezer Fletcher had brought his family north with such a rig.

Many of the settlers had nothing to sell or barter, and lived independent of the outside world, self-sufficient on their land for months at a time. If a good year brought a bit of prosperity, markets were far away. A day's trading at Canaan or Stewartstown occupied a man from dawn to dark. A trip to Colebrook, twenty miles south, was not to be thought of often, although the village stores offered a few of the manufactured goods shipped north from industries that had grown in southern New England to meet the shortage of imports during the war. As for Canada, it appealed as a market because Great Britain did not collect customs duties from settlers in territory it claimed was in Canada. Yet the nearest large town, Sherbrooke, was over forty miles away. Hereford, north of Canaan, offered nearer access to Canadian markets of the rural sort; its farm economy had few needs, and the profitable business of supplying British armies no longer increased the demand for beef and grain. The settlers at Indian Stream stayed home and worked.

They mowed with scythes the swale grass and English hay, the tall wheat, the rye, the barley, and the flax. A straight deadly sickle, called a corn cutter, laid over the stalks of corn for shooking. Farmers could raise flax on land now cultivated a few years in crops more tolerant of wild land. Their wives began to use the flax wheels and looms brought from their downriver homes. They wanted their men to raise more sheep for wool, but bears and wolves still raided the flocks, as did bobcat, lynx, and wolverine.

Interval lands produced forty or fifty bushels of wheat to the acre. Upland fields yielded twenty. The maize came to yellow ears in the fall; the small Canada corn—short, sturdy, quick-growing—produced forty bushels to the acre on good land in a good year. Farmers planted recently cleared land to winter rye, for of the grain crops it seemed to grow best in the forest mold of rotted leaves and vegetation, before repeated plowing had mixed the earth. If a new settler had to get a crop before he could plow, corn also grew well when planted between the burnt stumps and log ends. The piles of ashes could be spread around with rakes made of branches, or by chaining brush to the traces of a single ox and driving him over the land. A hoe was not necessary. Four or five holes could be drilled every few feet with a pointed stick, the corn dropped in, the holes closed by stamping on them. The land would then have the appearance of a lumberman's chopping, on which all the tops and limbs had been burned and the naked forest floor exposed. This floor went down a foot or more to mineral earth through ages of rotted leaves, like peat moss interlaced with fine rootlets into a broad mat. The black stumps and buttress roots protruded, the axe marks still denoting the axemanship of the settler: smooth for a skilled worker, gnawed for a clumsy one.

The growing of corn in new, unplowed, forest land had proved successful in Gilmanton as early as 1762. It became the accepted method of the new plantations. Girdling seems to have been taken over as a farm practice from the Indians, for their planting lands along the Saco near Conway included small areas of girdled trees near the natural meadows. It was not suited to the larger fields of the white men, who abandoned it by the time Indian Stream settlers faced the great trees along the upper Connecticut. Felling and burning trees took the place of chopping a ring around them to kill them. The openings in the forest made by girdling soon became a tangle of limbs and dead trunks uprooted by the wind as their roots lost their hold on the earth. The settlers discovered that the task of moving and burning the rock-hard, dead trees was more tedious, and exhausting, than chopping them down green.

Not only trees confronted settlers. Crops failed during the cold summer of 1816. That year came to be known as "1816 and froze to death." The snowstorm of June 17 claimed the life of at least one Vermont man caught in it. Crops refused to grow in the wintry air. Hail and ice storms destroyed apple blossoms, ruining the apple crop. Water froze in July. Snow fell a foot deep in the Berkshires. Birds froze to death and became scarce for several years. Sheep froze to death in exposed pastures. Farmers, dressed in their winter clothes, tried to fight the frosts with fires around their cornfields. This did little except to increase the smoke through which all summer the sun appeared to shine. In the fall, the fires escaped into the forests, tinderdry from the drought, where they burned till winter.

The almanac man, Dudley Leavitt of Meredith, attributed the cold to sun spots. He might have thought the eruption of Mount Tamboro in the East Indies the cause, had he known about it. A complete eclipse of the sun on May 26, and of the moon on June 9, caused fears and consternation in the minds of the superstitious, as examples of God's wrath, while reason itself could not but speculate that the sun was cooling.

The wheat crops surviving the frosts of June and July produced an inferior grain. It did not grind dry and smooth. Bread made from it was soft and sticky. Old Mrs. Pitkin of Colebrook said the only way she could get it out of the oven was to reel it out on a yarn reel. Northern humor could face up to starvation, and so they made bitter jokes, solemnly buried the corpses of the sickly, the aged, and the weaker infants, with tears and a prayer to an angry God, while some cursed Him in their hearts.

Men tightened their belts, and tended to their potash barrels and kettles. They leached out barrels of wood ashes with water "piped" from a nearby brook or spring in log troughs. The lye dripped through a screen of split withes, which formed the bottom of the barrels, into tubs that could be dumped or drained by troughs into huge iron kettles. Days of boiling reduced the lye to "salts." There was plenty of hardwood for the ashes. Spruce, pine, fir, and cedar were no good for potash; men chopped the deciduous trees covering the lower slopes of the ridges, and saved the ashes from hardwoods felled in clearing farmland. A large part of their cash money had always come from this work, but in 1816 cash meant nothing. Crops had failed all over New England. Cash could not buy grain that had not been harvested. The forest crops of moose meat, salmon-trout, rabbit, berries, and wild pigeons were their food, eked out by a little corn or wheat or rye from fields on protected high ground that escaped the freeze, and offered to neighbors by farmers contemptuous of the speculators who roamed the land trying to buy grain at tempting prices.

Cold weather held off that fall. A potato crop matured and was dug at a time when normally snow covered the ground. Some of the potatoes went to the whiskey stills, and this brightened temporarily the gloom of hard times. It also aroused comment about drink being a snare of the devil, especially when drink took food from folks near starvation. The purity of the product was no excuse.

The winter passed. Men and their families survived. They even looked ahead to better times. Not all had been impoverished.

The following year in September, John Haynes bought a thousand acres from David Gibbs for $1,000. This was common and undivided land without surveyed bounds, "situate in Bedel's and associates' Grant, North of Latitude 45 in the United States of America." John would choose and survey from the unallotted, unclaimed land the acreage which best suited him. He had the right to deed two hundred acres to each actual settler.

He lived and farmed on the pitch he had made along the deadwater of the Connecticut above Fletcher's Mills. Five years before the title to this hundred acres was confirmed by the Bedel Company in 1818, he had acquired land near Indian Stream, and soon became the settlement's most active dealer in real estate. Other settlers accumulated land for their own use; John Haynes made a business of buying and selling. He combined the acumen of a Yankee trader with a willingness to work on the land, for the company and for the settlement.

To his duties of clerk in the Bedel Company, 1815, he added those of justice of the peace. For a number of years he certified the oaths of acknowledgment on land deeds, and then recorded them in the Bedel Company ledger. The activities of farmer, land speculator, clerk, and justice in a less energetic man might have constituted full-time work. John Haynes also found days for surveying and exploration of the wilderness beyond his farm.

Another man of diverse abilities, Ebenezer Fletcher, took an interest in land as a sideline to his mills. He had invested as early as 1812 in the common and undivided land offered for sale by John Rowe. He paid $275 for twenty-two hundred acres—certainly not good farmland, at that price, but his mind may have been on the timber, worth very little to anyone who did not have a sawmill. A month later he bought four hundred acres from James Ladd. With the five hundred acres of his mill privilege along the rapids of the Connecticut, this made him the largest landholder of the settlers. He was clearing and farming, as well as building his gristmill and sawmill.

Among the other settlers, Nathaniel Perkins, on the west side of Indian Stream, held a greater acreage than most. When he first arrived from New Hampton he was thirty-three years old and had some money. He bought two hundred acres for $200 from John Rowe in September 1811, and later another hundred acres for $50. Finally, in November, he bought from Rowe the Nathaniel Wales farm on Indian Stream, with its great level interval, deep-soiled and devoid of stones, and its wide west ridge for pasture. This was a thousand acres, and cost him $1,000. With other less valuable land bought the same year his total investment reached $1,300, his acreage fifteen hundred. Fortunate on his land and capable in his farming, he faced with his wife, Dorothy, repeated tragedy in his family. Their son Joshua died in 1815, aged two years, one month, and twenty-six days, as they specified on the gravestone put up in the cemetery within sight of the farmhouse. Three other children died before they lived two years, but six children survived—three girls and three boys. Childbearing, continuous and full of risk, was the common lot of women, and the high mortality of infants a fact of life.

During these postwar years of 1817, 1818, and 1819, the Bedel Company continued to meet each October. Colonel Bedel and his associates were optimistic about the settlement and about a rise in land values. Although Bedel had been away during the war, and continued to live in Haverhill, he made frequent trips to the northern lands. He attended meetings, urged on settlers, and laid out roads. He directed the improvement of the road as far as Fletcher's Mills, two miles upriver from Indian Stream. With the other proprietors, he voted to tax their shares at five mills per acre for such internal improvements within the settlement as bridges, roads, and surveys. They wanted a flourishing community of good farms and valuable land.

Moody Bedel kept in touch with the doings of the settlement in various ways. He traveled a good deal himself, and he had agents looking after his interests. Sometimes these agents were not as reliable as he might have hoped. In 1817, a friend and fellow proprietor in the grant, John Tillotson of Northumberland, wrote that he had encountered in Canada a former agent of Bedel and had arranged for a payment in livestock or other goods on what the man owed Bedel when he absconded to Canada. On the other hand, Tillotson had been unable to collect from John Dean on Bedel's note. Dean did not vanish into Canada, but remained in Guildhall, Vermont, a stalwart, if impoverished, debtor to Bedel, and grateful.

The year 1817 brought to Bedel the request of Paymaster Hogan for an explanation or money for transportation charges. In 1818, the aftermath of the war continued to harass him. As legal guardian of the wife and children of his son Timothy, who died in the regiment during December 1812, Moody relinquished Timothy's right to federal bounty land. In its place he settled for the cash of a five-year, half-pay pension. He made no record of the transaction. His son John, his administrator after his death, had to learn of it through correspondence with the commissioner of pensions in Washington. Moody was an indifferent keeper of records as well as unfortunate in his agent who escaped to Canada.

Because of its liberal land policy, Canada appealed not only to debtors but to legitimate settlers from New Hampshire and Vermont. Canadians themselves found their way to Indian Stream. Migration by men of both countries across the border had an informality that went with the dubious nationality of the area north of the Forty-fifth Parallel and east of Hall's Stream. The Canadian government apparently never granted land there, after 1796, in the township it called Drayton. But Canadians invested in land. David Gibbs sold one hundred acres to a Canadian in 1814. By 1817, Gibbs had located in Hereford, Canada, just west of the territory. The valley of Hall's Stream, a productive farming section of flat interval between protecting ridges, led directly into Canada parallel to Indian Stream. It was accepted as part of the District of St. Francis, Province of Lower Canada. Its southern boundary, marked by the survey of Vallentine and Collins in 1772 along the Forty-fifth Parallel, terminated at the cedar post on the bank of the Connecticut River.

During these years, 1814 to 1819, Bedel and his associates far outdid the other claimant, the Eastman Company, in developing the territory. In 1817, they took from that company its agent since 1801, Jeremiah Eames, who gave up the Eastman job as hopeless. Bedel, Wales (who had returned to the group for a time), and Gibbs offered Jeremiah inducements: a loan of $2,000 and a thousand acres of land with the right to sell to settlers, and to give deeds for land cleared. In return Jeremiah agreed to relinquish his claim under the Eastman (or Philip's) title, and to support Bedel's title. He would assist with surveys, and promote settlement. This success in taking away the competitors' agent and only important representative in the north country (Thomas Eames seems to have become inactive in the company after burying Philip) must have appeared to Moody Bedel the final blow to his rivals.

These men of the Eastman Company, "proprietors of Philip's Grant"—Eastman, Cogswell, Bradley, and others—had found themselves unable to profit from their northern claim. After the early surveys in 1799 and the activity of Samuel Bradley, who, in the fall of 1804, took depositions to support their title, they did nothing. Their few settlers could not cope with the wilderness and left for easier land. A move among some of the proprietors in 1804 for a large sale of land, urged by the Bradleys, came to nothing. Meetings continued in Concord till 1812, without important business being transacted, and without a man emerging who was active, energetic, and interested enough to promote the settlement. The proprietors had varied business and political commitments. To some of them the land company was most definitely a minor interest, a speculation. Pearson Cogswell, a busy lawyer of Gilmanton, also took an active part in the militia and in politics. He became a colonel and a representative in the legislature. Stephen Ambrose, a merchant of East Concord, also in the legislature, was president of the Concord bank.

For seven years during and after the War of 1812, these men did not meet as a land company. Small wonder that their agent went over to Bedel. Suddenly in 1819, they began an active campaign to take over the territory. Their interest was aroused by the business depression, when any company might be valuable, and by the apparently imminent arbitration of the international boundary. Two younger men, Jonathan Eastman, Jr., and Pearson Cogswell, provided the physical drive: they went to the territory in person, although not to settle.

There seems at this time to have been no thought that they might, as a company, influence the legislature to grant them the land they claimed under Philip's title. The state could not be sure it possessed the lands until the commissioners under the Treaty of Ghent finished their deliberations and surveys. The validity of the Forty-fifth Parallel came into question along its entire extent. Was the fort at Rouse's Point in New York or Canada? Was not the survey by Vallentine and Collins astray to the north by about a mile? And where was the northwesternmost head of the Connecticut River? The commissioners and their astronomers would perhaps answer these questions. Astronomers determined latitude celestially, in contrast with surveyors who ran lines by compass.

CHAPTER 12

BOUNDARY CONFUSION, 1783–1817

In the year 1755, with the French and English about to engage in the final struggle for North America, John Mitchell published a map in London. He called it the "Map of British and French Dominions in North America." Six feet four inches by four feet four inches, clearly drawn, it became a standard reference until after the Revolution.

When Mitchell drew his map, the wilderness of the northern Connecticut valley extended south from the source a hundred and fifty miles to the most northerly English fort. The forests had for years sheltered the Algonquian allies of the French in their raids on the English settlements. The most extended, official, upstream exploration in New Hampshire had been carried out by Captain Peter Powers at the head of a scouting party sent by Governor Benning Wentworth. Powers turned back several days' march from the crucial eastward bend of the river, which Mitchell had omitted.

Like other mapmakers of his time, Mitchell relied on "the best information" (as Blanchard described it on his later map) about the uninhabited areas. This information came from hunters, from trappers, from rangers in the service of the province, or from captives ransomed back from Canada. These men also contributed information derived from the Indians themselves. Thus, across the territory between the upper Connecticut and the Kennebec Rivers, Mitchell printed the caption, "Carriages from Norridgenaok to R. St. Francis." This suggested Indian canoe travel, for he meant portages between rivers and lakes; it contributed little to understanding the geography of the area, other than the idea that Indians somehow traveled the maze of projected rivers and lakes.

The map's serious error lay, for New Hampshire, in the arrangement

Mitchell gave to the Connecticut at its source. The river did not run where he drew it on his map. He showed it leading north beyond the Forty-fifth Parallel—upstream—in a straight course, slightly east of the dwindling St. Francis river of Canada, to three lakes on three branches. His mistake had some accuracies in it. The river *did* have three lakes in this twenty miles, but joined by a single main channel. The river *did* flow into New England from the highlands, which tipped northern water into the St. Lawrence, but the river turned east, and much of the area was drained by the tributaries, eventually to be known as Hall's Stream, Indian Stream, and Perry Stream. The error might have been of no special consequence had not Benjamin Franklin, for the United States, and Richard Oswald, the British negotiator, referred to the map in preliminary discussions that led to the treaty concluding the Revolution.

There are other origins of the confusion. Twelve years before the shots fired at Lexington and Concord, the English king found himself, through the foolhardy but successful gamble of General Wolfe, in control of eastern North America. He issued a proclamation that established a northern boundary, east to west, between the old colonies and the provinces acquired by the conquest of Canada. This line was to be the forty-fifth degree of north latitude from the St. Lawrence River east across the northern end of Lake Champlain to the highlands dividing the waters of the St. Lawrence from those "which fall into the sea," namely, the Atlantic. No directions specified how to go from the Forty-fifth Parallel to the highlands in northern New Hampshire. None was needed; the territory was wilderness and all British. An unaccountable jog of twenty miles in the line had little importance.

Meanwhile, the provinces of New Hampshire and of New York began to quarrel over the territory that is now Vermont. Their conflicting claims went back to complications in original charters. New Hampshire's Governor Benning Wentworth granted townships as far west as Bennington and as far north as Maidstone. Under his direction, in March 1760 Joseph Blanchard of Dunstable surveyed up the Connecticut River on the ice from Charlestown, Old Fort Number Four, as far north as the present towns of Haverhill and Newbury in the section known as Lower Coos. Hubartes Neal continued the survey to Upper Coos above Fifteen Mile Falls, setting up markers of stones, blazing trees, and driving stakes in the riverbank six miles apart to indicate the townships. Governor Wentworth granted these surveyed towns to groups of men suitably equipped with money. He reserved land to himself, and had a tidy real estate business going.

New York objected so strenuously that the board of trade became involved. It established a north-south division between the provinces in 1764, the year after the king proclaimed the east-west lines of the northern boundary. The board decreed that the west bank of the Connecticut should separate the two provinces, from the boundary of the Province of Massachusetts Bay as far north as the Forty-fifth Parallel established by the king's proclamation.

Nobody knew exactly where this degree of latitude lay, though it formed so prominent a part of the proclamation, and though it appeared as a line on Mitchell's map. Obviously it lay midway between the equator and the north pole, but where was it on Lake Champlain? Where was it on the Connecticut River? Governor Wentworth's men had not surveyed that far upstream. What is more, nobody cared where it lay. Eight years passed before New York and Quebec undertook a joint survey. In 1771, under the direction of John Collins for New York and of Thomas Vallentine for Quebec, men began cutting a line through the wilderness.

On the first of October in the following year, 1772, John Collins wrote to Governor Tryon of New York from his camp on the Connecticut River. The completion of his work in that section, enhanced by the clear weather of October and by the red and yellow trees under a blue sky, put a note of satisfaction in his letter. He had fixed the boundary between New York and Quebec on the west bank of the Connecticut River, two miles and fifty chains on a direct line beyond the mouth of a small river flowing into the west side of the Connecticut, known as Hall's Brook.

Here, marking the eastern end of the survey that was to be known as the Vallentine-Collins Line, a cedar post became the focal point of a controversy, not between two or three of His Majesty's provinces, but between Great Britain and the United States of America, then a group of restless colonies. Probably John Collins supervised the setting of the cedar post. His name was carved on it. Besides marking the eastern end of New York's northern boundary, the post also indicated the spot at which the Forty-fifth Parallel intersected the Connecticut. Later determination that Vallentine and Collins had been north of the true latitude made no difference; it was accepted for thirty years before anyone questioned the astronomy of it. Today, because the international boundary negotiations of Webster and Ashburton settled on Hall's Stream, a granite monument stands in the approximate place of the cedar post, denoting the northeast corner of Vermont on the Canaan-Pittsburg town line. Maps show the Forty-fifth Parallel about a mile south.

At the time of the 1772 survey, no attempt was made to plot a route to the highlands, logically up the Connecticut River, or to follow the highlands east. New Hampshire, the province involved south of Quebec from there to the District of Maine, had no representative at the survey. This seems odd in view of a New Hampshire man's normal willingness to believe the Yorkers would steal him blind if given half a chance. Quebec, alone, could have surveyed on up the river to establish its claim on the route to the highlands, and to locate the highlands, a vague term in the king's proclamation. But wilderness was, after all, only wilderness, and for either side of the theoretical division, the forest and land came under the jurisdiction of His Majesty's government—if the moose and other furry inhabitants cared to know. More important was a survey at the head of that great north-south thoroughfare, Lake Champlain.

Boundaries to the highlands from other New England provinces had a similarly tentative quality about their northern ends. In 1764 the Province of Massachusetts Bay had sent a party to the Bay of Passamaquoddy in search of the St. Croix River, the eastern bound of its Maine lands. The line between New Hampshire and these Maine lands had been agreed on as the Piscataqua River at Portsmouth, then north from its source two degrees west, "till one hundred and twenty miles were finished from the mouth of Piscataqua harbor or until it meet with his majesty's other governments." Walter Bryant in 1741 measured and blazed about thirty miles of the line, but bad traveling and "alarms as to Indians" turned him back to the coast. Twenty-seven years later, in 1768, Isaac Ringe marked the line to Lake Umbagog but did not push on to the highlands, beyond which water flowed into the St. Lawrence.

These boundaries remained unchanged, except for annual growth of bark on blazed trees and for bushes springing up in the clearings around the stakes marking the miles. The colonies took more and more positive measures against England's policies, and embarked on their own independent troubles by revolution. The Continental Congress, clumsily prosecuting a war of doubtful outcome against a great power, yet looked ahead with sanguine forethought to a peace treaty. On August 14, 1779, it unanimously agreed to the north boundary that its peace commissioner must adhere to in negotiations. This would follow west from Nova Scotia, in the area now New Brunswick, along the same highlands designated in the king's proclamation of 1763. Here, more knowledgeable than the king's commissioners, the congressional committee specified the route across New Hampshire over the jog between the highlands and the forty-fifth degree of latitude, taken to be the line west along the survey by Vallentine and Collins. At the northwesternmost head of the Connecticut River, the line would turn down the middle of the river and follow it to the Forty-fifth Parallel. Here was a northern boundary for the United States (as well as for New Hampshire), to be demanded of Great Britain by a peace commissioner not yet appointed, in a treaty terminating a war not yet won, by a country that could scarcely claim the name of nation, in a territory never surveyed and most inaccurately mapped. Yet it was accepted: the detailed disputes came later.

Whoever the congressional expert coining the phrase "northwesternmost head of Connecticut River," he devised a term that was made for controversy. Had he described it as the source of Hall's Brook, the tributary running from the western end of the highlands, all would have come clear. Probably the British would have accepted it. They were in an accepting mood when, in 1782, Benjamin Franklin and John Jay met with the British peace commissioners, Richard Oswald and Henry Strachey, in France. After discussions about the boundary, Franklin and Oswald marked in red ink one of Mitchell's maps. Most certainly to them, the northwesternmost head of the Connecticut lay in the waters of Mitchell's western lake—which did not exist.

Rumors of this tentative claim by the United States—or of its intention to make the claim, for the negotiations had been secret—reached Canada, where the authorities realized that their new neighbor planned to seek a frontier on Hall's Brook, meaning the present Hall's Stream. Surveyor General Samuel Holland reported to Lieutenant Governor Alured Clarke that the idea of considering Hall's Brook as a frontier, instead of the Connecticut River, appeared to him new. The survey of 1772 by Vallentine and Collins crossed Hall's Brook to the Connecticut, and formed the boundary accepted by the provinces of New York and Lower Canada. Although Paris negotiations had been secret, as was the provisional treaty of 1782, this exchange in March 1783 indicates a knowledge of American plans and a suspicion of the outcome. The final treaty of September 3, 1783, did not clarify the problem, although a New Englander, John Adams, had joined the negotiations. The treaty specified: "along the said highlands which divide the rivers that empty themselves in the River St. Lawrence from those that fall into the Atlantic Ocean, to the northwesternmost head of Connecticut River, thence down the middle of that river to the forty-fifth degree of north latitude; thence by a line due west . . ."

And so the treaty was signed. The fifty-nine-year controversy began. Without even considering all the complications the treaty caused, such as the Aroostook War of 1839 in Maine, it is clear that the treaty's wording could be interpreted to suit two claims north of New Hampshire. Great Britain continued to maintain that the treaty meant that beyond the cedar post, the Canadian boundary should be the Connecticut. This would put the northwesternmost head at a tributary of Third Lake. To Americans this was not northwest at all. They maintained that Hall's Stream was the boundary, and its source was the northwesternmost head of the Connecticut. For New Hampshire this meant about two hundred thousand acres.

But the dispute at first remained undefined. Six years went by before anyone found time to go into the woods and locate the treaty points. General Washington had become president under the new constitution by the time the New Hampshire legislature at last appointed commissioners to survey the state's northern bounds. In 1789, Jeremiah Eames, the surveyor, then of Northumberland, and Luther Fuller, an early explorer of the upper valley, prepared to set out in March, that good month for woods travel. With them would go Nathan Hoit, another commissioner, later to be one of the men listed in the deed from Philip, Indian chief, and a Mr. Cram. Thomas Eames went along to supplement the wilderness knowledge of Eames and Fuller.

Fuller's account of the expedition indicates no hesitation about where the northwesternmost head of the Connecticut might be. He was testifying for the state in 1836, but his story is borne out by an earlier deposition by Jeremiah Eames. Men such as the Eames brothers and Luther Fuller—wide-ranging hunters and surveyors, associates of the Indians, in that time and place—had no doubts as to the lay of the land. They went up Hall's Stream, with packs and snowshoes, perhaps with a hand sled to haul over the crust. Sixteen miles from the junction they blazed trees, scribed them, and took bearings. This was close to being the northwesternmost head of the Connecticut by the American interpretation of the treaty. They then ran a line east-northeast to the highlands between the St. Francis River and the Connecticut, where they blazed more trees in the depths of the forest. Then they went home.

In the fall, the same group, again led by Jeremiah Eames, surveyed the eastern line of New Hampshire from Shelburne to the highlands, where water ran north. On a cloudy, stormy day, they blazed and marked a birch as the northeast corner of the state. They felled or girdled additional trees to mark the spot. Then they surveyed west with compass and chain for a total of seventeen miles, numbering a tree at each mile, till they reached their March line and a big fir tree on Hall's Stream. This was the final northwesternmost head of the Connecticut as they understood it, and so they carved "NH NW 1789" on the fir. They returned down Hall's Stream to Canaan and Stewartstown. Jeremiah kept a journal of his survey.

This was the fall when Nathaniel Wales and David Gibbs camped at Indian Stream to hunt and explore. Jeremiah and his party had surveyed around them.

The New Hampshire legislature made no prominent announcement that it had established the state's northern boundary. Had it instructed representatives at New York, the national capital at the time, to read excerpts from Jeremiah's journal, some national attention might have been given to that section of the Canadian line, and future confusion eliminated.

Canada disregarded the survey, or did not know of it. Samuel Holland, Quebec's surveyor general, in 1792 sent a party to lay out a township east of Hall's Stream. Starting at the cedar post of Vallentine and Collins, the Canadian surveyors ran a line north to mark off Hereford in the west and the new township of Drayton on the east. Drayton would include the fertile valley of Indian Stream, where Wales and Gibbs had begun to clear land and raise crops.

The Canadian survey party did not disturb the New Hampshire men. Neither did the Canadians make objections to the survey of 1799, which Jeremiah made to lay out a township for the Eastman Company.

In the next twelve years further settlement continued by New Hampshire men: John Haynes, Nathaniel Perkins, and Ebenezer Fletcher, among others. Disliking the War of 1812, they found no satisfaction from the national government in the Treaty of Ghent. Its article five could be regarded as a slick taking of the American commissioners by the British. Ebenezer Fletcher in particular kept up with the news, and John Haynes learned of downriver events from his friend, Colonel Bedel. New Hampshire men wouldn't expect much of a Kentuckian, Henry Clay, but they figured that since he wanted the war, at least he could get more than article five out of the British, now that the war was won. John Quincy Adams ought to have known, as a Massachusetts man, that the head of the St. Croix River, on the border of Maine, had been agreed to in 1798 by both Great Britain and the United States. He ought to have been informed that New Hampshire had marked the northwesternmost head of the Connecticut River. All the same, both Clay and Adams as well as others signed the treaty, which declared that these points had not yet been established. It further expressed the nonsense—to a New Hampshire man—that the forty-fifth degree of north latitude had not been surveyed, when everyone knew that the cedar post, where the road from Canaan came to the brow of the hill on the way to Indian Stream, marked the eastern end.

Some of the settlers figured they were in Canada anyway—and glad of it. Others figured they were in New Hampshire—and anyone who doubted it, a fool. Still others figured they were in a secluded, untaxed valley, where a sheriff seldom bothered, or dared, to penetrate, and they wanted it left that way.

A New Hampshire gazetteer, which Eliphalet Merrill published in Exeter three years after the treaty, supported those who claimed New Hampshire had a northern boundary on the highlands north of the Connecticut. According to the declaration on the title page, *The Gazetteer* was compiled from information by the best authorities. Eliphalet Merrill noted the birch on the highlands toward Maine, marked "NE NH 1789" and a line extending seventeen miles, two hundred and seven rods, to the head of the northwesternmost branch of the Connecticut River, where a fir tree was inscribed as the northwest corner of New Hampshire, and down that river to the forty-fifth degree of latitude: Hall's Stream and the Vallentine-Collins line, of course. As that put the cedar post into New Hampshire, so much the better.

The settlers all went back to chopping trees, to raising wheat, corn, cattle, and offspring, back to trapping marten, making potash, building houses of lumber to replace their log houses, and to shooting bears and wolves. A commission had been appointed to meet at St. Andrews, New Brunswick, for surveying and mapping the boundary. Maybe something would come of it.

CHAPTER 13

THE EASTMAN COMPANY COMES TO LIFE, 1819

At the source of the Connecticut River, the early days of October sometimes bring a rush of weather left over from the line storms of September. Clouds settle over the ridges bordering Canada. The mountains south and east lose their sharp fall colors under the gray sky, and they, too, vanish in a pall of rain clouds. The rain arrives suddenly. The sun is shining, then abruptly the light goes out. From the prevailing winds and clouds of the flat Canadian country to the northwest, the shower passes over the valley and becomes a steady rainfall beating down, bleak and soaking. After a day of rain, the wind rises. It blows cold as a chilled knife, and raises whitecaps on the lakes. The streams pour into the Connecticut. With the passing of the storm, frosty nights and sunny days bring the smell of fall into the air—the spice of brown ferns, the earthy fragrance of wet leaves on the ground. Clouds float high, on a still day, in a blue sky over the red and yellow woods. The air is quiet in the bright sunshine. Falling leaves, invisibly released, sift down with the whispering sound of a dry shower.

In October 1819, John Haynes, fifty years old, had an opportunity to go into the woods and be paid for it. Two men, having come up past the prosperous farms along Indian Stream, arrived by horse and wagon at the mills of Ebenezer Fletcher, the end of the road. The men wanted a guide to go with them into the woods. Beyond the mills, this meant going on foot.

They were Captain Jonathan Eastman, Jr., and Captain Pearson Cogswell—to use their militia titles—of East Concord and Gilmanton. John Haynes addressed them as Mr. Eastman and Mr. Cogswell. They explained that their business had to do with the old land company. They were interested in viewing the old survey lines, and in traversing the lands farther upstream. They wanted to see Lake Connecticut and to look over the tracts of land that had not been surveyed or settled. Mr. Cogswell seemed to be the leader and made their interest appear normal enough to John Haynes, who saw no reason for not guiding them.

As Haynes later learned, they did not tell him all their business. If they had, he would have informed them he was a friend of Colonel Bedel and held land by the Bedel title, as did all the other settlers. Mr. Eastman and Mr. Cogswell could get someone else to go into the woods with them. The two strangers were engaged in a devious undertaking that had its origin in the rehabilitation of the Eastman Company. They planned to entice and threaten the Bedel settlers into supporting the Eastman Company's claim to the land.

Jonathan Eastman, Jr., son of the Jonathan Eastman who was one of the friends of Philip named in the Indian chief's deed, had been a member of the company since he bought a 3/16 share of Philip's land in 1798 with Asa Crosby and Samuel Bradley, Jr., for $500. Pearson Cogswell represented the shares bought in 1791 for $5,000 by Thomas Cogswell and others. During the intervening years, Thomas Cogswell, moderator of the company's first meeting, had died. Pearson Cogswell took over, and helped instill new life into the company. A lawyer active in the militia in which he was later to become a colonel, he knew the influential Webster brothers, Ezekial and Daniel. He was a man of substance and initiative, polite in manners; his ability to deal with people surpassed that of Eastman, whose strength lay more in his knowledge of frontier life, of woods travel, of surveying, of farming, and of land.

The Eastman Company had held no meetings for seven years after the start of war with England. Before 1812, the annual meetings in Concord had been scarcely more than formalities. The older men of the company had lost interest in the profitless venture before the disruption by the war made the area still less valuable for land speculation.

By 1819, the pattern of events and circumstances had changed for the better—or so thought some of the younger men in the company, whose attention focused on the pending decisions of the boundary commissioners, on the rumors of improvements and opportunities in the settlement that were attracting more families, and on the decline of business, which made land appear a firmer investment.

The boundary dispute with Canada did, indeed, appear to be nearing a solution, should the provisions of article five of the Treaty of Ghent continue to be followed. Moreover, the astronomers working for the boundary

TABLE 1
Early Settlers at Indian Stream

The first column lists family names of individuals arriving between 1790 and 1820 along with the year of arrival. Also included are a few post-1820 arrivals who played major roles in the dramatic events of 1835. Column two identifies the place, if known, from which the family migrated. The third column shows the number of households named in the 1829 land claims records. The last column links families to the two competing land development companies. See map 3 for many pitch locations.

Applebee (1819)	Franconia, N.H.	3	Bedel
Barnes (1822)		2	Both
Bedel (1811, 1820)	Haverhill, N.H.	1	Bedel
Blanchard (1820)	Haverhill, N.H.	1	Eastman
Blood (1820)	Temple, N.H.	3	Eastman
Brockway (1819)		1	Eastman
Carr (1819)	Lisbon, N.H.	2	
Cummings (1820)	Temple, N.H.	2	Eastman
Danforth (1819)		3	Eastman
Eaton (1819)	Plymouth, N.H.	1	Eastman
Flanders (1819)	Warner, N.H.	3	Eastman
Fletcher (1811)	Charlestown, N.H.	3	Both
George (1820)	Newbury, Vt.	2	
Gibbs (179?)	Haverhill, N.H.	0	Bedel
Haynes (1812)	Lisbon, N.H.	5	Bedel
Holt (1820)	Temple, N.H.	2	Eastman
Hyland (1816)	Bradford, Vt.	3	Bedel
Judd (1813)	Piermont, N.H.	3	Eastman
Ladd (1805)	Hereford, Canada	0	Bedel
Mitchell (1821)	Bath, N.H.	2	Bedel
Orsborn (180?)		1	Bedel
Parker (1820)	Temple, N.H.	3	Eastman
Perkins (1813)	New Hampton, N.H.	3	Bedel
Perry (1811)		2	Eastman
Rogers (1819)	Windsor, Vt.	2	
Rowe (1813)	Lisbon, N.H.	0	Bedel
Sawyer (1821)		2	Eastman
Tabor (1820)	Bradford, Vt.	6	Bedel
Tyler (181?)		5	Bedel
Wales (179?)	Haverhill, N.H.	0	Bedel
Wright (1820)	Bradford, Vt.	2	

commissioners had relocated the Forty-fifth Parallel about a mile south. This added some land to the Eastman Company claim, the area known as "The Gore," south of the southwestern corner of present-day Pittsburg.

Settlers along the streams and rivers, particularly along Indian Stream and in that vicinity, had greatly increased the value of the area. The sawmill and gristmill of Ebenezer Fletcher helped the older settlers prosper; to men searching for a new farm and home, the mills were an inducement for pitching in the territory. A dozen or so of the farms had lost the roughness of the early years. Houses were being built for comfort rather than for primitive protection. The good land along the Connecticut, upstream from Fletcher's

The Eastman Company Comes to Life, 1819

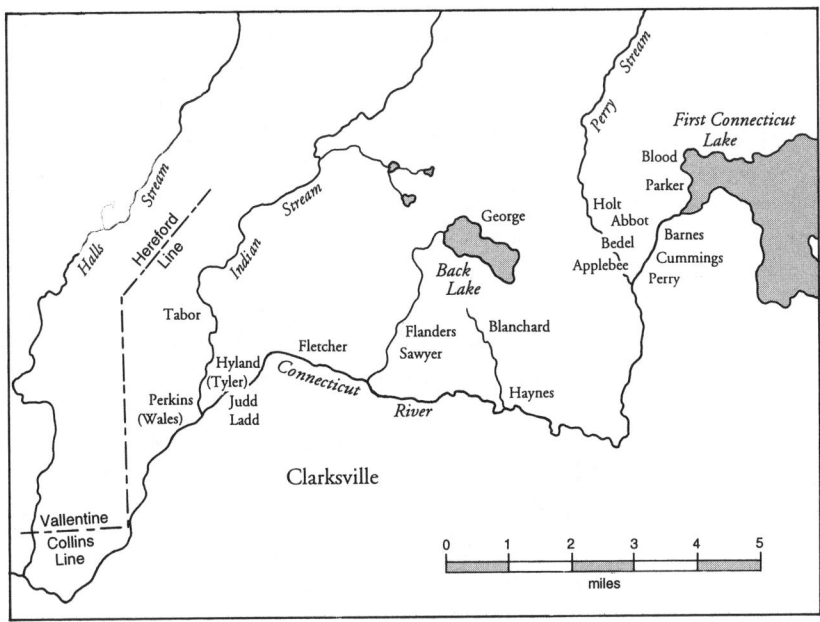

3. Pitch locations for Indian Stream's earliest settlers. See also table 1.

Mills, would follow this same course of clearing and cultivation. Eventually, if the settlement continued to develop under the Bedel title, the Eastman claim would disintegrate by default and neglect. When the state held jurisdiction over the land, the legislature might very easily recognize the title of the group in actual possession, the Bedel Company and its settlers. The younger men of the Eastman Company had no intention of allowing this.

To their considerations of a boundary decision and of growth in settlement and land value, thoughtful men of the company added a justified uneasiness over the business situation. The first great panic of the new industrialism might well continue to weigh heavily on the country for years. Prudent men should preserve land claims whose value might rescue and anchor other ventures of more doubtful security

The proprietors of the Eastman Company talked and exchanged letters. Some of them felt a sense of outrage that Colonel Bedel and his associates should make a claim to land, and encourage settlement on land, that the proprietors themselves had "reserved for that purpose" and surveyed twenty years before. The time had come, they felt, for quick and decisive action. They agreed to meet at the inn of William Smith at Concord on June 3, 1819.

Changes in the organization brought Archelaus Cummings of Temple to represent Ebenezer Edwards. Cummings would in time become the only Eastman Company man to settle on the northern lands. Pearson Cogswell took the place of Thomas and Nathaniel Cogswell, both of whom had died. An aggressive merchant and banker from Concord, Stephen Ambrose, assumed control of the shares of Richard Everett. He favored prompt and strenuous measures against Bedel. He was voted treasurer and clerk; Bradbury Cilley, moderator. The meeting chose a committee for surveying the remaining lands in Philip's Grant, as they termed the area. The word "remaining" aroused discussion of Bedel's settlers squatting on lands rightfully and originally included in Philip's deed. Another survey was necessary. The previous one, in 1799, had been made by a man now with Bedel, Jeremiah Eames. In twenty years, trees had grown up, no doubt obscuring the lines; they should be renewed, and additional wild land surveyed.

Captain Pearson Cogswell was chosen for the committee, and Jonathan Eastman, Jr., and a John Eastman, who took no active part. Jonathan Eastman, Jr., could carry a compass in the woods and could supervise the work of a chainman to measure the distance. He could take charge of packmen to carry equipment and food. Expenses would be covered by a tax of $15 per share on each proprietor. Ambrose and Eastman would assess the tax and make the collection. So it was voted. The problem of the Bedel settlers had not been solved, but could be taken up in the August meeting at Smith's Inn.

That meeting devised a solution and authorized Eastman and Cogswell to put it into effect. They were to circulate among the settlers and acquire legal acknowledgment of the Eastman Company's title, by a document that the settlers were to sign, stating they held their land by virtue of that title. In return, Eastman and Cogswell were to give the settlers assurance of not over two hundred acres.

This amounted to bribing them away from the Bedel Company. The settlers' deeds from Bedel gave them only a hundred acres for settler's duty as defined in common by both companies—five acres cleared and a log house built. Many settlers had bought additional land, but this also came from Bedel or from a member of the Bedel Company. If the settlers were convinced that Bedel's deeds would eventually be worthless, they might—pointed out the thriftier members of the Eastman Company—come over without the incentive of extra land. In the end a compromise measure met the approval of the proprietors. It was embodied in a document for the settlers to sign. An additional fifty acres, over the hundred to be received for settler's duty, would be allowed for fifty days' work on the roads.

The Eastman Company Comes to Life, 1819

Acting for the committee, Jonathan Eastman, Jr., laid in supplies that would help establish cordial relations with the settlers. Naturally he went to the store of Stephen Ambrose on the east side of the Merrimack River in Concord. The store offered broadcloths, "cassimeres," and calicoes. It displayed furniture, nails, glass, brass kettles, and teapots. Useless to Eastman for the northern trip were the black, white, and colored silk gloves, the umbrellas, and the straw bonnets. He bought his supplies from the assortment of West India Goods and Groceries, which included a choice of New England whisky, West India rum, brandy, Holland gin, port or Madeira wines, brown sugar, coffee, chocolate, rice, salt cod or pollock, figs, and teas. Eastman selected four pounds of tea, ten and one quarter gallons of West India rum, one pound of powder, and four pounds of shot. The tea and rum were to be given to the settlers; the powder and shot were for the wilderness exploration. Stephen Ambrose had his clerk make out the bill for $17.19, and agreed to take later payment from the company.

Eastman and Cogswell laid in a large supply of tobacco, packed their goods in a wagon, and left Concord for the north country on October 5, 1819. They stopped at Cogswell's hometown, Gilmanton, where Peter Folsom supplied half a gallon of brandy for $1.00. Then they swung north and west to the Connecticut valley.

They reached Indian Stream a few days later. The farmers of the valley and on adjoining lands along the Connecticut appeared industrious and intelligent, as well as hospitable in offering accommodations in the houses on their well-cultivated farms. The men from Concord saw the country and the people through the rosy glow common in all times to land speculators and real estate developers.

At this point in their excursion they began to look for a guide. When they found John Haynes, they did not explain the entire background of their plans and intentions, nor did they tell him about the rum, tea, and tobacco. Because of this reticence about their motives, he saw no reason for not going with them into the woods, and agreed to guide them for a dollar a day. He would also provide four loaves of bread and a pound of butter. With salt pork and brandy from Eastman's wagon, with partridges, rabbits, and trout from the forest and streams, they would eat well during the four days of their trip beyond civilization. John Haynes arranged for the horses to be fed for ten cents a day. The wagon and other supplies they left at Fletcher's Mills, the jumping-off place, and shouldered knapsacks for the eight-mile hike over the rough track to Lake Connecticut.

John Haynes showed the younger men the clearings along the river, after they crossed Back Lake Brook. They passed one or two cabins and stopped at his own log house for the bread and butter. There the Connecticut flowed slow and still through flat land. The track became a trail as they pushed on to Emor Applebee's new clearing, where Perry Stream dropped swiftly from swamp and beaver meadow into the Connecticut. The man who had been in the area since 1811, John H. Perry, used his cabin and clearing as a home camp for hunting and trapping more than for farming. Farther on, as they neared the lake, the land was claimed by Colonel Bedel.

Because Eastman and Cogswell were interested in the old survey by Jeremiah Eames of a proposed township, John Haynes showed them that the witness trees still existed, and that the lines could still be followed by the blazes on the forest trees. The lines also indicated that some of Bedel's settlers, in the view of Eastman and Cogswell, had no business being where they were.

From the steep rapids at the outlet of Lake Connecticut, they could see the sweep of water beyond the bay, although the southern expanse was hidden by a marsh and wooded ridge. Jonathan Eastman studied the rapids as a possible mill site. The strong head of water and the high banks made the location a valuable part of the land his company claimed. He had heard rumors that a certain Simeon Eastman of Landaff, no close relation, was planning a mill here under the urging and title of Colonel Bedel. Something would have to be done to stop that, but it meant that the wild land above Fletcher's Mills would inevitably develop. Eastman thought that a road would greatly improve the location and would induce settlers to come in.

John Haynes confirmed the increased interest in the new land. Several men from Temple had been looking around. Various young men asked about the land and explored for a few days, feeling disposed to come north another season if they found the right place to make their pitch. The country was opening up—no doubt about it.

In the next three days, John Haynes guided his men through the woods along the north ridge above Lake Connecticut, paddled them up the inlet in a canoe for two miles, and led them on foot toward the next lake. In spite of the weather, which turned stormy, Eastman and Cogswell admired the tall sugar maples, beeches, and birches, which reached up high above the scanty underbrush of moosewood and hobblebush. After their return to Lake Connecticut, they paddled in the canoe down the middle of the lake from the inlet to the outlet, a distance Eastman estimated at eight miles. They could see the great forest through which they had walked.

This they later described to the proprietors as beautiful, with excellent, deep soil suited to farming, rising in gentle swells without mountains or stony ground that made cultivation difficult elsewhere in New Hampshire. Three or four townships could be located in the entire territory, whose fertility of soil and pleasantness of situation would not be exceeded by any town in the state.

They neglected to mention the snowflakes that in all probability came down the last of October with the cold wind, and dusted the tops of the distant ridges. They neglected to mention the height of a mountain eastward toward Maine, which came to be named after the river beyond it, Mount Magalloway, 3,360 feet above sea level. A series of ridges, spruce-topped and steep, extended south into the distance, but seemed remote enough to be in the College Grants rather than in the Eastman Company territory. The ridges north of the lake, 2,300 feet above sea level, would protect the nearer land from north and west winds, would reflect the sun in winter, and would reduce the seasonal cold.

So they returned to the settlement. John Haynes stopped at his house. Eastman and Cogswell went on to Fletcher's Mills after arranging to pay Haynes as soon as he submitted his bill.

CHAPTER 14

RUM AND TEA AT FLETCHER'S MILLS, 1819

John Haynes caught up on his farm chores, and made out his bill. It came to $5.17, the seventeen cents being the charge he made for the pound of butter he took into the woods to spread on the four loaves of bread, which he valued at 50 cents. The guiding he called "Four days deep in woods," for which he charged $4. Care of the horses cost 50 cents ("Horsekeeping 5 days"). He made out the bill to Mssr. Cogswell and Company, for he still was not aware he had dealings with the Eastman Company, or, as they called themselves, the Proprietors of Philip's Grant.

He dated the bill October 25, 1819. He would stop to collect it from Eastman and Cogswell at Fletcher's Mills, then go on to the annual meeting of the Bedel Company. When he arrived at the mills, he learned the true intentions of the men he had guided.

Around Ebenezer Fletcher's massive buildings were gathered many of the men of the settlement, with their wives and children. They stood in groups talking, or sat on the great logs in the mill yard, or on the piles of lumber. Some of the men looked over the large barn Ebenezer was framing of hardwood timbers. They held dippers and mugs of rum, smoked tobacco in pipes, or chewed, as might be their habits, removing the pipes or tucking the cuds in cheeks, and spitting before drinking the rum. Their wives held packets of tea, and sipped at their husbands' rum, or gathered in strictly feminine groups to share news and a draft of water and rum mixed in a cup.

John Haynes noted the festivities of his friends and neighbors. He noticed, also, a few new faces. Eastman and Cogswell were passing out the rum, tea, and tobacco. John Haynes asked them what the prices might be. They said they had nothing to sell, and continued to pour out refreshments for the settlers who arrived at intervals. News of the openhanded men from Concord had reached remoter cabins and clearings.

The significance of the gathering became apparent to John Haynes when he saw Eastman and Cogswell circulating with a document, which most of the settlers signed. Cogswell took him aside, away from the talk and laughter and beyond reach of the rollicking boys and girls, away from the noise of the river pouring over the milldam. Cogswell had with him the document. Politely he asked John Haynes to sign, speaking of the Philip's title, which a signature on the paper acknowledged. The document did not specify what settler's duty was expected, but a signature bound a man to perform it, for which he would receive one hundred acres, and fifty acres more for fifty days of work on the roads.

Said Cogswell, in a flattering way that John Haynes did not like, "You're the very man we want to see to our business here. You'll be well paid."

John Haynes at once told Cogswell that he understood the title or claim based on the land deed of the Indian known as King Philip, and did not want to become a settler under it. Cogswell, joined by Eastman, transferred his attention to the mill builder, Ebenezer Fletcher.

John Haynes walked among the settlers whom he knew to hold land by deeds from members of the Bedel Company. He found that some of them didn't realize what they had signed, some had signed because they were afraid of losing their land, some because they thought it good insurance, as Bedel's title might not be recognized by the state. Various newcomers had signed; they could not yet properly be called settlers, for they had just started their pitches, or were still exploring and might pitch another year. The interest of a few of the young men centered on hunting and trapping; their names did not signify more than intentions.

On Bedel's behalf, various settlers long in the territory, as well as John Haynes, refused to sign. Nathaniel Perkins did not, nor did Samuel Orsborn. Against these, Nathan Judd, although undecided, favored the Eastman title. John Perry and William Hyland actually signed the document.

Although John Haynes was unaware at the time of the extent to which the settlement would be affected by Eastman and Cogswell, he later dated in his own mind the disunity from that October. The bribery and coercion certainly came under discussion at the meeting of the Bedel Company later that day. It was held at Abner Hyland's house, which David Tyler had sold him in 1816. John Haynes presumably went from Fletcher's Mills to the meeting, taking with him the news of the Eastman document. The meeting, under previous circumstances, would have been certain of signing newcomers as settlers. Now four new men—Burleigh and Seth Blood, Abial Holt, and Joshua Parker, all of Temple, New Hampshire—had signed the Eastman paper. Seventeen other men of accepted standing as Bedel Company settlers also had signed. If John Haynes placed this news before the meeting, the proprietors neither made no mention of it in the record nor took any specific action to meet the threat of Eastman competition. They probably relied on the established position of their company in the territory, and pushed forward various improvements for the settlement. The twenty-four members again voted a tax of five mills on each acre they held, to be used in cutting roads, building bridges, and making surveys. They chose John Tillotson for assessor and Nathaniel Perkins for collector. The total tax, when computed, came to $847.21. Collection was more difficult. Perkins and Tillotson had the task of allotting labor against the assessments among the inhabitants. The nonresident proprietors were expected to pay cash.

The following year these measures proved inadequate to oppose the Eastman Company. John Tillotson, who traveled about the state on business of the Coos County Probate Court, heard the news of Eastman activity during the winter, and he realized the danger.

Meanwhile, Eastman and Cogswell completed their business at Fletcher's Mills. They gave up trying to appoint Ebenezer their agent, for he remained undecided. Instead they solicited another longtime settler, John Perry, who agreed to represent them and to continue getting signatures on another document.

The day had worn along. The rum, taking hold of some men, caused the usual problems for wives in getting their husbands home to chores.

An argument between William Hyland and Eastman and Cogswell had causes other than rum. Emor Applebee joined in. Both Hyland and Applebee demanded that their names be scratched off the paper.

William Hyland and his father, Abner, had come to the territory in March 1816. The elder Hyland considered himself a settler under the Bedel title, having bought land from David Gibbs, and later the farm of David Tyler, where the Bedel proprietors held their meetings. When the son, William Hyland, realized what he had signed, he insisted that his name be taken off. Emor Applebee's reasons were not so clear, but "hard words" began to fly. Eastman and Cogswell would not, beyond a point, threaten or antagonize. They scratched out the names, leaving two inky blotches on the document.

Rum, tea, and tobacco had not been sufficient inducements to some of the settlers, nor had the talk of Eastman and Cogswell about a road to Lake Connecticut, a bridge at Fletcher's Mills, and a new mill at the outlet of the lake. Eastman and Cogswell, leaving to John Perry the job of convincing more men, went back to Concord.

John Perry concentrated on the new men in the territory—even those who were merely looking over the settlement and the land. Luther Parker and his older brother, Joshua Parker, Jr., signed. A carpenter and sawyer, appropriately named Elija C. Sawyer, signed. After careful thought, Nathan Judd signed; he had the improvements of six years' labor to protect.

From the former hometown of Moody Bedel, a man explored northward, looking for a way out of his business difficulties, for a new home, or for both. David Mitchell signed Perry's list because the Eastman Company promised a deed to land in return for settler's duty, and David Mitchell suddenly found himself without money. A year or two before, he could have bought all the land he wanted; soon he would be penniless. In Bath, his store and tavern dated back to 1807, when the selectmen issued him his first tavern license. Thereafter he prospered in land, buildings, stock-in-trade, and bank stock. He drove a horse and chaise. He served the town as sealer of weights and measures, was chosen selectman in 1811, and then for five years was voted town clerk. The details of his business failure remained unexplained; he probably was caught, like many others, in the first great panic to seize the nation's new industrialism. During the year or two after 1819, he became a total bankrupt. He and his wife moved north to clear the forest with their own hands, in 1820 or 1821. Twelve years later David Mitchell helped to write the constitution for the settlement.

Of the men on Perry's list, Ebenezer Fletcher finally came around to supporting the Eastman Company by acknowledging that he held his land and mills under their title. More realistically, his signature, and the conditions he laid down, indicated he was hedging his bets on which land company would win the title contest. He held a deed from Bedel for his five hundred acres at the mills. Now he wanted the Eastman Company to vote him the same five hundred acres. He didn't care a row of beans for the hundred acres they offered, and as for working on the road to get fifty acres more, that didn't appeal to a man who had about twenty-six hundred acres of common and undivided land from the Bedel proprietors.

On the back of the paper that Eastman and Cogswell had given John Perry, and on which Perry had taken fourteen signatures acknowledging the Eastman title, Ebenezer Fletcher clearly specified the location of the land to be voted him by the Eastman proprietors, if they wanted his support to their title. It lay for three hundred rods on the north side of the river adjoining the mills, for which privileges of water and falls must be included. It was bounded on the east by the land of Samuel Orsborn, and on the west by the land of Simeon Wright.

The Eastman Company did vote him his land, in 1822, three years later. By that time the State of New Hampshire had brought suit against him as a squatter.

CHAPTER 15

COLONEL BEDEL LOOKS NORTH, 1820

In the winter of 1819–1820, deep snow came early. Under this insulating cover, the first thin ice of the lakes and streams thickened too slowly for safe travel over these winter roadways into the back country. Travel on them remained dangerous. By January, two feet of snow blanketed the country beyond Indian Stream. Spruces carried white drifts in their branches, yet the streams flowed dark and open between white-mounded banks.

John M. Tillotson, a proprietor of the Bedel Company who lived in Northumberland, having been to Indian Stream, wrote of these obstacles to woods travel in a letter to Moody Bedel down the river sixty miles in Haverhill. Plans for a winter survey must be postponed: no use to attempt running lines through the snowy woods till spring.

Tillotson, who at this time held 13,333 acres of the Bedel Company lands, for which he had been assessed $66.66 for the survey and roads, had come into the group of proprietors as early as the meeting in 1811. He then controlled 1/12 share and 1/24 share, under Wales's title. In 1816, Colonel Cutts of Saco in York County, Maine, who bought from Wales in 1804, appointed Tillotson attorney to act for him in handling his 1/12 share. So Tillotson had a big stake in the territory, and reason to be anxious about the activities of the Eastman Company. From his office as register of probate in Lancaster, and from his travels through the state, he heard reports about the determination of Eastman, Cogswell, and Ambrose to take over the territory, to control all the new settlers, and to cajole or coerce the older inhabitants. At the settlement itself, fifty miles north, Tillotson learned through John Haynes the temper of the men in the farmhouses and log cabins. They were restless.

John Dean, the farmer and woodsman of Guildhall, Vermont, across the falls of the Connecticut from Northumberland, who had once owed Bedel money, wrote also about the deep snow. He had expected from Bedel's earlier letter that a surveyor would arrive to begin work at Indian Stream. This would have been impossible in the deep snow, so it was well that Bedel had not sent anyone. Dean personally found himself enduring hard times. Although he had settled the business of the "furrs" to his satisfaction, he needed a "cheep horse," which Bedel might be able to get him. He had heard from Bedel's daughter, Mary Bedel Quimby, and the family was in health. He also had talked to Benjamin Coon up in the territory and learned that Bedel expected to move his family up there soon.

The Bedel Company's survey was held up while rumors persisted about Jonathan Eastman's plans for a spring survey in behalf of his company. Persistent, too, were rumors of easy terms on Eastman deeds and of new roads and bridges to be constructed in the summer of 1820. Tillotson reminded Bedel by letter of his pledge to move to his northern land, and of his promises to the settlers about improvements in the area beyond Fletcher's Mills. Tillotson emphasized the importance of Bedel's presence and influence in the settlement, necessary to secure the claim and title that they based on the deed from the St. Francis Indians.

As the winter dragged on, Tillotson wrote again, in February 1820, offering to go down anytime and take Bedel's family to Indian Stream. He had talked with one of their settlers, who had recently seen Jonathan Eastman. Tillotson thought Eastman's plans for the spring and summer sounded like humbug, but nevertheless, he wanted Bedel to come up by March 1 at the latest. Bedel should take John McDuffee to start the survey. In the complications of the land deals, McDuffee had acquired a voice in the business of the company. David Barnet had appointed McDuffee as his attorney to act in his behalf at the meeting in November 1815. Barnet, then living at Topsham, Vermont, held his land from Hobart Spenser, who had bought it in 1804 from Nathaniel Wales.

Tillotson wrote to Bedel that the cost of the survey should not deter them. He would be responsible for his own share in the expense and for that of Colonel Cutts. Woodsmen to carry the packs and the measuring chains could be hired for a dollar a day. John Dean would help on the survey. Bedel ought to come north by March 1, for Jonathan Eastman planned to start his survey the middle of the month.

They must get ahead of Eastman, repeated Tillotson in another letter. They must prevent his seizing their lands. The settlers were counting on

Bedel, but if he failed in his contract with them, more of them would acknowledge possession of their land under the Eastman Company. This would mean losing the mill privilege at the outlet of the lake as well as the best of the unclaimed land. Possession was an important part of the title.

In the pleasant and busy town of Haverhill, Colonel Bedel opened the letters from the north with a sense of being committed, yet with an inclination to put off his obligations to the settlers and to the company. His assessment for improvements up there was $266.66, a large sum not easy to raise. His 53,333 acres sometimes seemed almost a dream. He had other plans and projects. There were certain bounty lands due him and his father's estate for service in the Revolution, but the War Department had ruled that his father's regiment was eligible only for the year 1776. He kept up a difficult and losing exchange of letters with the Pension Department while old soldiers of his father's regiment appealed to him for help.

The town of Haverhill itself had its hold upon him. He liked the white, square-built, and elegant houses surrounding the snowy common, the red brick academy building, where upstairs were held the sessions of the Grafton County Court. He had seen the town grow; it was home. Reluctant and undecided, he weighed the possible risks and profits of the move to the clearing in the forest up near Lake Connecticut.

His experience in two wars, in politics, in land speculation, and in town organization seemed to increase his reputation at the expense of his fortunes. Now with the national prospects of commerce and credit failing, he hesitated. He knew that the organization of a new settlement was not necessarily profitable. When he was thirty-three, as one of the proprietors of the new town of Coventry, later Benton, east of Haverhill, he had served on the finance committee. He had represented Coventry and Haverhill in the legislature, and he knew the problems of both struggling and prosperous towns. Of course, Coventry was largely mountainous, including the great peak of Moose Hillock; the clearing of land and efforts of farmers in the rocky soil had not increased the value of holdings there to any great extent, except for lumber. In the north, a similar small-scale growth and improvement might leave him without profits again.

The best land had largely been taken up at Indian Stream. And the title from the St. Francis Indians—he had no illusions about the problems of getting the legislature to recognize it as a legitimate claim to state lands, an undertaking that he could not, would not, attempt. Familiar with the political influence and abilities of Eastman, Cogswell, and Ambrose, he knew he might well lose to them through political maneuvering. And the British:

would they make good the line they contended for along the Connecticut? Their Commissioner Barclay was said to be a stubborn bargainer. What a blasted, everlasting shame that the invasions of Canada had failed to settle the boundary for all time.

Besides the considerations of business, he had personal reservations about a move north. He was fifty-six years old, fathering a second family with Mary. Their second son, Hazen, was not yet two years old. This young wife, to whom he had been married ten years, did not think highly of frontier life. All her family ties and friends were here in Haverhill or nearby Bath. The projected move to the upper Connecticut made him think of these things, as well as of the fortune that seemed ever to elude him.

Where was the money from early land sales? Some of it he had turned back into the settlement for work on roads and bridges and for surveys. Accounts and figures were never his strong point, and they became more complicated with the years. Perhaps he should be there in person to promote the company's stake in the settlement, to secure his own share. Perhaps if he lived up there and really looked after his interests, he would realize a permanent return on his money and labor. The boundary decision, whether in favor of the United States or of Great Britain, could be treated as immaterial; indeed, should the land become Canadian, his claim might be better regarded by their authorities than by the New Hampshire legislature.

And he had promised the settlers he would live with them, would organize them into a coherent, secure town that offered new lands for farms and mills. Many of the men were his friends. John Haynes, Ebenezer Fletcher, Nathaniel Perkins would greet him at the end of the long winter journey. John Tillotson had offered transportation, probably sledges and horses over the winter roads, to carry furniture for the log house, bedding, grain, pork, firearms—a thousand things he must tend to. He might postpone the move till summer, possibly ship his household goods on a flatboat above Fifteen Mile Falls. He would talk to Mary. He must first go up there with McDuffee, and take advantage of the good forest travel in March, to make the survey near Lake Connecticut ahead of Eastman. He must stop at Landaff and convince Simeon Eastman that a mill at the outlet would be a profitable venture.

In the next few weeks, he would do well to make other arrangements for concluding his affairs in Haverhill—an agent to see to the farmlands, lumber lots, and wild land in Haverhill, Bath, and Coventry, and to sell the house, if he should make a permanent move north. He would delegate the necessary authority to handle the business of the militia; next year they could elect someone else. He must personally try to collect money due him—a poor year for that!

To the north in less than a month? The thought and the prospect appealed to him more and more. New country, new opportunity. As Tillotson had written, possession formed a large part of the title: all right, he'd take possession. Perhaps he might convince one or two young men that they should go with him and bring their families later. He would talk to a few possible settlers over cigars and mugs of toddy at an inn, but not at Jonathan Sinclair's—his bill there was of too long-standing. And he would write letters to the proprietors about their assessments and about the costs of the survey. Tillotson would help. Then there was Gibbs. David had an interest in these doings. Also John Rowe and James Ladd. He'd get busy.

CHAPTER 16

JONATHAN EASTMAN'S SERIOUS TASK, 1820

In April at Indian Stream, Jonathan Eastman sought someone other than John Haynes to go with him into the woods. Haynes aligned himself more than ever against the Eastman interests in favor of Bedel's group. So, arriving early in the month, Jonathan Eastman talked with the company agent, John Perry, about the list of signatures on Perry's document acknowledging the Philip's title and the Eastman Company.

Among the fourteen names were signatures of men not yet actually settlers on the land. Perry had approached them the previous fall when they were hunting and looking over the country. They fully intended to return this season. The young men especially were interested. These included Luther Parker, his older brother, Joshua, Jr., and Burleigh Blood, all between the ages of twenty and twenty-two, young and strong, who probably would bring others from Temple, in southern New Hampshire. Then there was another young man who signed at the rum and tea get-together the previous fall, Richard I. Blanchard. He would be twenty-one this year, and due to arrive early from Haverhill. David Mitchell, although he might not actually move this year, planned to make a pitch. The territory was attracting men—no doubt about it—and some of them had money. A well-to-do man, Archelaus Cummings, one of their proprietors, thought he might move up from Temple.

Eastman visited around with Perry and met a newcomer named Zebulon Flanders, who seemed to be enterprising and energetic and glad to sign as an Eastman settler. Jonathan boarded with Flanders for two weeks while signing up twenty more men, including Reuben Sawyer, Miles Hurlburt, Samuel Danforth, and John Dinsmore, who had trouble signing, whether from rum or from fingers more used to an axe than a pen, Eastman didn't inquire. The total last fall and this spring reached fifty-four, or fifty-five counting Ebenezer Fletcher's conditional agreement on the back of Perry's document. Jonathan Eastman had a right to feel reassured and more than confident.

All the same, he found that his presence in the settlement did not please everyone. Rumors of threats reached him from men claiming their land under Bedel's title. The suggestion that he head downriver was made by some of the more obstreperous citizens. Others didn't want *any* land speculator threatening the hunting and fishing and trapping—not to mention the freedom of the woods—with schemes for populating the area. Eastman felt capable of handling his opponents. He was a man of courage and determination. Also, there were in the settlement men like John Haynes, on the opposite side in the land controversy, but sober and law-abiding. As a precaution, however, and as a record for the company files, before going into the woods, Eastman wrote to Stephen Ambrose in Concord, describing the serious task he faced this year, and the possible violence.

For a guide to replace John Haynes, Eastman chose Nathan Judd. Younger than Haynes, thirty-four, he had the qualifications, for he had known the territory for ten years, finally settling in 1813 on land he had bought from John Rowe before the second war with Great Britain. By making a pitch, he acquired two hundred acres more, for a total of three hundred. To Rowe, a proprietor with Bedel, Gibbs, and the others, Judd had paid $100 for his first hundred acres. From Rowe, also, he had received the certification for having done the required settler's duty for the two hundred acres. He was definitely a Bedel settler, but now, looking toward greater progress and security, skeptical of Bedel's intentions and ability, he had signed Perry's list supporting the Eastman title and company.

Eastman also hired Zebulon Flanders and Hezekiah Peck to cut timber and haul rock for the new bridge at Fletcher's Mills. This project, approved by the proprietors of the Eastman Company, would be a summer's job that Eastman could not stay to supervise. He would get it started, although actual construction must wait until the snow melted and the ground thawed.

To him the bridge was an important part of the development of the territory. He and Pearson Cogswell had examined the site the previous fall. A bridge over the Connecticut at Fletcher's Mills would link the settlement more directly to the south through the Dartmouth College Grants and Stewartstown to Colebrook—when a road was cut. Should the Forty-fifth Parallel be established a mile south, the bridge would attach this new land to the older settlement. Already men were taking up land on that side of the river, in the College Grants actually, yet considered part of the Indian Stream settlement.

At present, the survey up near the lake must be undertaken, and not in the best weather, for snow still lay in the woods. Although April was more than half gone, the temperature of the nights continued below freezing, sometimes far below. The sunny days had melted the snow from the south sides of buildings and trees, and from open fields with a southern exposure. In sheltered corners, green grass, encouraged beyond the season, waited for spring. The wheat stubble in the fields along Indian Stream had a flattened appearance from the weight of snow pressing down on it all winter. Snow still lingered, coarse and granular, in drifts on the western ridge of Nathaniel Perkins's farm. Cold and sere, hay fields stretched beside the overflowing stream banks.

The ice was out of the other streams as Eastman and Judd carried their packs up the rough track from Fletcher's Mills toward Lake Connecticut. In the low places, tamaracks with their bare branches gave the old beaver meadows an autumn emptiness; an odd tree, the tamarack. In summertime it looked like the spruce or fir; in autumn its short needles formed a yellow torch before they fell; and in winter its twigs stretched out as bare as any elm.

With snow in the woods, the robins and sparrows seemed hardly to belong. They had mistaken the season, but in the clearings they appeared fat and happy, and over the meadows swallows skimmed, looking for the rare insects that hovered in the cool air. A sparrow hawk skimmed the tops of the dead ferns along the edge of the river. From an alder, a blackbird with red wing patches called in a queer, hoarse, fluted note that yet had in it a touch of spring.

Eastman and Judd did not always meet with friendly greetings at the log houses. Perry had not made converts of all the settlers. At the outlet of the lake, Eastman would learn whether Simeon Eastman of Landaff had really started to build his mill under Moody Bedel's title. Stephen Ambrose, as clerk and treasurer of the Eastman Company, was to warn him off unless he agreed to build under the Eastman title.

In the late afternoon a cold wind blew down the trail. Eastman and Judd came to the rapids at the outlet, and to the frozen lake. Ice stretched away across the bay toward the snow-covered ridges of spruces. The wind blew chill, bringing the barking call of ravens from the east. As the sun lowered, a howl came downwind, faint and distant. Timber wolves were in the moose yards. At dusk the howling changed from the wailing, high-pitched, drawn-out tones descending to a moan, and became the quick, eager, growling cries of the hunting wolf family.

Stories of the great gray woods dogs persisted—of their attacks on lone hunters, on cabins in which women and children had been left alone—but the real woodsman had no such fear or belief that the wolves were dangerous. New Hampshire offered a $12 bounty for a wolf head. Wolves attacked sheep and young stock as readily as they dragged down a moose calf or deer, or even a bear when woods hunting was poor, but with uncanny intelligence they kept out of a hunter's way and usually avoided his traps.

But if not needed for protection from wolves, a log shelter is warmer than the open woods, and a fire of birch bark and spruce twigs, set aflame by flint and steel and tinder, can be built up to a roaring bonfire. A man can skewer a slice of pork on a stick over coals raked from the big fire and catch the drippings on bread. He can heat a ramrod for a rum toddy when the wind blows colder. Watch a big hare, still in his white winter coat, hop into the firelight—and away again with a leap as a rifle hammer clicks . . .

The next day, Eastman found no mill at the outlet of Lake Connecticut. He noticed little change since the previous fall, when he had been there with Pearson Cogswell. A few blazed trees, a clearing and burned stumps, with the best logs piled on a ramp, and ox tracks in the snow, melted, old, beside those of boots, might mean the beginning of Simeon Eastman's works, or they might mean that a settler had cut logs, which he would float down the river to Fletcher's sawmill. There were no signs of a mill frame or of a foundation, although the latter might be hidden under the snow that lay deep beside the rushing water.

With Judd carrying the chain, Eastman held the compass and directed him as they set up stakes, blazed trees, and took bearings at the corners of lots. They managed to survey ten lots of one hundred acres each, in a hurried and inaccurate way, through the snow and rough country. Late the following day they started back down the river.

At the settlement, Eastman found a letter from Stephen Ambrose, acknowledging his account of conditions in the territory. Violence, wrote Ambrose, was a typical expedient of men trying to seize the property of others unjustly and unlawfully. "Your opponents seem determined to supply the deficiency of their title by violence and intrigue." Ambrose added that he had no doubt a prosecution would be commenced after the June meeting.

Also, he had written to Simeon Eastman, and hoped that Simeon would "not be impetuous enough to plunge himself into difficulties in this business." Jonathan Eastman did not see the actual letter to Simeon. It was a masterpiece of diplomacy. First, Ambrose warned Simeon against trespassing on Eastman Company land at the outlet. If Simeon built under the authority of Bedel, they would "contest every inch of ground," because they had a prior and better title. On the other hand, if Simeon wanted to make his improvements under the Eastman Company title, they would "feel pleased to find you amongst the number that contribute to turning the wilderness into a fruitful field."

Jonathan Eastman could do little more in the territory, and his spring planting awaited him on his farm in Concord. He paid Nathan Judd $2.34 for going to the lake with him, and 25 cents for the bread and pork that Judd supplied. To John Perry he owed, and paid, $1.50 for boarding and "five knights horsekeeping." This last seemed rather high, compared to Haynes's 10 cents a day for horsekeeping the fall before, even adding the board bill. But Eastman paid. The company proprietors might have something to say when he presented the bill. If they did, he could mention that it was a small hardship for them to endure, compared to his, here in the territory of Indian Stream in Bedel's Grant . . . in Philip's Grant . . . whatever it was called. Jonathan Eastman was ready for home. He had been away almost thirty days—plenty long enough! He would pay Zebulon Flanders for board and lodging, and then be on his way.

He made one stop going down the valley, at Stewartstown, to arrange with William Tirrill for payments on the bridge that Flanders was to build at Fletcher's Mills. Because the leading citizen, Jeremiah Eames, had gone over to Bedel, Eastman could not approach him to act as agent, and for some reason, he did not appoint John Perry again. So Tirrill would act as agent in the bridge enterprise, paying Flanders as the work progressed. Eastman could spare only $31.65 in cash, but it was enough to start the bridge, and represented his good faith. Tirrill signed an agreement, which was also a receipt for the money. Eastman's horse had cast a shoe; Tirrill provided a shoe and nailed it on for 34 cents. Eastman set out for Concord.

The proprietors in their June meeting approved his bill. It came to $272.96, for the thirty-five days, and covered his wages and all expenses, including the bridge payment. None of his associates offered to go north to see how the bridge progressed. Archelaus Cummings was planning to go up later, after the crops were in, and take with him a few men from Temple, perhaps in mid-September. The other proprietors, having been assessed for the cost of the work and the survey, had paid their tax—most of them—and considered that enough.

After harvest time, Jonathan Eastman himself returned. He found the bridge built near Fletcher's Mills, the first span of the Connecticut in the settlement. Looked at one way, it was an achievement to be proud of; another way, it wasn't. Had he been there himself, he would have insisted on better stonework and higher piers, to put the timbers up above the highest flood level. Any fool could see the old scars on the trees, which marked the high water of years back—not recent, but still possible.

He thought of the bill he had received for the bridge, a labor of sixty-five days at a dollar a day. Zebulon Flanders and Hezekiah Peck had worked together, so that sum represented about a month's work, or a little over five weeks. They had used oxen for thirteen days, which figured to $9. And a gallon of whiskey for "getting on things" came to $1. The total bill was $75. Not much for a bridge, really, and the structure might last a good many seasons, if an unseasonable hot spell in the spring didn't melt all the snow at once and pour it down the river with a flood of ice slabs before it.

Already the bridge had been used. Marks of muddy sledge runners crossed the logs and planks. Oxen dragging against the yoke had sunk deep into the mud of the new track leading to Fletcher's sawmill. A man came out of the woods on the opposite slope, carrying a bag of grain on his shoulder, and stamped across the bridge, his boots making a series of hollow thumps audible above the rushing water. The bridge demonstrated to the settlers that the company meant business in developing the territory. Seventy-five dollars was cheap enough for such an advantage over Bedel.

For his fall survey, Eastman hired Reuben Sawyer to carry the chain. Sawyer charged only fifty cents a day, for he was anxious to help this representative of a company that would make something of the territory. He lived in a log house on five cleared acres, to become part of the hundred-acre lot Eastman surveyed for him. David Wells, another newcomer and signer of the Eastman paper, provided victuals and lodging. They surveyed ten lots in the area to be known as the Hill Settlement, up the river from Fletcher's Mills and west of the long deadwater where John Haynes had his farm. To Eastman's mind, the land belonged to his company. Sawyer agreed, and some of the other settlers acknowledged the title of the Eastman Company. Others did not, and threatened both gunfire and lawsuits in the name of Bedel, whose surveyors had already been over the area. The gunfire threat might be disregarded as mere show and talk. New Hampshire men seldom resorted to firearms in personal quarrels. The threat of lawsuits could be considered empty because of lack of cash to undertake them, and because court jurisdiction in the area was vague to the point of not existing. Eastman kept on with his survey.

And yet, times were changing. Men who had never thought to look toward the north since the War of 1812 now spoke of the vast territory there. They began calling attention to the claims of Bedel and his associates, to the Eastman Company claims, to Canadian claims. Where did New Hampshire stand among all these claimants?

In the month of November, following Eastman's return to Concord, the prediction Ambrose had made in April came about. The legislature listened to a motion brought by Jeremiah Mason of Portsmouth. Mason, one of the lawyers who had joined Daniel Webster at Exeter on behalf of the trustees of Dartmouth College three years before, now as chairman of the Judiciary Committee of the New Hampshire legislature, recommended legal action against the squatters north of the Forty-fifth Parallel.

CHAPTER 17

MOODY BEDEL IN THE LAKE SETTLEMENT, 1820

Meanwhile, to the north, Moody Bedel took stock of the unpromising, late-summer crops in the new clearings. The meal barrel in his house was almost empty, and harvest still weeks away. In tune with the hard times of the nation, Bedel's settlement beyond Fletcher's Mills struggled against time, poor crops, and the surrounding forest. The area that Bedel was developing included his own clearing and log house, as well as most of the land from Back Lake to Perry Stream, up to Lake Connecticut, and along the northern shore. He had laid out a road to take the place of the old trail from the mills. The work of cutting trees and pulling the stumps went slowly, for there wasn't enough man power. In time it would be passable to ox-drawn sledges, and later to horses and wagons. Logs and grain would go to the mills and return as lumber and meal. Time—that was the problem; all work took time—the surveying, the farming, the clearing of land from the vast forest. For Moody Bedel there were also the trips down to Haverhill, to Concord, the meetings with the settlers, and always talk—talk of organization, of hard times, of bad debts, of labor required for the road, of failing markets, and always of whether they really owned their land. Bedel's many obligations and activities kept him far busier than the average settler, but they contributed no provisions to feed his family.

In August, he wrote to John Tillotson asking for some corn. Tillotson was surprised that John Dean had not told Bedel about the crop problems around Northumberland and Guildhall. Of forty bushels of corn expected from a man named Pike, Tillotson had received only twenty. He could send one bushel of corn and two of rye. John Dean would send a bushel and three-quarters of corn. Tillotson thought this would carry Bedel and his family until he harvested his own grain in the fall.

In the territory, particularly up by the lake, mid-August constituted, very nearly, early fall as John Tillotson knew it fifty miles south. Any crop not ripening before mid-September was in danger of a killing frost or even of snow. This short season in another year or two—with better-cultivated land after the first crops, with manuring and spreading of wood ashes, with earlier planting—would not be so critical. Also, cattle would thrive better on good hay raised in fields and stored in barns than they did having to survive on swale grass scythed in wild meadows and put up in stacks open to the weather. Living would be easier, food plentiful, cattle fatter.

Bedel accepted the grain, although it put him in the odd position of taking one and three-quarters bushels of corn from John Dean, a man who had that spring been laboring under "poverty and opposition," and needed a "cheep horse." It could be considered as payment on an old note. Collections were almost impossible, and all debtors seemed hard up.

Then in September, Tillotson rode up the Connecticut valley and visited Bedel, deep in woods, as Haynes had phrased it, though not so deep now, with the new road a-building. The land along Perry Stream, interval land, and the slope along Lake Connecticut, facing the sun, looked suitable for farms. Plans of the lands, which he claimed with Bedel, would enable them to place the new settlers.

The settlers arrived soon after Tillotson returned home to Northumberland. On his way he bought provisions in Canaan and Stewartstown, leaving them with Jeremiah Eames at his inn, for Bedel or one of his men to pick up: shot, powder, pork, a quart of West India rum, crackers, and $2 in cash, to be used in the settlement and in the fall surveying.

The new men who stopped to see Tillotson were from Temple, New Hampshire. Of the ten, several had been in the territory before. Archelaus Cummings led the group. He was forty-two years old, a representative from Temple in the legislature, and a shareholder in the Eastman Company. He had worked with the settlers' list the year before, when Eastman presented it to the December meeting. His farm in Temple was one of the best in town, for he followed in the steps of his prosperous father of the same name.

Cummings, despite his close association with the Eastman Company, stopped to talk with Tillotson, and said he planned to see Moody Bedel up at the Lake Settlement. Some of his men—including the three Parkers, Joshua, Sr., Joshua, Jr., and Luther; the two Holts, Abial, Sr. and Jr.; and Seth Blood and his son, Burleigh—had signed as Eastman settlers, although more as an indication of intention and as insurance than as actual settlers. They were a closely knit group bound by ties of blood and background. The young men had grown up together in Temple. Seth Blood had married Archelaus Cummings's sister, Betsy, so Burleigh was Archelaus's nephew. They had explored the territory and favored land near the lake, no matter who owned it, claimed it, or could make it available to them.

Tillotson loaned them his land plans before sending them along to see Nathaniel Perkins on Indian Stream. Perkins favored the Bedel title and was certain to deliver a few arguments in its behalf. Then the group would go on up the Connecticut past Fletcher's Mills to see Moody Bedel himself. Bedel, forewarned by a hurried letter from Tillotson, must show them the best land, whether it lay in his division or Tillotson's: thus they might convert ten of Eastman's settlers to their cause and to their land.

Still later that fall, in October 1820, Tillotson was asking Bedel, at about the time Jonathan Eastman again arrived in the territory, to find out where Mr. English, "the old Doctor Astronemer," would establish the international boundary line. Also, other men were coming to settle or look about. Mr. Quimby and some men intended to settle and bring up their families that winter.

During that depression year, such families, because of the proximity of the territory and because of friends or relatives preceding them, trekked north from the main flow of westward migration. Twenty new clearings and log houses were chopped out of the forest by new settlers. The number of improvements had doubled in a year, and the number of inhabitants accordingly.

In the remoter clearings, settlers clung to the edges of the forest by lonesome grit or by hope in the future. Some must stay because they had sold out and had no place to which they could return. Some lived in the rudest of log shelters and hoped for a big catch of furs to bring cash: marten in the spruce forests of the ridges, beaver in the upper brooks, wolves, moose, bear, raccoon, wildcat, weasel, muskrat, fisher, mink, lynx, deer (a few, for they did not become plentiful until the 1830s), and sometimes caribou over on the Magalloway. They not only counted on the forest animals for money in the form of fur, but for food, and to some extent for clothing. Also they caught the trout in the streams and trapped the myriad wild pigeons, which sometimes nested on the northern ridges. But when the meal barrel was empty and game scarce, men—and particularly women—longed for the old days in the lower valley.

Young, unmarried men sometimes went back to their parents' homes for the winter. Family men, hoping to move north in a season or two from poor, stony farms, or from land mortgaged beyond saving, would work on their clearings and log houses for two months in the fall, and return south to spend the winter with their wives and children. By the following March, they might all head north with ox sled and household furnishings, axe and rifle. Three of the young men who stopped to see John Tillotson that fall, Abial Holt, Jr., and two of his friends, planned to marry and return with their wives in the spring. Luther Parker had large plans for the future, of which this venture in the new settlement might be a minor part, a speculation.

And John Tillotson, by a messenger named Kemp from Orford, sent Moody Bedel two pairs of ladies' shoes for his wife, Mary.

CHAPTER 18

NEW HAMPSHIRE JURISDICTION AT INDIAN STREAM, 1820

Down in Concord, during the autumn days of November 1820, the legislature adopted a motion to investigate the settlers north of the Forty-fifth Parallel. Proposed by Jeremiah Mason of Portsmouth, a former United States senator and present chairman of the Judiciary Committee, who towered six feet seven inches tall, the motion resulted in the appointment of an investigating committee, with Mason in charge. Of the four men appointed to help him, two were Eastman Company proprietors: Archelaus Cummings, recently returned from Indian Stream, and Stephen Ambrose, who that spring had warned a Bedel man from the outlet of Lake Connecticut, and had written Jonathan Eastman that he had no doubt a prosecution would be commenced after the June meeting. The committee's report recommended legal proceedings against the settlers.

Whereas it has been represented to this legislature that sundry persons have unlawfully entered and intruded upon certain lands belonging to this state situate in the County of Coos and northerly of the tract of land which was granted to Dartmouth College,

Resolved: that the attorney general be and he is hereby authorized and required to institute due proceedings in law against such of said persons as he shall deem proper in the name and behalf of this state and the same to prosecute to final judgment, to the end that the said persons in case it shall be found that they have unlawfully entered and intruded upon said lands may be removed therefrom.

The legislature passed the resolution on November 27, 1820. The Eastman Company, in its December meeting, appointed Archelaus Cummings agent to sell land, but the next day voted to await the results before proceeding because it was "inexpedient for our agent for selling Lands to sell any until after it is ascertained what Course is pursued by the State." The following June, the company appointed Pearson Cogswell to defend any of their settlers against suits by the state. At this time, Ebenezer Fletcher and Abner Hyland were not settlers under their title. Ebenezer's conditional signature on their document had not been accepted. Abner Hyland had never signed it, and his son William had made Eastman and Cogswell scratch off his name. By an odd coincidence, the attorney general chose Ebenezer Fletcher and Abner Hyland to prosecute for trespass on state lands.

Intrigues to discredit the Bedel title and to force out his settlers may have been the ulterior motives of the Eastman Company proprietors. Jeremiah Mason had a larger problem in mind: the northern boundary of New Hampshire. An adjustment could be expected from the work of the committee negotiating under the terms of the Treaty of Ghent. The American agents, Bradley and Ness, were holding out for Hall's Stream or Indian Stream, whereas the British continued to claim the Connecticut from Third Lake to the Forty-fifth Parallel. A legal proceeding that established New Hampshire's jurisdiction over the disputed area—including Moody Bedel's recent improvements, John Haynes's farm, Ebenezer Fletcher's mills, and Abner Hyland's farm—should strengthen both the claim of the United States and of New Hampshire, for Canada had never attempted or enforced jurisdiction over the territory.

Attorney General Sullivan, of the silver-toned voice and moving oratory, drove to Lancaster and filed informations in the May term of the Coos County Superior Court. This most northern court, a county division established in 1803 from the earlier county of Grafton, represented the law nearest to the disputed lands and settlers (or squatters, as they might be). Although Coos County had no positive northern boundary, the Coos sheriffs were sometimes called upon to penetrate into the area above the Forty-fifth Parallel, which might or might not be Coos. An excursion of the law into the territory of Indian Stream required sufficient courage on the part of the sheriff, backed at times by firearms.

Sullivan named in his two informations Ebenezer Fletcher and Abner Hyland as trespassers on state lands. The cases dragged along for six years, the court again and again declining to rule on Sullivan's repeated accusations. During this litigation (the details of which were consumed by a fire in 1886 at the Lancaster Courthouse) three major consequences developed beyond the immediate question of the guilt or innocence of Fletcher and Hyland of technical trespass. First, the New Hampshire legislature defined its view of the boundary. Second, the Eastman Company turned from legal intrigue, which had backfired, to attempts to push confirmation of their title through the legislature. Third, the legislature by resolution granted to the settlers lands in their actual possession.

Attorney General Sullivan, or at his instruction, the county solicitor, brought into the case testimony from the early surveyors, with a view to establishing New Hampshire's earliest claim and jurisdiction. Jeremiah Eames, Thomas Eames, and Luther Fuller were summoned to the Lancaster court. They testified concerning their survey of 1789. They had surveyed north between New Hampshire and Maine, from Shelburne. (At that time, Maine was a district of Massachusetts, but by the time they testified, after the Missouri Compromise, it had become a separate state.) They had reached the highlands bordering Canada, where water drained north. They had then struck out west along the height of land to what they interpreted as the northwesternmost head of the Connecticut River—Hall's Stream—and down it to the Forty-fifth Parallel.

This testimony brought out in court and for the records that New Hampshire had surveyed the disputed area. Whether the evidence would influence the boundary negotiations seemed doubtful, for they were approaching a stalemate; it was a legal bulwark to a more aggressive claim in the future.

The Eames brothers and Luther Fuller did not get paid for their trouble. The legislature refused to honor their accounts of expenses until 1837, at which time Jeremiah was no longer alive. A committee had to review for the legislature the circumstances surrounding their testimony. Thus speedily did events leave behind the first decision of the court, in 1823.

During the May term that year, the court returned a verdict against Abner Hyland. This Bedel settler, after seven years' work on his 320-acre farm that he had bought from David Tyler for $700, found himself legally a trespasser, according to New Hampshire law, on land that might not, however, be within the state. The Superior Court ruled that the Indian Stream lands belonged to the state, and rendered judgment against "the intruders on that ground," as Attorney General Sullivan described the cases to Governor Badger in 1835. More involved legal maneuvering followed in the case of Fletcher, against whom a verdict was finally returned in the November term of 1827.

Meanwhile, the Eastman Company began petitioning the legislature in June 1823 to grant it the lands it claimed. A legislative committee appointed by the House, headed by Ezekial Webster, Daniel's brother, recommended a grant of the lands for 2 cents an acre. In spite of the influence of Ezekial

Webster, and of Pearson Cogswell, a senator in the New Hampshire legislature, the resolution on the report was postponed indefinitely in the House.

Planning and consultation between Cogswell and the Websters continued. For political reasons, they abandoned a scheme for a grant from the United States Congress. The New Hampshire legislature turned down a petition sponsored by Ezekial Webster and Archelaus Cummings, but the Eastman Company *did* press close to success. The June and November sessions of 1824 *did* consider the petition at length. A committee *did* report favorably. The northern men who had not signed as Eastman settlers were living on the brink of ruin, as was the Bedel Company, for their claims might become the property of the Eastman Company. If that happened, the settlers would be reduced to the poverty of owning only the personal belongings they could salvage, and the Bedel Company's title would be destroyed.

During the June session of 1824, the petition of the Eastman Company reached a committee whose chairman, Jeremiah Mason, had originated the court cases against the settlers. His committee now recommended that the House postpone action on the petition until the courts gave a final verdict on the northern lands. To provide firsthand information at the November session, the House should appoint an investigating committee. This was done.

At the fall session, three representatives, headed by Wilson of Lancaster, reported on their study of the territory. They sidestepped the questions of jurisdiction and land companies, but covered the subjects of land values, population, farms, and boundaries. They believed that about half the land had no crop value. Much of the good land seemed to them as fine as any in the northern part of the state. They set a value of $5 an acre on such cleared land and estimated another hundred thousand acres to be worth $1 an acre. They had gone into the woods along the northern boundary surveyed by Eames, and down the Maine line to the land granted to Atkinson and Gilmanton Academy, then returned to the Connecticut along the line of the Dartmouth College Grant, which had not then become Clarksville.

Their report was at first tabled by the House, until a representative from Exeter, William Smith, Jr., who had presented the Eastman petition in June, made a motion that it be taken up by Ezekial Webster's five-man committee. This committee, about the middle of December, returned a version of the northern situation that showed the Eastman Company as the active benefactor of the territory, encouraging settlement, building roads, bridges, and mills. Webster's committee recommended that prosecutions of the settlers be stopped.

Several days of legislative discussion and maneuvering followed. Webster's committee finally offered three resolutions. These were to the effect that: (1) the land north of the Forty-fifth Parallel, and outside Maine, Vermont, and Lower Canada, be incorporated into New Hampshire; (2) the land in the possession of actual settlers be given to them, up to two hundred acres; and (3) the remaining land be turned over to the Eastman Company.

On December 22, 1824, the legislature passed the first two resolutions. Opponents of the Eastman Company, unconvinced of its benign intentions and benevolent past, rallied and voted down the third.

The men of the Eastman Company, noting the delicate balance of votes, remained hopeful. They continued in the following years to petition for the remaining land. They also realized that their company required such a grant for its existence, because the state now claimed the land that had not been allotted to settlers.

The case against Fletcher continued also. The Eastman Company, having agreed to his conditions for his support of their title, had voted him in 1822 the five hundred acres he claimed. It took upon itself the defense of his case, with legal advice from a future secretary of the navy, Levi Woodbury, who had been governor in 1823. The final verdict against Fletcher in 1827 did no more than confirm the state's jurisdiction; the legislature had already secured to him by the Resolve of 1824 an area of two hundred acres along the Connecticut at his mills. Abner Hyland, not so fortunate because of his earlier conviction of trespass, had not "owned" his farm for a year, until the Resolve of 1824 restored two hundred acres of it to him. Later, Attorney General Sullivan never instituted proceedings against Hyland or Fletcher based on the judgments, because a resolve of the legislature prohibited it without a further order from that body.

Four years of litigation, petitions, and legislative moves resulted in New Hampshire's confirming itself in its jurisdiction over the territory. The tactics of the Eastman Company had crystalized the state's policy in the north.

All this time, Great Britain maintained that the area was part of Canada. In the debate, British Commissioner Barclay held out for the northwest stream emptying into Third Lake, thence down the Connecticut to the new Forty-fifth Parallel. One American commissioner, Van Ness, was willing to settle for Indian Stream as the international boundary, but the Vermonter, William C. Bradley, to whom fell the principal advocacy of American claims, would settle for nothing less than Hall's Stream and the Vallentine-Collins Line. Along the boundary in Maine, similar conditions of stalemate developed. The commissioners returned the problem to their governments. Four years of surveys, debates, and conferences had resulted only in the division of the islands in Passamaquoddy Bay. Although the Treaty of Ghent's fifth article provided for such disagreement through arbitration by a friendly sovereign state, five more years went by in negotiations that finally laid the tangled question before the king of the Netherlands.

In the meantime, the settlers at Indian Stream received whatever benefits they could from the Resolve of 1824. It became a landmark in the history of the territory, without actually settling the land controversies. On the positive side, it established a precedent in state policy, a general "right" of the settlers to their land, which formed the basis for a legal title that might be evidence of ownership to Canadian authorities, should the boundary be run to the south. On the negative side, the Resolve seldom secured to a settler all of his claim, because of the limitation to two hundred acres, and because of incomplete surveys. The deeds given by the Bedel Company, and the few from the Eastman Company, pointed up the injustices and inequalities caused by the Resolve.

Nathaniel Perkins and Jeremiah Tabor, farmers of the fertile Indian Stream valley, profited more than the other settlers. The Resolve granted Nathaniel seven hundred acres, and Jeremiah four hundred acres. These grants, however, represented less than half of the land each man had bought.

Jeremiah was not satisfied, with good reason: he had paid $700 to Nathan Smith of Stratford for one thousand acres. His farm lay a mile from that of Perkins, where the northern ridge protected the rich meadowland along Indian Stream. The soil was dark and without stones, until it rose into the pasture and timberland that extended west to the Hereford line and north to the ravine that came to be known as Tabor Notch. From his fields, Jeremiah could look across the Connecticut valley to the hills of the College Grants. Technically, six hundred acres of this fine farm by law no longer belonged to him.

Other men had complaints, often originating in the faulty practices of the two land companies. Their claims were not confirmed by the Resolve because the land had not been surveyed, because surveys conflicted, or because deeds were not clear or had not been given by a company at all. Settlers in the area above Fletcher's Mills found their claims unconfirmed because the surveys of the Eastman Company and those of the Bedel Company overran each other. The state ruling was strict: no accurate survey, no land.

And beyond the uncertainties caused by New Hampshire's administration of the Resolve lay the unanswered question of international ownership. The settlers uneasily awaited the outcome.

CHAPTER 19

MOODY BEDEL, 1820–1823

By a combination of bad luck, poor crops, and a wife unhappy with frontier life, Moody Bedel lost the benefits of the Resolve of 1824.

After his first winter in the north, 1820–21, in the spring he found himself short of hay for his cattle. He planned to expand his hay fields, and John Tillotson had located some grass seed for sale by a man named Sargent who lived in Colebrook, two miles back of Judge Loomis's farm. But the seed did not fill the bellies of his cows and oxen. A month of snow and cold remained before he could put the cattle out to pasture. Tillotson wrote that Jeremiah Eames, whose barns usually contained plenty of extra hay from the meadows along the Connecticut at Stewartstown, could not spare an ounce. Eames would let Bedel have some grain against what he owed Bedel but had no spare hay. Ebenezer Fletcher, however, had hay. He would take Bedel's oxen and keep them till warm weather—might buy them, in which case he'd let Bedel use them that spring.

Wheat seed for spring sowing was scarce. Equally scarce was any grain—wheat, corn, or rye—for grinding into meal. In June, Tillotson sent up a bag of corn from John Morse, who wanted to be remembered to Bedel and might go up later and make a pitch. John Dean left Bedel two bushels of wheat at Judge Ingham's in Canaan. Tillotson sent three bushels of wheat to Eames, for Bedel and his settlers, from Jesse Hugh and others who had learned of the scarcity and wanted to encourage the settlement. Would Bedel please return the bags.

In that spring of 1821, the trespass cases at Lancaster had begun against Hyland and Fletcher. Pearson Cogswell, appointed by the Eastman Company to defend the settlers under the Philip's title, had more concern for the interests of the company in its relation to the jurisdiction of the territory than he had for the fate of the settlers as individuals. Besides, originally Hyland and Fletcher had been Bedel settlers.

The question of title again came to the front. Bedel and Tillotson were aware of this. A man from Maine provided them with a sworn deposition that Philip the Indian had no right to convey land to the founders of the Eastman Company. John Whittemore of Rumford swore that forty-five years ago Philip had been "cashiered and banished by the Indians and forfeited all rights as a chief or brother."

The Eastman Company determined on a policy that would play down its Indian title, having through its legal advisors come to the conclusion that they must correct the legality of the flimsy conveyance, which they well knew was outlawed by the federal government and by state legislation. The general interest in the court suit, and in the prospects of the territory, gave the company a prominence that forced discretion. Moody Bedel stayed clear of the controversy. Attached for the time to the land and to the people, he counted still on the actual organization of the settlement eventually carrying the legislature in his favor.

Other problems continued to bedevil Moody Bedel. In March 1822, after another long winter, he learned from Ira Young, a lawyer who had been practicing law for two years in Bath, that Jonathan Sinclair had become restless about a bill Moody owed at his inn. Young, a friend who had visited Bedel at his wilderness farm, regretted having to accept the action. Sinclair's bill covered items of minor importance from between 1816 and 1819—from the viewpoint of a man with Bedel's background and experience, ones almost too minor to list. They were part of the larger purchase of sixteen bushels of salt.

With salt at the price of $2.00 a bushel, Sinclair could easily have thrown in the day's labor of a man and cart and oxen, but no, he charged Bedel the sum of $1.00. He also charged 60 cents for twenty Spanish cigars, probably a legitimate charge. But as to the item of a half mug of toddy and a cigar for 15 cents . . . what a small way to do business! The cash advance of $2.00 was correct. But Sinclair had allowed him only $2.24 on the 280 feet of clapboards Bedel had given Sinclair against the bill.

The price of salt, $2.00 a bushel, might be called high. Times were changing, but all the same, salt once sold for $1.00 a bushel on the coast of Maine. But that was forty years before. Values a man learned in boyhood were his measure of commodities, property, and possessions all his life.

Bedel owed Sinclair $39.87. Everybody owed someone those days. Even prospering John Haynes—industrious, shrewd in his steady way, and careful—owed money. According to Ira Young, a promissory note from Haynes formed part of a widow's estate. The widow needed the money. Would Bedel spur Haynes up a little? Mr. Haynes, commented Ira Young, being out of reach of process, would consider that in itself an inducement to pay.

With no illusions about the difficulties of serving a writ near the source of the Connecticut, Young understood also a quality in Haynes's character, a sense of honor. Haynes might indeed be out of reach of normal legal action and might remain in the security of his remote farm along the Connecticut above Fletcher's Mills, a farm that might be in Canada, where a bear could raid the sheep or a moose come from the woods to feed on a haystack. There a sheriff had a dubious right to penetrate, and a still more dubious reception would await him from some of Haynes's neighbors. Yet Haynes was a man who paid his just debts, without a sheriff making attachments. His own conscience was his sheriff and writ.

Moody Bedel knew John Haynes's character. Other men in the territory might find themselves visited by sheriffs of Coos County, particularly in the future if the case against Abner Hyland proved that New Hampshire had jurisdiction. A man such as Horace Loomis, down at Colebrook, was a sheriff capable of going into the woods after his man. That man would never be John Haynes.

To Bedel, Ira Young seemed hardly more than a boy, for he was only twenty-five. Ira's father, a Revolutionary soldier, and his mother lived in Lisbon when Ira was born. A lad still, to Bedel, but capable and amiable, and a good lawyer already. He had become active in the militia. Ira liked the north country. Bedel had no way of knowing the future, but Ira liked it well enough to move to Colebrook a few years later, and in another few years would find himself in command of the 24th Regiment when the adjutant general called out the militia to subdue the men of Indian Stream—which had nothing to do with the debts of the moment and was still thirteen years off.

Other personal matters at home occupied Moody Bedel's mind. Mary was carrying another child, due late in June or early in July. She missed her relatives and friends in Haverhill. She did not like the Lake Settlement. The cold emptiness of the land in early spring made the days drag, as though summer would never come. The mud of the cart track past the rough house, the bark and logs and ox sled in the dooryard appeared as flotsam from the endless winter. Distant smoke over the bare trees might reassure her that people lived in the wilderness—the Holts, the Parkers, the Bloods—but it was not Haverhill, with its people walking across the common to get their mail or to trade in the stores, with its children going to school over the green grass, with its elms budding above the white houses and the brick academy.

Moody Bedel had also occasion to think about his father in that spring of 1822. A hearing to be held on bounty lands stirred Bedel to search for papers to prove his father had served to the end of the Revolution. He traveled to Bath and Haverhill for the purpose. He never accepted the ruling that his father's regiment was in the "continental establishment" only during the year 1776. His father, whose commission had the signature of John Hancock, had served at the capture of St. Johns on the Richelieu River in 1775, of which Israel Morey of Orford had written to the Committee of Safety at Exeter that Colonel Timothy Bedel "behaved exceeding well in that affair etc. and that he Does honor to ye Colony of N.H. etc." His father's conduct the following year at the Cedars brought down the wrath of Arnold but caused no official damage to his record, because he was acquitted and recommissioned. Of course Arnold's name subsequently became synonymous with traitor. His father had continued to be active in the militia, had served on a committee to prevent the transportation of grain from Haverhill in 1780, and in 1781 had represented the town at the General Assembly at Windsor, Vermont. If trouble arose in establishing his military service to the end of the war, it would be during these years. Moody Bedel might never prove his father's right, and his as heir (or as a member of the regiment himself) to the bounty lands Congress had voted.

His father's men continued to write him about their service records. The men would be old now, their claims obscure. The problem brought back memories of horror: smallpox, starvation, mud, flies, blood, scalped heads, hatred, and fear. So much to think of from a short letter by John Dean reminding him of the court session dealing with bounty lands for that old war.

The growth of the settlement itself absorbed Moody Bedel. In 1822, for the first time, the inhabitants met and organized themselves into districts for roads and schools. "Surveyors of Highways," chosen at the meeting, supervised the volunteer workers. They had more impact on the swamps and woods than did the 25 cents that Jonathan Eastman paid Samuel Danforth for filling in a mud hole near Gage Brook.

On July 8, 1822, Mary Bedel had a baby boy. Mother and child survived, and the baby was named John—a simple name and a remote start for a brigadier general in the Civil War. Like all his generation, at his birth the world was not very different from earlier centuries. The task of plowing for wheat was no faster than in the days of pharaoh. By the time of his death, steam tractors rolled across the prairies, and iron horses on rails sped across the continent. The minds of men had seized the theories of Darwin with less enthusiasm.

No solution to the land claims of the two companies appeared that summer. John Tillotson continued to investigate on behalf of the St. Francis title, which he shared with Bedel and the other proprietors. He acquired a copy of "Ben Wentworth's Commission" from the crown, and thought it favored them. Ill though he had been since May, and "with scrip on my side," he went to Concord. Back in Northumberland, he wrote to Moody Bedel in August 1822. In his opinion, the state was "sick of their job . . . and the resolve would have been repealed this session, could the matter have been brought before the house." A committee had been appointed to investigate. Thus, the group in the legislature that opposed the Eastman Company's petitions for land during the following years appeared strong enough to Tillotson to discontinue the prosecutions of Hyland and Fletcher.

Tillotson sent his letter by a millwright named Elisha Abbott, who had tended for many years the Phelps Mill in Piermont, New Hampshire. Abbott now wanted to help build and operate mills at the outlet of Lake Connecticut. Tillotson thought a sawmill, at least, could be completed by fall. Simeon Eastman was perfectly willing that Bedel have the privilege of building, as the proprietors had voted.

This was the origin of a land controversy that continued through the years. Bedel in 1822 had arranged or agreed that another man take over the mill site, whether for cash or for building the mill is not clear. Peter Barnes did build a combined sawmill and gristmill. A few years later he claimed between five hundred and seven hundred acres, a parcel stretching up the ridge from the lake in an area cross-hatched with the survey lines of both Bedel and Eastman. Barnes claimed in 1830 half of Archelaus Cummings's betterments, more than half the land of Huggins, all of Abbott's, and that of some others.

Elisha Abbott, in spite of the controversy, stayed on. He was a powerful man, as attested by a mention in 1842 of the physical strength typical of the Abbott men in a diary kept by the historian Francis Parkman. A younger Abbott, probably Elisha, Jr., guided Parkman to the valley of the Magalloway and, in a log canoe, down to civilization. Parkman had then completed his sophomore year at Harvard. He described the younger Abbott as having complete self-confidence, mentioned the traditional great strength of the family, and noted that he was an accomplished axeman, who was well-read in history and various other fields but disliked fiction. Abbott was "resolute and independent as the wind."

The year 1822 brought further cares and sadness to Moody Bedel when John Tillotson died. Bedel lost Tillotson's friendly interest and encouragement; his death also weakened the company and the prospects for unification in the settlement under one title.

The Eastman Company had not given up entirely its projects in the north. Hesitating while the cases against Hyland and Fletcher remained in the Coos Court, the company instructed Archelaus Cummings, now living in the territory on the Connecticut below the outlet of the lake, to refrain from pushing land sales. It did send Pearson Cogswell north to promote a road to Maine. He took the names of forty settlers who were willing to work on the road. Most of them signed to work out $10, but Rufus Brockway subscribed $20 and Ebenezer Fletcher $25. This scheme appeared later, during the days of the area's "independence." It did not succeed then, although once again there was interest from the citizens of Maine, who agreed to cut a road from their side of the wilderness. Cogswell's document described them as "the inhabitants of that country." The road from Lake Connecticut was to leave Burleigh Blood's clearing and run northeast around the lake, then southeast over the height-of-land and (probably) down the valley of the Dead Diamond River to the vicinity of the Maine line above Lake Umbagog.

Pearson Cogswell made a true copy of the original document when he returned to Concord in June. The original bore the date of May 16, 1822. Blackflies then were not out in force at the settlement, for snow lingered in the deep woods and along north slopes, with ice still in some of the lakes. Mud, thin and slippery on claybanks or bottomless in the swamps, turned the roads into ribbons of muck, bridged in the worst lowlands by a slippery corduroy of logs whose bark had been peeled by hoofs and sled runners to a shiny, treacherous footing of inner wood. Rain, snow, and sleet were in season. Carried by Pearson Cogswell through such weather and terrain, the document needed copying; worn and weathered, written on by forty hands, it was unfit for presentation to the legislature with the other records of the Eastman Company's public works in their northern lands.

Rufus Brockway helped Pearson Cogswell tend to the business of the company. For three days' work he charged only $1.50. Rufus would run afoul of Sheriff Loomis in a few years. A signer of the 1819 Eastman paper, he had been settled for three winters in the territory. He was a woodsman given to travel and letter-carrying. He had been on the British survey party of Tiarks and Carlisle about 1820, searching for the northwesternmost trickle of the Connecticut River system draining into Third Lake. He and John Hughes of Canaan disagreed about the distance to the St. Francis River in Canada. They stood on a steep ridge above the lake, surrounded by hardwoods rising into the upper spruces that topped the ridge toward Canada. Tiarks and Carlisle decided they had found the ultimate point of the British claim and went back to Stewartstown.

Moody Bedel's wife left him in March 1823. She returned to Haverhill with John, not yet a year old, a daughter, Annaugusta, and Hazen, who was five.

Bedel stayed on in the Lake Settlement with a son and daughter, Moody, Jr., and Marion. He felt stricken with grief, deserted, and old. He was fifty-nine.

One evening in April 1823, he was sitting by the fire in his house when his son Moody came in with a letter brought by a neighbor, or perhaps by the carrier Rufus Brockway. The boy told his father it was a letter from "Mam." The father read it with an expression of hope that turned to agitation, which he tried to conceal from his son. It was his first news of his wife and the younger children since she had left him. To cover his emotion, he busied himself giving his son bitters and supper, then sent him to bed. The out-of-doors seemed to offer relief, and he wandered in the cold April night under the northern stars before returning to the house.

The letter had not been from Mary but from her nephew, James Hunt, at Bath. Mary and the children were staying at Moody Moor's house. The baby, John, had been very sick; under the care of Aunt Moor he seemed to be improving. Annaugusta had the ear ache for one or two days; otherwise the older children were well and having good care. James Hunt offered an opinion: "We all think they are better ovit then they ware up there with you." Hunt also thought it would be better for Moody Bedel to come down to Bath "then it will be to stay up there in that cold climate."

This bland assumption and advice by his nephew-in-law enraged Moody Bedel. Who was the "we" meant by Hunt? The welfare of the children was Bedel's concern—his and Mary's—not that of some vague family members.

As he read on, he became convinced the children were not merely living on family charity, but were to be paupers on the town. James Hunt wrote that Elija Hunt wanted young Moody to live with him till he was twenty-one. Daniel Bedel wanted Marion to live with them until she was eighteen. These offers meant town care to Moody Bedel, for he could not believe that family charity would extend so long. Yet James Hunt had the temerity to write that "we" think them better off!

Hunt offered further advice, that young Moody and Marion ought to come down so they could go to school during the summer. And in the last sentence he urged Moody Bedel to write to "Mrs." as soon as possible.

When Moody sat down to answer the letter, he thought not of James Hunt but of Mary and the children. His thoughts were incoherent. He had no paper, could find none, and wrote on the back of Hunt's letter, carefully avoiding the outer fold on which Hunt had addressed him, "Gen. Moody Bedel—Indian Stream," before sealing the letter with red wax. Words rushed off the tip of his pen. He had to reread and make inserts for clarity, because one subject led him directly into another.

Coming to cheer his Father Spirits and make him forget his Troubles and advanced years. Alas Alas, Dear Children, a town charge or Town's Poor or Paupers, Situated thus by an Unfeeling, Cruel Mother unnecessarily, but I respectfully pray God to forbid it . . . If the children are supported by the Town of Haverhill, why not let the support come here with them, where they can be a-earning something in order to enable me to Pay the Town again, for there they are doing nothing but an Expence—if I had them with me you could go to work and Earn Sumthing towards their support. You told me that Mr. Goskins offered you a Dollar a Weak (this was occationed I suppose by one of your unreasonable conversations), but if he will, you could Do with One-Third of it if you were prudent, and you ought to be, and the rest could help Support the children, and as you have had luck in hoping to get to Mr. Goskin's again in order to have an opportunity to take your last Degree where you had your first, and now if you will have Patience—I say have Patience—I will help you there so that you can take your last degree while you are capable of receiving it . . .

Moody Bedel went on to write in a confusion of distress, love, entreaty, regret, and hope—a flood of words forming essentially a love letter. He was plagued by grief, tears, and sleeplessness. He felt that their differences in age and temperament—her sensitivity, his irritability, her homesickness, his preoccupation with the settlement—had been more the cause of their separation than the bitter life in the north.

Moody Bedel could stay no longer at the Lake Settlement. All the land in northern New Hampshire was not worth the loss of Mary and their children. He moved to Bath and gathered his family together.

By doing so, he lost his chance to receive a deed from the state for two hundred acres of his land by the Resolve of 1824. One of the requirements was actual possession—meaning personal residence on the land. Perhaps he thought the parcel too small and trivial compared to the thousands of acres he claimed. Perhaps he felt insulted—angry certainly, for he was human—or amused when he learned of it. The irony, that he should be denied a share in the settlement he had promoted! But in his heart, he did not intend to relinquish his third of the territory.

CHAPTER 20

ENTER LUTHER PARKER, 1819–1828

Another settler, of another generation, also happened to be away when the New Hampshire legislature adopted the Resolve of 1824. Luther Parker might have received a deed securing two hundred acres on which he had worked since 1820, but he was in New York State teaching school near Albany.

Luther, like most of the settlers, had a complete New England background. He was born in 1800, the second son of Joshua and Polly Parker. His family went back to a Thomas Parker, who had arrived in Massachusetts from England in 1635. His parents moved from Reading, Massachusetts, to Temple, in southern New Hampshire, before he was born. His father was a farmer in the standard New England tradition of freeholder or yeoman. This Parker tradition included independence of action when pressed; Luther's grandfather, Asa, joined a kinsman, Captain John Parker, one early morning at Lexington, Massachusetts, on a day of history, April 19, 1775. This independent spirit took shape in Theodore Parker, unorthodox Unitarian, transcendentalist, and ardent abolitionist, who was born ten years after Luther in a different line of the same family.

Luther's father apprenticed him to a shoemaker in Stoneham, Massachusetts, when Luther was sixteen. This may have been a legal and binding arrangement, a virtual indenture with papers signed before a justice, or it may have been (more likely) an apprenticeship, during the winters only, for several years. Shoemaking at the time was winter work, for farmers or fishermen during the snowy months. Friends, relatives, and neighbors worked in a central shop on leather put out to them by local merchants and tanners.

Often these men hired a student or young scholar to read to them in history, politics, law, and philosophy. The saying came about that a Lynn shoemaker was fit to be a United States senator. One from Natick, Henry Wilson, did become vice president. Perhaps such readings and an awareness of a wider world sent Luther back to school. He learned his trade and took it, with his kit of tools, back to Temple. He abandoned neither the skill nor the kit during his lifetime, for he was to spend his years on the borders of civilization, and he had need of all the crafts of artisan, woodsman, farmer, and trader, as well as of book learning.

He enrolled in the academy at New Ipswich, five or six miles from Temple toward the valley of the Souhegan River. New Ipswich had a more flourishing past and a more promising future than the surrounding towns. There a lad might think beyond a life on a hill farm. The academy had been established in 1789, almost thirty years before Luther went to classes. New Ipswich had also attracted industry. A waterwheel in a cotton mill had started to turn there in 1803, one of the first in New Hampshire. More prosperous than nearby areas in both farms and mills, New Ipswich benefited from a soil of greater fertility and from the mill privileges along the Souhegan.

Temple at this time had an agricultural population whose members found the land difficult to cultivate. This was common; indeed, it was the ordinary lot of the New Hampshire farmer outside the fertile valleys. Yet Temple flourished in spite of its moderate productivity. During Luther's boyhood, almost 1,000 inhabitants lived on the rocky and hilly farms—941 at one time, of whom 139 paid polls. The principal road from Amherst to Peterborough passed through the town. A Congregational Society had built a meetinghouse. Four gristmills and three sawmills provided food, lumber, and employment along some of the streams that ran down from the Temple Mountains to the west and north. The farmers worked with 167 oxen and 107 horses. They grazed 750 head of cattle on their uneven uplands. Of these, they milked 377. They mowed hay in the fields tediously cleared by their ancestors who settled there before the Revolution. They pruned and harvested the trees of 84 acres in orchards.

By the time Luther grew to manhood, the town had reached a population level that left a young farmer little choice but to move away. The attraction of more fertile land also began to catch the interest of older men; a number of farmers, including Luther's father, began to listen to tales of better land to the west and north. Particularly they heard rumors of free land— "free" for settler's duty—from men connected with a Concord land company. Archelaus Cummings took over the share of Ebenezer Edwards and in 1820 was appointed agent for the sale of the company lands. He talked about the northern territory to his neighbors in Temple. It was former Indian land, unorganized, untaxed, and also practically beyond reach of legal process on debts, an attraction to more and more men as hard times deepened. But the attraction that caught young men was the chance to earn their own land by clearing the wilderness. Joshua Parker, in 1819, took his two older sons north with him to look around.

The effect of this trip on Luther, then nineteen years old, must have been one of release and excitement. The ride up through the fruitful Connecticut valley during those October days could have been only an invitation and a revelation. Fields stretched for miles along the winding river in the older towns of Charlestown, Lebanon, Hanover, Orford, Haverhill, Lancaster, and Northumberland. The fields that Luther saw required no years of backbreaking work with oxen, chains, and stoneboats to clear the stones, or the agonizingly slow laying up of walls at the rate of sixteen feet a day. The valley soil showed deep and clean where streams ran down from the hills in the little ravines and vales, cutting through pine lands (pine trees now remained only on untillable slopes). The soil showed smooth and without a stone in the furrows of fall-plowed fields. The pine trees had given their dead roots and stumps to fences between the fields, where the wheat, oats, corn, and hay had been harvested. Maples flared red and yellow along the roads and on the hills; syrup and sugar came from the spring run of sap.

On the Connecticut River, men steered flatboats loaded with barrels of pork, bags of wheat, barrels of potash from the northern forests, bundles of shingles and clapboards, bales of wool. Men steered with long sweeps, poled over shallows, sailed when the wind was fair. They floated on rafts of lumber, watching the current, maneuvering the clumsy craft with poles and sweeps. The roads also carried produce to market, wagons pulled by oxen or horses, and droves of steers, sheep, geese, and turkeys moving along under the care of boys and dogs and men in smocks and with broad hats on their heads, the boss drovers on horseback.

The river itself would fascinate a young man headed north. It moved slowly, wide and powerful, and its source in the distant wilderness of forests and lakes and streams signified adventure. On the river the necessities of that distant country went upstream: salt, gunpowder, lead, traps, firearms. As the valley narrowed, these goods were transshipped to smaller boats, their cargoes of more civilized use: steel and iron for blacksmiths, kegs of cutlery, boxes of pots and pans, small tools from the shops of Connecticut, barrels of dishes and glasses packed in straw, barrels of molasses and of salted fish. Also included were castings and forgings and machined parts such as mill irons for up-and-down saws, ring gears, bevel gears, and turned shafts, not to mention plows, harrows, scythes, axes, hammers, handsaws, window glass, looking glass, desks, bureaus, bedsteads, and rum—always barrels, kegs, and jugs of rum.

The crews of the boats—aided by the rum—would shout songs and would drop the sails, then pole the boats into the landings near the villages. Their twenty-five tons of cargo, the rivermen boasted, had left Hartford in Connecticut a fortnight before, and would reach Wells River, opposite Haverhill, New Hampshire, in a total of twenty days. The men were ruddy, strong, often bearded.

Always the north country beckoned to Luther Parker, past the falls at Stewartstown, past Indian Stream—free land, all wilderness across into Maine; moose, bear, beaver, marten, fisher. Land.

Luther may have seen himself as a leader in the settlement along the upper Connecticut, for he seems always to have been drawn in two directions, to the freedom of the wilderness, and to the controlled freedom of law and order under self-government.

In 1819, no cleared road led from Fletcher's Mills to Lake Connecticut. The Parkers probably left their horses at the mills, as did Eastman and Cogswell that year, and proceeded on foot with packs. They talked to Eastman and Cogswell, and to John Perry. They passed the house of John Haynes, and those of other settlers holding under the Bedel title. They saw the miles and miles of forest along the river, along the bays and coves of Lake Connecticut. They met—may have traveled with—Burleigh and Seth Blood, and Abial Holt and his son, of Temple. They talked of a little neighborhood near the lake settled by Temple folk.

The following year Luther and Joshua, Jr., were in the party led by Archelaus Cummings when it stopped in September to see John Tillotson in Northumberland. As a result of this second trip, Luther and Joshua pitched on land beyond the outlet of Lake Connecticut. The area lay east of the mill privilege later developed by Peter Barnes, beyond the land of Moody Bedel and Archelaus Cummings, yet not as far as Burleigh Blood's pitch a mile beyond the outlet. Fronting the lake and extending north and east, Joshua's claim of ninety-seven acres bordered those of his father, of Luther, and of the Holts. The brothers began chopping down trees and clearing all three claims.

That first winter the elder Parker went back to Temple, as his sons possibly did also, although Luther later considered them all as settlers from 1820. In Temple, another son, Edwin, at thirteen, needed help with the farm work. A fourth and youngest son, named Asa after the grandfather who had rallied at Lexington, was only ten, yet his imagination caught fire from tales of the north, and his work at the woodpile slowed almost to a standstill in the next few years whenever Luther came to visit, for he was torn between showing what a worker he could be and listening to his favorite older brother.

Asa dreamed of wolves and bears, of Indians (for there were still Indians in the territory), and of salmon-trout in Lake Connecticut big enough to swamp a canoe. He dreamed of trapping fisher and marten in the forests. He could see the moose in their winter yards on the south ridges, stripping bark from the mountain ash trees with their long, flexible, upper lips and then gobbling it. He would be on snowshoes, with a rifle, and with a knife in a sheath at the belt around his blanket coat—a knife to skin out the moose hide, which he would form into a sledge that would freeze hard almost at once and onto which he would load the meat he would butcher into quarters, loin, and rib roasts. That was the way north country settlers brought in their meat.

Luther's thoughts and plans had a more practical and serious trend. He began to teach school in the years after he and Joshua pitched on their land. In this occupation, he was away during the adoption of the Resolve of 1824. He may have continued his studies at the academy in New Ipswich; he certainly continued to read widely.

During this time his brother Joshua stayed on at the Lake Settlement. It had become a backwoods community that included cabins and clearings over across Perry Stream toward Back Lake, down the Connecticut past Peter Barnes's mill, past the clearings of Archelaus Cummings and Moody Bedel, past John Haynes's farm on the deadwater, and there joined the older area centered about Fletcher's Mills and the Back Lake Brook junction with the Connecticut. The settlement included in a wider sense such sidehill clearings as that of Richard I. Blanchard on the slope south from Back Lake.

Log cabins now sometimes sheltered cows, oxen, or horses, while board houses brought to humans a new level of comfort. Men rived out the long clapboards from cedar logs, using a froe and a maul. Thinking of the easy, shorter shingles they had rived for their cabins, they joked about Ma and her fussing for a new house, but they were proud all the same to be well-off and able to afford the boards, strong enough to cut the logs and to work for the mill owner, or sharp enough to trade for the boards. Many families still lived in log cabins—log houses, they called them.

Abial Holt's wife bore her first baby in a log house, which Abial had built the previous fall. He and his bride had come north by ox cart from Temple. Abial walked with his goad at the head of the nigh ox; his bride rode in the wagon.

The claims of the Holts, Abial, Sr., and Abial, Jr., stretched over toward Perry Stream and Back Lake from the Parkers' land—large holdings, if such tenuous possession could be called a holding. Their relationship as father and son was similar to the Parkers': the father a nonresident whose land the son cleared. Abial, Jr., worked long hours on both claims only to find that neither could be secured by the Resolve of 1824. His father was not a resident settler. His own land had never been properly surveyed. The state did not recognize either claim.

Abial and Luther Parker talked of ways to secure their land. Gradually they had less and less hope of legal title through the land companies. Moody Bedel had moved to Bath. John Tillotson was dead. John Haynes kept up a pretense of the old Bedel Company business but could not provide a sound title. The state claimed jurisdiction and had found Abner Hyland guilty of trespass, yet it could not formally annex the territory till the boundary was negotiated with Great Britain. Meanwhile, the Eastman Company continued to petition the legislature for the land. If the Eastman Company won over the legislature, Abial, Luther, and all the other settlers not secured by the Resolve of 1824 would be on land belonging to a group of men who, except for Archelaus Cummings, lived to the south, mostly around Concord—speculators, land-gamblers. There seemed to Abial and Luther no immediate way out.

During the conferences, Abial's wife, a small, frail girl, would sit in a chair by the cradle and rock the baby. In the daytime, she might be up in the loft spinning the flax Abial had managed to raise. Like Mary Hunt Bedel, she endured the discomforts of the wilderness but never felt at home. She thought often of Temple and of her friends and relatives there, of the dances and bees she went to before her marriage. She remembered them especially when she was alone on the nights Abial had to stay away, usually when he went to Fletcher's Mills with grain to be ground, in the days before Peter Barnes built the mill nearby at the outlet of the lake.

Home thoughts of Temple helped to keep her from worrying about the wolves. One night they did come howling weirdly around the cabin in the moonlight. She sat at the foot of the ladder to the loft, holding the baby and thinking the creatures might jump onto the roof. If they did that, she'd go down in the small root cellar. At daylight, she crept to the window and saw the great, dog-like, gray shapes still lurking among the trees at the edge of the clearing. Each had a price of $12 on its head in the State of New Hampshire. Samuel Danforth and others claimed the bounty and pocketed the money, whether or not they believed New Hampshire had jurisdiction in other matters. If the wolves had only come when Abial was at home with his rifle, they would have represented quick money.

Joshua Parker did not marry while at the Lake Settlement, and Luther continued for seven years without the comfort of a wife. Then on February 27, 1827, Luther married Alletta French. She had been one of his pupils in Stratford, forty miles downriver from his pitch on Lake Connecticut. He had taught school there in 1825 and 1826. Alletta was three years younger than he.

Boys of similar age and more formidable size and disposition also had attended Luther's classes. The school might not have been as primitive as the one the Willey boys attended over near Conway. (Through the cracks in the floor of that school, bristles protruded from pigs rooting underneath, an invitation to the larger boys to start the pigs squealing by pulling the bristles.) But it was primitive enough. Luther, never one to suffer fools gladly, had developed a firmness that controlled his impatient temper. This together with his position of schoolmaster—that cloak of traditional authority—made him an awesome and imposing young man when aroused by an inattentive or insolent backwoods boy.

Alletta French had both gay and shy moods. She was quick of wit and retort among friends and in the family of the Baldwins, with whom she lived. Her folks, on the farm across the river in Vermont, had nine other children. She had stayed with the Baldwins in Stratford since she was ten. Her shyness came out with strangers. She first met Luther's father when he stopped for a drink of water as he was going up to the pitches. Joshua, Sr., said that his son had told him about a girl named Lettie French. She almost dropped the cup and, blushing, ran from the room.

Deep snow lay in the forest when Luther and Lettie went north to the cabin on his claim. It prevented the customary welcome to newlyweds and casual visits between neighbors—between Mrs. Holt and Mrs. Parker, both young women and not separated by any great distance, judged by wilderness standards.

Mrs. Holt longed more than Mrs. Parker for talk and feminine companionship. Winter had a deadly grip on the land, yet the sun came out hot and bright some days, brilliant on the white snow, and made the chickadees go "Dee-dee-dee," with a spring lilt. Jays—both the crested, blue-and-white kind and the other kind, the soft, grayish ones with the long tails, almost hatched tame, it seemed—would flutter about in the trees at the edge of the woods where they fed on the remains of a moose or on the carcasses of skinned marten and fisher. Trappers said that sometimes a fearless gray jay, which they called Moosebird, would tamper with a wolf trap and lose its head.

March settled the snow and crusted it over. The men spoke of traveling easily in the woods. Out in the shed, Abial Holt's young horse felt the confinement and pounded the log walls with his restless heels. The Parkers didn't keep a horse. Luther had a yoke of oxen, a cow, and four acres of mowing, as shown on his tax bill. (The inhabitants had voted to tax themselves for roads and schools; collection was another matter.) But no horse.

Mrs. Holt knew how difficult the first year or two could be without a horse to ride. She had walked to Sunday meeting barefoot, carrying her shoes till almost at the meetinghouse. Then she put them on. After meeting, on the way home, she took them off again and went barefoot, watching her footing on the rough path. Shoes were hard to come by. The mud and stones of the trail ruined them in no time. Feet didn't mind the mud, except when it hid a sharp-edged piece of slate or broken branch or gnarled root, and feet would heal. Meeting was irregular, held in folks' houses, and preachers didn't stay long in the territory. School was the same way. In 1821 Betsy Roger kept school for the first time in a log house, but soon probably there'd be a real schoolhouse.

Now, when spring came, the Holts could ride the horse when there was Sunday meeting, and the baby would snuggle in the knapsack on Abial's shoulders—a knapsack she had made from the flax Abial raised, the linen cloth of her own weaving.

At the end of the long winter, Indians had a way of hanging around begging for food. This was of no importance when the man was home—provided the house contained adequate food—but the Indian who came while Abial was away had the audacity or hunger to demand food. Mrs. Holt tried to control her shaking hands while she cooked a meal for him. The silent Indian ate greedily and messily, then went away. Mrs. Holt thought he might tell his beggar friends in the woods about this lone girl who set such a good table. Suppose they arrived full of rum or potato whiskey? Abial returned at last and told her not to worry. She had done just right, except maybe for cooking so much, though the old folks said to feed Indians hearty. Anyway these weren't dangerous Indians.

Abial was right. In the fall the Indian returned with a woven basket and gave it to Mrs. Holt.

Luther Parker worked hard that spring and summer and fall. He traded for another cow. He seeded down three acres of hay, out of the land that he had been pasturing, and pushed his pasture back into the forest, girdling, felling, burning. There were no fences. His two cows ran free. Lettie tended them, watched them, milked them, till she became too heavy and awkward with the child she was carrying.

His brother worked the adjacent pitch, and that of their father. Joshua lacked Luther's drive and, for that matter, the ambition of Abial Holt, who planned to have thirty acres improved in another two or three years. Joshua seemed content with the two acres of mowing on his claim and his two oxen, which he used in hauling logs and plowing his corn piece among the stumps. He and Luther joined up for haying. In the dewy mornings they scythed around and around the rough fields, working from the edges of the woods in to the center. They raked the hay after it had dried in the sun and wind, then tumbled it into cocks with wooden pitchforks. They loaded it on the hayrack fastened to a sledge and pulled by oxen. The best hay, with the least ferns, wildflowers, and brush sprouts, they packed into the lofts of the low log barns. The remaining hay had to be stacked outside. They scythed their father's four acres of mowing and shared the hay.

Before half the work could be done, the days grew shorter and colder. Early in November 1827, a cold wave spread across the territory and New Hampshire. November 9, 10, and 11 were the coldest days in memory at that time of year. Lakes, streams, and rivers froze iron-hard. Luther thought of shooting a moose for winter meat. He chopped more firewood and thought of the stove he would someday have instead of a fireplace, in a snug home of timbers and boards instead of in a log house.

Two days after Christmas, Lettie bore a son. They named him Charles Durham Parker, another child of the settlement who would grow up elsewhere—Wisconsin, in this case. He also would become active in public affairs as lieutenant governor of that midwestern state.

Luther began to look ahead to the future of the settlement, to a town organization that would provide roads and schools. There was talk about a schoolhouse centrally located above Fletcher's Mills, maybe on Gage Brook near the road over through Hill Settlement. It would be a "center" schoolhouse, and so it came to be called after it was built in 1828. Center Schoolhouse served as a school, town hall, courtroom, church, and legislative hall.

Luther also looked ahead to the future of his land and its dubious title. He kept thinking of land controversies in other parts of New Hampshire. Invariably the settlers who had done all the work of subduing wild land got the short end of the deal. This had happened in Lisbon, forcing most of the farmers to buy back their holdings from the company that finally secured title through the courts. There were other towns in which the settlers had become embroiled with contending companies, grantees, and proprietors, in the end finding themselves squatters on land they had considered their own. Luther made up his mind that this would not happen to him if he had the power to prevent it.

He had been taxed $2.50 that year, including his poll tax and the tax on his cow, the oxen, and the mowing land. Next year it would be more, with the additional cow and the new hay field. For roads and schools, the tax was important and necessary—and fair, if everyone paid or worked out his share. The tax had been voted at the annual meeting, held each March, as were all the New Hampshire town meetings. Yet the territory was not a town. The meetings had derived from those of the Bedel Company proprietors at David Tyler's house. Real authority was lacking. The men could vote this or that but then had to rely on voluntary goodwill or a little pressure from leading citizens to enforce their vote. This lack of authority and organization troubled Luther Parker.

The other problem, which weakened his land title, seemed no nearer solution than it had been when he first made his pitch. Indeed, the boundary solution seemed farther away, in the hands of the king of the Netherlands, than it had been when entrusted to the commissioners after the Treaty of Ghent. Perhaps his land was not even in New Hampshire. He made up his mind to fight for New Hampshire's claim.

The ruckus that occurred when Sheriff Horace Loomis from Colebrook tried to serve a writ against Rufus Brockway came as bad news. Luther knew that friends of Rufus had rescued him, but that was no way to meet the law. Sheriff Loomis proved it by getting special papers and raising a posse, which he brought to the territory. He collared Rufus and jailed him down at Lancaster. Some folks said the sheriff overstepped his authority. Others said the territory belonged to New Hampshire, and Sheriff Loomis had the right. Luther understood that New Hampshire was exercising the jurisdiction it had claimed in the Resolve of 1824, as upheld by the Coos court when it found Hyland and Fletcher to be trespassing on state land (if it was state land).

During this uneasy time, Luther knew two things for sure: his land *was* wilderness (his neighbor, Abial Holt, shot a bear that tried to steal a hog), and the territory *was* disputed. Word came from Alexander Rea, a magistrate in Hereford, Canada, that their land claims could be guaranteed under the Canadian system for settling new territory. Canada would grant not a mere two hundred acres to each settler, but twelve hundred! Hereford was the nearest Canadian town, north of Canaan, Vermont, and west of Indian Stream. It lay, so to speak, a few jumps of a buck deer west of Nathaniel Perkins's back pasture, where the Canadian boundary ran north from the cedar post on the bank of the Connecticut. Moreover, Canadian surveyors had laid out a town across Indian Stream and called it Drayton. This sort of talk from Alexander Rea made a number of men think long and hard about that twelve hundred acres, and about the authority of Canada, backed by the might of Great Britain. Everything would be simple if Canada took over the territory, from this point of view. The next step was to join Britain in claiming that the Connecticut was the boundary intended by the Treaty of Paris.

Thoughtful, inclined to action, and ready to regard such men as traitors or numbskulls, Luther watched his corn grow, hoped for a long season, worried a lot because he could do nothing, yet managed to laugh with Lettie when Charles began to crawl along the cabin floor. He also visited around the settlement to learn news from Concord of the doings in the legislature by the Eastman Company.

Archelaus Cummings had expanded his holdings along the Connecticut in 1826. He bought from John Haynes the hundred acres near the mouth of Gage Brook where Haynes had pitched in 1812. Archelaus Cummings was still the agent for the Eastman Company, although the company had ceased all attempts to sell land while the state cases against Hyland and Fletcher were dragging through the court at Lancaster. Archelaus, then, was both a neighbor to Luther—four or five miles away, on the way to Fletcher's Mills—and a source of information about the land company.

In 1827, the House had voted down, 112 to 78, a bill to grant the northern lands to the Eastman Company. Now, in 1828, a motion to postpone indefinitely such a bill favoring the Eastman Company had caught in a shift of political wind and had failed. Supporters of the Eastman Company rallied, 105 to 64, on a motion to reconsider the grant in 1829. The balance of power seemed teetering, variable, unreliable.

Luther had reason to fear that the Eastman Company would eventually push its bill through the legislature. Rumor said that Moody Bedel was considering a merger with Jonathan Eastman, combining their claims and companies. That might swing the legislature toward granting them the land. He, Luther Parker, might someday wake up and find that the Eastman Company owned his clearing in the woods, his cornfield, his hay fields, and his pasture. All the other settlers not secured in their claim by the Resolve of 1824 could also be put off their land.

Circumstances were swirling Luther along into a controversy similar to the one in which Litchfield, Maine, had existed for so many years. There, because of repeated and contradictory grants, not one of the 1,044 inhabitants in 1800 had a legal right to the land on which he lived. He might want to buy his land from a legal owner but could find none. Meanwhile, if he sold his farm, he could convey title to the improvements only: cabin, barn, fences, crops, all probably more valuable than the land itself, but basically valueless without the land. Although the courts were inclined to uphold the squatter against a tenuous proprietary title, at least to the extent of his improvements, they also might not favor his claim.

Luther began to think about an extension of the Resolve of 1824. In some way the claims of the settlers should be put before the legislature. In some way a true statement should be made to correct the fraudulent assertions of the Eastman Company about having developed, promoted, and aided the settlement beyond anything it had actually done.

Another and more immediate problem haunted the families in the clearings that fall of 1828, one that drove men to check the priming of their rifles every day, and women to almost impossible trips accompanying their men rather than to be left alone in the cabins. A man named David Robbins, a trapper and hunter from the Magalloway valley, having quarreled with his partner, Hinds, had the previous year burned their cabin and made off with the furs. Robbins had experienced a change of heart, "great penitence" (after his arrest), and had settled with Hinds for $350. Incredibly, this fall Hinds had gone into the woods again with Robbins, this time taking his son.

The bodies of Hinds and his son were found covered with brush in a brook near Little Kennebago Lake.

David Robbins lived near the mouth of the Diamond River, two days' tramp, for an able woodsman traveling fast, from settlements to the east. A mad murderer such as Robbins might turn up at the Lake Settlement or at Fletcher's Mills. He might raid the remote log houses for food and supplies, in Stewartstown, Colebrook, or Milan. People said he had killed a child in Maine and used the body to bait his traps.

The entire north country was roused up. Jurisdiction fell to New Hampshire, because Robbins's house was west of the Maine–New Hampshire line. Warrants were issued to Coos County sheriffs. Public subscriptions provided Sheriff Hezekiah Parsons with twenty-four pounds of pork, fourteen pounds of cheese, and $34. Parsons took with him into the woods, as his deputy, the champion wrestler Lewis Loomis.

For thirty-three days, Parsons and Loomis searched the woods along the New Hampshire border, toward Maine. They traveled as far east as Farmington to get legal authority to take Robbins in that state. The people in the settlements were in terror all during the month of October. Tension increased in November when Parsons and Loomis returned to Colebrook without their man. Later in the month, word came from the Magalloway that Robbins had been seen again at his home near the junction with the Diamond River.

Sheriff Parsons and Loomis set out again, in snowy weather. Apparently Robbins had laid in winter supplies, for he had gone back up the Magalloway toward his wilderness trapping grounds. Parsons and Loomis caught him portaging traps and provisions around Aziscoos Falls. Loomis jumped Robbins before the trapper could grab his rifle from his sled or pull his knife. They tied him up and slung him into the boat, then paddled down to the Colebrook Road east of Dixville Notch.

Jailed in Lancaster, Robbins never stood trial, for he managed to escape and disappear into the woods toward Canada. Supposedly he died in the forest that winter, although later a story reached the settlements of his having been hanged in Canada for another murder. Months passed. In lonely cabins, men, women, and children continued to start up at the sound of scratching among the leaves outside, or at a haunting call among the snowy trees. The man would say it must be a coon or an owl, as he moved closer to the axe by the door or to the rifle over the fireplace.

CHAPTER 21

THE COMMITTEE OF SAFETY PETITIONS THE LEGISLATURE, 1829

Luther Parker's neighbors—some of them—joined him in the belief that the intrigues of the Eastman Company and the disintegration of Bedel's group created a danger to the settlement and to their land claims. Abial Holt came naturally to Luther's thinking, being young and ambitious. John Haynes had opposed the Eastman Company for ten years. He was the leader of a family that included four sons. Clark J. Haynes, thirty years old, and John Langdon Haynes, twenty-five, had themselves become settlers. Clark was secure in two hundred acres through the Resolve of 1824. (His second wife was Adeline Bedel, daughter of Moody Bedel.) John Langdon Haynes's claim had not been recognized in 1824 because it had not been surveyed. The two younger sons, Timothy and Ross, twenty-one and eighteen, had yet to take up land. Their father talked with young Luther Parker—twenty-nine seeming young to sixty—about various other men who could not call their land their own. He also spoke about Moody Bedel throwing in his title with that of the Eastman Company.

In January 1829, Moody Bedel had agreed to negotiate with Jonathan Eastman. He and the two remaining active proprietors of the Bedel Company, William Quimby and Simeon Eastman (warned from the lake-outlet by Ambrose), signed a pact to abide by the settling of claims between them and Jonathan Eastman. They met and signed the paper on January 14 in Landaff, a hill town northeast of Bath. William Quimby was to go to Indian Stream with Jonathan Eastman, if Eastman would accompany him, which was a condition of the agreement, and define their share.

Despite Bedel's apparent joining with the enemy, John Haynes considered himself still a friend and associate, and agent still for the Bedel Company at Indian Stream. He felt that his duty lay in helping the settlers secure their lands. His personal interest also lay in a firm and equitable solution of the problem: he claimed more than fourteen hundred acres, to which his title was hardly better than that of a younger, struggling settler, excepting the two hundred acres he held through the Resolve. With his records and memory, he would help compile a list of the claims that Luther Parker wanted to submit to the legislature.

Another solid citizen, Jeremiah Tabor, joined them. His claim of seventeen hundred and fifty acres, acquired mostly along Indian Stream through various purchases, was valuable real estate. New Hampshire had secured to him only four hundred acres of it in 1824. He wanted a clear title to the rest. Leader of the Tabor clan, he represented Elisha, Jeremiah, Jr., Paul, and others.

A third older man held similar opinions. David Mitchell, the former bankrupt merchant and chaise owner from Bath, had been active in the affairs of the settlement since his arrival in 1821. He claimed two hundred acres, of which none had been granted him by the state in 1824 because the boundaries had not been surveyed. Now his son, David, Jr., had taken up land and cleared five acres for a house and for crops. He claimed one hundred and fifty acres but could get no title because the Resolve did not provide for young men maturing after 1824. Neither did it recognize later arrivals. The Resolve had been a politically expedient stopgap. It should be altered, continued, corrected.

The tradition of town meeting, which lay behind all the settlers, had for several years taken the form of annual gatherings. Now these meetings could be held at the new Center Schoolhouse on Gage Brook. Notices of the meeting were posted at Fletcher's and Barnes's mills.

By 1822 the annual meetings had gradually developed from the early neighborhood "bees" and voluntary get-togethers for road building and maintenance into more formal meetings, probably organized through the efforts of Moody Bedel. Inevitably taxation came, in 1827, mostly paid in labor on the roads. The town organization was voluntary and without sanction from the State of New Hampshire, but it satisfied an innate need of men who were descended from generations of New Englanders and Englishmen. The less cooperative of the inhabitants sometimes needed a little urging from the more civic-minded men, who took the position that anyone living in the territory ought to behave himself and anyone using the roads and bridges ought to help maintain them. These men of property and probity sometimes visited the happy-go-lucky woodsmen who were content in cabins and small clearings handy to the best fishing, hunting, and trapping; such visits were occasionally met with quiet independence, humor, or blasphemy.

The majority of the inhabitants favored the rituals of New England town organization and politics. With an active, perhaps selfish interest, the men determined to create a law-abiding society in which property and personal rights would be respected. This met with the approval of their wives, who, as women, were always in favor of secure institutions. Although without the vote, they did influence their men.

Settlers came to the March meeting through snow and mud. They adhered to the pattern of town meetings in their old homes. They chose a moderator and voted on committees and rules. They organized districts for schools and roads, assessing themselves for taxes to construct and maintain both.

In contrast with this civilized attitude, many otherwise reasonable men hated sheriffs and writs of attachment with a passion that would have pleased Daniel Shays himself. They had been afflicted for most of their lives by a currency of dubious and fluctuating value. Often they acquired debts no matter how hard they worked. Judgments of the courts in cases of delinquency appeared always to favor the man with money and power. They had hoped to be clear of this on the northern border. Intention to pay might have been lacking in some, but always with the qualification that the debt was unjust. Most men fully intended to pay their just debts, and did so when they could.

Therefore, they resisted the sheriff who tried to attach the cow that produced milk for the children's porridge, the sheep and wool to clothe the family, the hog for winter meat, and the oxen to raise crops for food. No, said the Indian Stream men, no, by God, not without a fight.

As for customs inspectors along the border, in general the settlers grouped them with the sheriffs of Coos County and avoided them when necessary. Canada did not impose any import duty on the produce of Indian Stream. Wagons of grain, potash, furs, hides, shingles, and lumber could rumble north through Canaan, Vermont, into Hereford, Canada, with the drivers hardly more than shouting a greeting to the Canadian customs officer. Cattle could be driven over the same route. If any doubt existed about the ownership of the cattle—half-wild stock caught running loose in the woods and not always identified by an earmark—then a backcountry trail into Canada avoided unpleasantness.

The travels of Canadians southward, roundabout the United States Customs, aroused in the Indian Stream men more sympathy than opposition. Reporting such deviations from the law seldom occurred to the settlers. They were in the habit of dismissing difficult laws of New Hampshire and the United States as not applying to themselves. Hard times required taking what steps were necessary to live; the law might call it smuggling, but it did not reflect on a man's character in the disputed territory and, in fact, took on something of the standing it had in eighteenth-century Scotland. Also, many of the men considered themselves to be British subjects on British soil. These the Coos sheriffs regarded as involuntary exiles, with shady pasts, from Canada *or* the United States.

Actually, outside authority took little notice of the settlers. Each March they made their own rules and regulations, which could not be called laws. The three judges chosen had no penalties to enforce the rules. Penalties were hardly necessary. Most of the people were law-abiding and honest. Their roots were in New England, the home of honesty and unlocked doors, the wellspring of legal process for redress of all grievances. Yankees carried the heritage across the nation, and here in the northern tip of New Hampshire (if it were indeed), they started governing themselves in a society of their own formation.

Not that all was sweetness and light. A legend still exists about some vague, mild coercion. The story of the potash kettle used as a jail in later, more difficult times continues to crop up. But in these early days of political youth, the settlement accepted a committee of solid citizens talking to wayward souls. Perhaps it was, as David Blanchard, son of Richard I. Blanchard, later described it, a mild form of lynch law.

However it is described, the committee of five—chosen on March 17, 1829, by the inhabitants convened in General Meeting—took the name "Committee of Safety for the General Security." It consisted of Luther Parker, John Haynes, Jeremiah Tabor, David Mitchell, and Abial Holt. They at once undertook their principal duty, drafting a petition to the New Hampshire legislature.

Dissenters there had been. Men lately connected with the Eastman Company still remained faithful to it, hopeful of it, and assumed (credulous dupes, in the view of the Committee of Safety) that it *would* secure them their lands. These men included Zebulon Flanders (he of the 1820 bridge, which had since washed away in high water, probably in the spring of 1824 when floods destroyed many bridges and milldams in New Hampshire); Reuben Sawyer, who had carried the chain for Jonathan Eastman in 1820; Southwood Sibley, a signer of the 1819 Eastman list of settlers holding land by that title; Elija C. Sawyer, a carpenter and, true to his name, a sawmill operator; David Eaton, an Eastman settler since 1819; and John Perry (who usually signed himself with his middle initial, H), the company's agent in the territory before Archelaus Cummings. All these men, a good dozen or more, opposed the proceedings of the meeting and of the committee. Archelaus Cummings, who had a farm on the Connecticut, not only protested; he moved to Canaan that March. Alanson Cummings, his son, born in 1803, also protested but stayed on his claim near Back Lake. He had bought his place, adjoining Abial Holt's, in 1826 from Langdon Haynes for $65.

The Committee of Safety went ahead. A suggestion of obstinacy and determination appeared in Luther Parker's character, traits that thrived on opposition and on the conviction that he was doing the right thing.

Spring came to the north country. Sap from the maples trickled into wooden buckets. Bright sun on crystalized snow made the sap gatherers blink as they came out of the dark and steamy sheds, where they boiled the sap into syrup and sugar. Hard crust in the morning would bear the weight of a man carrying a shoulder yoke and two buckets of sap. By noon it softened in the sun and let him down in hip-deep drifts, till he went for his snowshoes. In the clearings around the log cabins, chipmunks sunned themselves on stumps for the first time in four months. Coons moved about during warm nights, leaving tracks in the damp snow, which showed the sap gatherers the following day where the den trees were among the big hollow maples and yellow birches. Nuthatches flitted from tree to tree and ran down the trunks looking for larvae in the bark. They had been around all winter, but now they called with their persistent spring note; small boys, irritable and restless after the long winter, threw snowballs at them.

Deer were on the increase at this time, 1829, with a consequent increase in wolves. Settlers talked of deer drives to exterminate them, for the wolves preyed on sheep and young cattle and colts. With the deer gone, the wolves would go, or so the settlers reasoned, and there would always be moose in the back country. Woodsmen such as James Minor Hilliard told of caribou in the Magalloway valley. Hilliard that spring took nine wolf pups from a hollow log, tied them up, and packed them home to Colebrook. Two of them lived. Asked what he would have done if the she-wolf had attacked him while he was in the log, he said, "I'd have kicked her to hell!"

Bears came out of dens as the snow fell back in the deep woods. Trappers took up their bobcat traps from the sets made at the openings of hedges woven from evergreens along the shores of frozen ponds. They began their spring muskrat trapping, made sets for wolves, made last rounds of marten deadfalls, and planned what they would do with their fur money. The ice went out of the rivers. The roads thawed from frozen ruts to slushy mud. In April, the birds returned, and then in May the ice went out of the lakes.

Word had spread through the settlement about the petition that Luther Parker and the other men on the Committee of Safety had written to the legislature when it met in June. The contents and statements were known and discussed, approved and scorned. It became the most important topic of argument, and sometimes of heated controversy. To accompany the petition, the committee had compiled a list of settlers and their claims. Luther Parker continually went through the settlement, talking, checking old deeds and bills of sale, noting down recollections of old-timers and comparing them to those of John Haynes, and making inquiries about acreage granted to the various settlers by the Resolve of 1824 and about reasons why their titles had not been recognized. It was a tedious and often thankless task, but Luther persisted. It might secure the property they had chopped out of the forest.

The opening words of the petition outlined the origin of the committee and its intentions.

A petition of Luther Parker and others, Committy of Safety in behalf of the inhabitants of Indian Stream. To the senate and house of representatives, we the undersigned . . . a committee of safety chosen by the inhabitants of Indian Stream at a meeting called agreeable to our rules held March 17, 1829 . . . and given the duty to take measures to secure them in possession of their lands . . .

Then Luther outlined the background of their problems. Paraphrased, the petition stated: in this territory claimed by the United States and Great Britain but governed by neither, the custom being to meet from time to time in General Meeting, each individual has felt duty-bound to obey our laws, and they have generally been observed and the inhabitants have enjoyed peace and security . . .

Until now.

Jonathan Eastman and other claimants are trying to obtain a grant from the legislature. If the legislature shall grant their petition agreeable to a resolve reported by the standing Committee on Public Lands dated January 15, 1829, the inhabitants of this place will suffer great loss in their lands and be embarrassed by many long and tedious lawsuits with said claimants.

And why should they so suffer and so be embarrassed by lawsuits?

Jonathan Eastman did not give deeds as promised for settler's duty. Only three deeds were given (at $5 consideration) covering one hundred acres each. The inhabitants have so often been deceived by the above-named proprietors that they have lost their confidence in them. If the legislature should grant these proprietors all the land in this place, every settler who is not secured by the Resolve of 1824 would be left at the mercy of the proprietors, and be obliged to pay them whatever sum they are pleased to ask for the land, or leave it.

Luther outlined the probabilities of what would result from the international dispute over the territory: should the boundary be settled on Hall's Stream, the land will probably belong to New Hampshire, and we believe that it will conduce greatly to the security of the inhabitants of this place if the legislature should authorize some person to release to each settler, individually describing the bounds to their particular claim, agreeable to their several surveys, all the right which the state of New Hampshire hath or may have in the same, before this tract of land shall be conveyed to any set of proprietors . . .

. . . such a conveyance, we imagine, cannot be construed as jurisdiction, or cause any collision between the two Governments . . . but if the boundary be established on the Connecticut River, as claimed by the British, the conveyance would enable the settlers to adjust their claims with that Government on more favorable terms.

Luther knew, from appeals made earlier by the Eastman Company to the legislature, that it would try to establish its important role in the development of the settlement. He carefully listed the work of the settlers themselves: . . . we believe that by cutting roads and making bridges and other facilities for making new settlements, the inhabitants have rendered wild lands not claimed by them more valuable than the whole would have been, to have remained in a state of nature . . .

. . . since 1822, districts for highways and schools [have been] set up . . . Surveyors of Highways chosen yearly . . . [and] inhabitants worked under the Surveyors by voluntary contribution . . .

. . . 1827: $300 assessed by the inhabitants for Building Bridges and making and repairing roads . . .

. . . 1828: $375

. . . 1829: $300

. . . inhabitants have built four large bridges, one over the Connecticut River near Ebenezer Fletcher's, connecting this settlement with the College Grants, over Indian Stream, and Perry Stream.

. . . cut and worked forty-one miles of roads . . . no assistance except $75 paid by Jonathan Eastman to Zebulon Flanders in 1819 toward building the bridge near Ebenezer Fletcher's, and twenty-five cents paid Samuel Danforth by said Jonathan Eastman for filling in a mud hole near Gage Brook, and the assistance received from inhabitants of the College Grants in rebuilding the Bridge across the Connecticut . . . estimate of $3000 put into roads and bridges by the inhabitants . . .

. . . inhabitants have borne the cost of surveys except the ten lots of 100 acres for which Jonathan Eastman carried the compass, in the Lake Settlement, and six lots of 100 acres in the Hill Settlement already surveyed by the Bedel Company, "which rather produced confusion among the settlers than any beneficial effects."

. . . the Resolve of 1824 by the legislature was satisfactory to the inhabitants as far as they could avail themselves of its provisions. From various causes, many inhabitants were not secured as was supposed to be intended by the legislature . . .

"We therefore pray that the Legislature authorize some person to release the right of the title the state hath or may have to each settler describing bounds per attached schedule, or take such measures for the security of the Inhabitants of Indian Stream in their claims as the Legislature in its wisdom may see cause and as in duty bound will ever pray."

Luther Parker   Committee
Jerm. Tabor   of Safety
John Haynes   in behalf of the
David Mitchell   Inhabitants of
Abial Holt   Indian Stream

CHAPTER 22

THE CLAIMS OF 1829

The scrupulous honesty that Luther Parker tried to preserve in the petition, in which he held back his contempt for the Eastman Company as best he could, carried over into the list of settlers and their claims. Here John Haynes could help with an accurate accounting of acreage and exact dates, through the records dealing with shares and sales of the old Bedel Company.

The task of collecting information occupied the committee all spring. They had to consult with settlers about land granted them by the Resolve of 1824. They had to check old deeds. They had to investigate property lines and old survey plans. This was to be an honest and complete record of all the inhabitants who held or claimed land. After each man's name would be the date of his settling, his improved acreage, his whole claim, and the acreage secured by the Resolve—or not secured, and the reason for lack of title.

Luther put the mill owners, Ebenezer Fletcher and Peter Barnes, at the head of the list. He wrote a marginal note stating that Mr. Fletcher and Mr. Barnes were entitled to more land than common settlers, although each held two hundred acres by the Resolve. Fletcher claimed five hundred and Barnes five hundred.

Luther continued down the list: Sampson Rowell, settled 1823; improved land twenty-five acres; whole claim two hundred acres; secured by the Resolve of 1824, two hundred acres.

In much the same fashion followed the names of Samuel Orsborn, Simeon Wright, Ephraim C. Aldrich, Paul Tabor, Nathan Judd, Nathaniel Perkins (700 acres), and Clark J. Haynes, whose 60 acres of improved land topped even Perkins, with 52, and spoke clearly of Clark's energy. The land of all these men had been granted to them by the state in 1824, and they claimed no more than they had received—a pleasant, straightforward start to the list.

Then came David Eaton's name. David opposed Luther's petition. His claim of 170 acres had been granted him by the Resolve. Some of his neighbors had managed to get 30 acres more from the state, the maximum allowed by the Resolve, except for the 400- and 700-acre grants to Tabor and Perkins. Most of the men put their claims at the figure of 200 acres. Not David Eaton. He held his 170 acres legally, and he didn't want more, didn't want to bother the legislature at all. Let sleeping dogs lie. He was content with his property. He wanted no fight with the Eastman Company. Next on the list, Benjamin Coon held 190 acres by the Resolve. He didn't think highly of the petition; he didn't want more land. The next man, Samuel Huggins, held 160 acres by the Resolve; they were enough for the time being and kept him busy, for he had been in the territory only five years.

At this point, Luther reached the end of the simple listing. Next would come the conflicting, unsecured claims. He might well have paused and considered the odd meanings hidden in the figures he had put down after the names of the last two men. Ben Coon had cleared eight acres in nine years. Ben lacked ambition. He tended toward carelessness in his house, which was evident in those bare figures. Sam Huggins had cleared twenty-five acres in five years; that he was a man working to get ahead was evident in those figures.

At the bottom of the page, Luther saved space for Jeremiah Tabor's name. The largest landholder by purchase and settler's duty, Jeremiah now claimed 1,750 acres. His improved land amounted to 167 acres. Of course, Jeremiah wanted all his claim.

Following Tabor on the list, Luther wrote the names of men less fortunate: Southwood Sibley, Jonathan Hartwell, Samuel Danforth, Enoch Carr, Moses Thurston, Richard I. Blanchard, and John McConnell. They all claimed two hundred acres, of which only half had been granted to them in 1824 because of incomplete surveys. After them Luther listed other men who, for reasons of absence, later arrival in the settlement, total lack of surveys, or coming of age after the Resolve, had received no grant or only a portion of their claims.

All this information went down on the list. The seventy-three men of the settlement appeared clearly through their property: rich and poor, ambitious and easygoing, industrious and lazy, hunters and farmers, young and old. They would take an active part in the following years of contention, violence, conflicting loyalties, and frustrated ambitions. All hoped for, and some needed desperately, the security of owning their land legally. This was a right and security many of them had taken for granted as a condition of manhood. As yet they had not aligned themselves into factions or begun to think of their independence, with a separate government. In their names and properties on Luther Parker's list were the signs and portents.

One of the controversies displayed itself in the last four names, put down with the honesty Luther required of himself, although he knew the men were against him. He wrote a note to inform the legislature that their names were put down without their particular request, a vast understatement but certainly true. Archelaus Cummings's name, and the phrase "one of the Proprietors of Philip's Grant" (meaning the Eastman Company), preceded his claim to two hundred acres, sixty of them improved. Cummings also claimed a lot of one hundred acres with a mill commenced on it at the outlet of Back Lake. The other three names were Zebulon Flanders, Reuben Sawyer, and Alanson Cummings.

Whether or not they wanted to be on the list, Luther put them down. If the legislature should act on his petition, he did not intend that it should neglect these men because he had been spiteful and had not included them. As for others he knew to be against him, he put them down without comment.

The list revealed for the first time an orderly picture of the property in the settlement. It showed the farms, clearings, and pitches in their confused extent. The men of the territory claimed 17,618 acres, if John Haynes's claim is estimated at 1,400 acres. (Probably it was more; because of its length, Luther wrote it on a separate paper, which has vanished.) The men had cut down trees and improved the land on 1,413 acres. Weighing the labor and investment as constituting rights to their lands, they felt that their claims were a small part of the 200,000 acres sought by the Eastman Company.

The list revealed other facts. Only nineteen men of the seventy-three held two hundred acres from the state through the Resolve of 1824. Five of these claimed larger tracts through earlier, supposedly legal purchases. Ten men held fewer than two hundred acres, because the state would not recognize the unsurveyed balance. This situation could be blamed on the careless methods of both land companies. Forty-four men held their lands only as squatters. None of these squatters admitted to this classification. A few had paid money and had received company deeds not recognized by the state. Others had done settler's duty in the wide domain of the companies' "common and undivided land"; they had never received their deeds, nor had the companies provided surveyors. Almost half of these men had arrived in the territory after 1824, or were sons of settlers and had pitched on wild land after 1824. Others, including Luther Parker, Moody Bedel, and Burleigh Blood, had been away in 1824. Moody had, of course, moved away for good. His agent was improving the farm. Some of the older men, including Abial Holt, Sr., and Joshua Parker, Sr., had been working their claims with the help of sons or agents, and as nonresidents they received no land by the Resolve.

Thus the list revealed four groups of men, classed by their land: (1) those who arrived or matured after the Resolve, and not secured; (2) those actually on the land in 1824 but with faulty titles and surveys, or none at all, and consequently not secured; (3) those who claimed more than the state had secured; and (4) those secured to their entire claims.

The first three groups made up 80 percent of the men in the settlement. They might have worked together effectively; however, selfish and contentious traits of character appeared. Two men took upon themselves the duty of warning the Eastman Company about the petition and claims list.

CHAPTER 23

JONATHAN EASTMAN LEARNS ABOUT THE COMMITTEE OF SAFETY, 1829

The month of May brought green grass and occasional hours of warm weather. It also brought cold rain and gusty winds that blew away the white petals of the shadbush flowers, scattering them through the newly leaved woods. The land waited for the sun's full warmth. Mud and soggy earth clung to the carts and plows of men accustomed to earlier seasons at their old home farms. Unable to fit their land for crops, they could only curse the mud and cold.

Old-timers in the territory scoffed, saying, "Up here we have ten months of winter and two months damn late in the fall." A real cynic might laugh sourly and say, "Up here we have eleven months of winter and one month of poor sledding." Talk would continue among the longtime settlers: "After all, we get pretty near four times the snow we had down home. Thirty inches down home—ten feet here. They told us early snow keeps the ground from freezing. So it does, and then piles up till you figure it'll never melt. Damn near don't some years. Hangs on like an unwanted guest. The weather won't warm up till the snow melts on the hills. Snow on the hills won't melt till the weather warms up."

Always the weather at Indian Stream was good for a few words. If you didn't like it, wait a minute. (The man who so phrased this New England phenomenon had yet to be born—six years after the spring of 1829—into the Clemens family of Missouri.) Or travel a few miles. Taking the territory as a whole, weather at Indian Stream could exhibit ten kinds of rain, snow, cold, sun, wind, fog, and sleet, all at the same time. Great country for weather.

Zebulon Flanders and Reuben Sawyer had in mind certain matters other than weather. Their interest lay in upsetting the plans of Luther Parker and the Committee of Safety. They both felt a kind of loyalty, based on self-interest, to Jonathan Eastman.

Both men were settlers of almost a decade. Sawyer had pitched on land promised him by Eastman a year after Flanders built the bridge at Fletcher's Mills in the summer of 1820. Flanders had taken up land, also through Eastman, northwest of the junction of Back Lake Brook and the Connecticut in 1820. This put him on the plateau area upstream a mile or so from Fletcher's Mills. He held two hundred acres there by the Resolve of 1824. Sawyer had been granted only a hundred acres of the two hundred he claimed. Both men thought that interference by New Hampshire was unnecessary. Flanders regarded New Hampshire's attempts at jurisdiction as an infringement of Canadian rights in the township of Drayton, which belonged to Canada. He understood that Luther's petition would lead to more interference by New Hampshire. He also felt a good deal of respect for the men he had worked for in the Eastman Company. Luther's petition belittled their expenditures in developing the territory; to Flanders, such statements were lies. Sawyer supported Eastman because he wanted a deed from him that would, he thought, assure him of his two hundred acres. They knew that other men in the settlement felt as they did. Ebenezer Fletcher did not like the stirrings of trouble he saw in the petition. Archelaus Cummings had moved away, but opposed the Committee of Safety, and had the right to, for he still kept his claim and betterments on the Connecticut River and at Back Lake.

When consulted at his home in Canaan, Vermont, Archelaus advised Flanders to write to the proprietors of the Eastman Company. Flanders sat down and wrote a letter on behalf of himself and the others who didn't like the actions of the committee. He addressed it to Stephen Ambrose, a member of the Eastman Company certain to take action, as he had nine years before when Simeon Eastman planned the mill at the outlet of Lake Connecticut. Flanders continued with a letter addressed through Ambrose to Jonathan Eastman, whom he knew personally. Only some of the people were backing the petition to the legislature, he wrote, and and went on to name Luther Parker, David Mitchell, John Haynes, and Jeremiah Tabor. Flanders continued: "We deny their assertion. If they do present a pertion not that I think it will have any more wait than a lief I wish you would write me the particulars. Yrs. with esteem, Zebulon Flanders."

He took this letter to Fletcher's Mills, where he talked with Ebenezer. The mill owner, thinking slowly, by careful stages hedged into a middle route. Luther Parker had the appearance of a young radical compared to the wealthy and powerful men of the Eastman Company. On the other hand, Luther had put Ebenezer at the head of the claims list, with a special note about his deserving more acreage than a common settler. The Eastman Company had voted him his five hundred acres and had hired lawyers to defend him (and at the same time the interests of the company) in the Lancaster Court. He had been granted two hundred acres by the Resolve, yet the court had found him guilty of trespass on state lands (if the state owned the land).

In the end he signed Flanders's letter. He added in a note that he wished Eastman would send him newspapers, after Eastman had read them. Ebenezer would pay the postage and be grateful. The note might be taken only as a communication about newspapers, not as backing Flanders. The uncommitted miller, man of substance, upright, careful, a builder of solid mills and a huge barn, then went back to work.

Flanders went up the road toward Lake Connecticut, turned off to the north, and arrived at Reuben Sawyer's twelve-acre clearing northwest of Captain John McConnell's half-wild twenty-acre field dotted with stumps and patched with grass turning bright green over the fertile ashes of vanished tree trunks.

Sawyer had been promised a deed by Jonathan Eastman when he first settled in the territory in 1821. He still counted on Eastman's giving him the deed, although Eastman had put him off at the time Sawyer completed his settler's duty. Sawyer also had worked his fifty days on the roads, for which he had been promised fifty more acres by Eastman, making a total due him of one hundred and fifty. The state had secured to him a hundred acres in 1824, yet he wanted no part of the appeal to the legislature for more. He clung to the promises of Eastman with an innocent faith, backed by a sense of outrage that anyone should question the motives or promises of Captain Eastman.

He felt so strongly about the matter that he agreed with Flanders to write an additional letter to Ambrose, which many of his neighbors would sign. As he began to write, his anger and resentment that anyone should go against the great Eastman Company emerged, tinged with awe—not fear, for at this time he was not a man to fear anyone. And he knew Captain Eastman. He had carried the chain for him while he surveyed. Therefore Sawyer was loyal as stoutly as John Haynes was to Moody Bedel and the Bedel Company. (Sawyer and Haynes had been on opposite sides for almost ten years.) Outrage flowed in the words that his pen scratched on the paper, not easily but with sincerity:

> ... there is a party in this place who stile themselves a Comity and they have under taken some thing which we are not in favor of nether have we authorized them to take the measures they are taken for they are a Bout to address the Legislater in the name of the People of this Place which thing we Disalow and certify ourselves to be setlers as at the first and look for our setlers sites from your honorable company. Therefore we think fit to address a few lines to you. a word to the wise is enough.

Having composed this letter, he went about the settlement during the next five days getting men to sign under his name. Fourteen men agreed that the Eastman Company should be warned. Their motives were mixed. Ben Coon had been secured in his 190 acres by the state, but he signed. So did David Eaton. Also signing were Southwood Sibley, Alanson Cummings, Elija Sawyer, Enoch Carr, and his son, Osmund. Some signed because they were urged to. Some signed to put themselves on the side of the bigger guns. Some signed from sincere belief in the policy and integrity of the Eastman Company. Some signed to spite Luther, whom they thought interfering and overbearing, or to spite others of the Committee.

Over at his place at Sucker Brook, north of Back Lake, Alanson Cummings of course signed the document. His father was an Eastman Company proprietor. And an old-timer, John Perry, once agent for Eastman and Cogswell, signed. He might well have been against state interference because his land had been designated as unsurveyed and ineligible for a grant in 1824, although it lay in lot number thirteen of the Bedel plan known as Ladd's Survey. Young Sam Danforth, Jr., and Rufus Hartwell both signed. Luther had listed their claims in the petition. Jonathan Hartwell signed, and Nathaniel French. Of the fifteen men (counting Reuben Sawyer himself), seven had been secured in all or part of their land by the Resolve. They were just against the Committee.

Reuben, aware that the letter must be sent, stopped calling on his neighbors. May had almost slipped by. The legislature met in June. Stephen Ambrose and Jonathan Eastman would need time to rally their forces. Reuben sat down in his house on May 23, 1829, and wrote Ambrose another letter,

> staten the reason why we send this enclosed paper knowen that the afore named Comity has undertaken some thing injurias to the proprietors as they think and as we know that your company has expended a considerable sum on roads bridges and

in surveying lands in this place and considering ourselves holden to your company as setlers and hope you will consider us as such we therefor take this opertunity to show ourselves hopen in that these ill composed lines will meat with a cordial reception by you and believe us your sincear friends and please sir to rite to me and let me know what there petition does afect So I remain Yours with Esteem, Reuben Sawyer. If nessary make use of our names as ocasion may Require.

CHAPTER 24

THE LEGISLATURE HESITATES, 1829–1830

Although the New Hampshire electoral vote had gone to John Quincy Adams in the election of 1828, many men favored the winner, Andrew Jackson. Traditionally, Adams stood for wealth and power, Jackson for the common man. The proprietors of the Eastman Company were in all likelihood proponents of the former, yet a contradiction existed in the support they received from the less educated and poorer men of Indian Stream. This contradiction comes into focus at once when the prose and thinking of Parker, Mitchell, Haynes, Tabor, and Holt are compared to those of Flanders and Sawyer. The men protesting the petition saw not a glimmer of the obvious logic that they would be at the mercy of the Eastman Company if the company managed to play politics both forcefully and subtly enough to win a grant from the legislature.

At the same time, a similar contradiction existed in the policy of the Eastman Company. Led by merchants, bankers, lawyers, politicians, well-to-do landowners—Adams men—they hoped for support from Moody Bedel, a known Jackson man. They were attempting a land grab of the kind Adams condemned in those who eyed public lands "with the thirst of a tiger for blood."

The letters to Ambrose from Flanders and Sawyer had the desired effect of arousing and preparing the men of the Eastman Company. Ambrose and Jonathan Eastman laid the letters before the company lawyer, Pearson Cogswell. They learned that the Committee on Public Lands considering their petition for a grant was also debating the Parker petition. Cogswell outlined a strategy to discredit Parker's statements. At the hearing, which Cogswell probably could not attend because his mother was very sick, he advised Ambrose and Eastman to hold their fire until Parker's petition had been read and discussed and its proponents had "put in all their strength." Then Ambrose and Eastman could deny the charges, reiterate the figures of their expenses already in their petition, and read the letters from Flanders and Sawyer. The plan was successful.

The Committee on Public Lands responded with a report favoring the Eastman Company. On June 23, 1829, just a month after Sawyer wrote his second letter, the committee reported to the House that Parker's statements about the miserly expenditures of and neglect by the Eastman Company were false. It recommended that the House, in settling the question of ownership in the territory, bear in mind the company's services to the settlers and its efforts at improving the northern lands.

All the same, reported the committee, casting a figurative glance at men backing the settlers and at various representatives from northern towns, the settlers had taken the land in good faith, many of them counting on the state to provide title; their rights must not be disregarded. Because the international boundary dispute might soon be settled by the arbitration of the king of the Netherlands, the committee advised that the problem of land claims be put off until the territory was officially, legally, and internationally part of the United States. If it became part of Canada, the land problem would not exist, at least not for the New Hampshire legislature.

The House debated the advice, then followed it. Action on the petitions was postponed until the next session, leaving both the men of the Eastman Company and the settlers at Indian Stream frustrated and exasperated.

The failure of the legislature to act upon Luther Parker's petition, and its rejection of statements he believed to be accurate, placed him in the irritating position of having failed his neighbors after convincing talk, logic, and much hard work at his writing table. The men in the territory who favored the Eastman Company never hesitated to point out his failure. Their company's failure hardly bothered them. Next year would bring success, they thought, with Eastman in control of the territory, ready to reward his henchmen and punish his enemies. Parker might as well prepare for his medicine—Tabor, too, the land-rich farmer of the Indian Stream meadows. David Mitchell, John Haynes, and Abial Holt could all watch out.

Luther passed the frustrating days in hard work on the farm that he did not own, in planning, planning. The very work seemed at times a stupid waste of energy on property without a title. His mind turned toward trading, where a chance for profit did not hinge on ownership of land. A little store in his house might be the way to start, one room and a counter and shelves. Money was scarce, but fur still ran in the woods. The days of forty years ago were no more, when an Indian would trade twenty pounds of beaver for a blanket, ten pounds for a shirt; still there was money to be made taking furs in trade, also grain, lumber, maple sugar, potash, and hides. Luther made up his mind not to drive himself forever against the wall of land claims.

The settlement was now divided. Men grew nervous and took sides. The legislature's postponement had been based on the boundary dispute. Would the territory become finally part of Canada or the United States? The king of the Netherlands sat in judgment on their nationality. Some men asked, "What's wrong with Canada? Use you better than the Coos sheriffs." This was the feeling of men with Canadian property and background, and those who saw an end to indebtedness, if the boundary were established on the Connecticut River south of their clearings. New Hampshire men, neighbors, born and expecting to die in New Hampshire, laughed. Of course the territory was New Hampshire. Luther didn't; he knew the problem wasn't that simple.

Word arrived in the winter of 1830 that the Eastman Company would definitely bid for the support of Moody Bedel. Opinion on this, too, divided the settlement. Some of the older men thought Bedel might well receive a grant himself if he applied to the legislature. To others his position suggested horse trading and politics, for the sole benefit of Moody Bedel. A few loyal supporters—and Bedel himself—believed that they would be better off merged with Eastman. The settlement would be unified under one title. The merger would result in a company with more power to influence the legislature. With Moody Bedel to defend his old settlers, they would not be in danger of reprisals from Eastman and Cogswell. Luther Parker, John Haynes, the other members of the Committee of Safety, and a few old settlers maintained that their only hope was to discredit the Eastman Company and put before the legislature the virtual self-government of the territory; in other words, to seek again with all possible means the approval of the previous year's petition.

So dissension ran through the clearings in the winter woods and lurked in the shadows about the fireplaces of the log houses.

Archelaus Cummings (how odd that he carried the name of the son of Herod, himself so tyranical that Augustus banished him to Gaul), having removed himself from the scene of the controversy, could view the settlement with a certain amount of calm disinterest. He had resigned himself to a mistake in judgment on his own part, though he hoped to retrieve something from his claims in the territory. He continued to sponsor the Eastman Company's interests from his farm in Canaan and listened to settlers favorable to the title he and the other proprietors held. He understood the split among the inhabitants and believed that his company's cause would succeed that summer of 1830. He thought that an agent need not be sent into the settlement; the problem might resolve itself. Many settlers favored the Eastman Company. Of those opposed, Archelaus thought that some were beginning to waver. Two were going to move out, and others talked of moving. They were worried about reprisals when the Eastman Company, as seemed likely, pushed through the legislature its petition for a grant. Peter Barnes, the mill owner at the outlet of the lake, opposed the company loudly but nonetheless had begun to tremble a little. This pleased Archelaus, for Barnes claimed half his betterments—his improved land—on Archelaus's claim, which adjoined the mill privilege.

Archelaus had seen a petition signed that winter by many of the inhabitants, which a member of the group had shown to him for his approval. Archelaus advised against sending it to the legislature. Of course he so advised; the petition requested that *all* the territory should be granted to the *settlers*. On the other hand, Archelaus was willing to help promote a petition asking that the land be given to the Eastman Company. Many of the settlers would sign such a petition. It might help next June in the legislature, although Archelaus believed their success was assured without it, and that circumspect quiet might be the better policy now.

He was, beneath his business interest, discouraged about the land development. He had sold his farm in Temple after moving to the Lake Settlement and estimated that he had lost $1,000 by that transaction and by his northern venture. The Lake Settlement appeared of doubtful value. Most of the settlers there wanted to get away. It was a cold country, and the crops were generally light. He wished some of the other proprietors would come up to see him. A good road for chaises led from Guildhall Bridge—the best crossing into Vermont if the Connecticut was flooding—past his house. "I should think some of the proprietors would like to take a ride and see the country and the fine territory of Indian Stream."

Thus he wrote to his friend Joseph Blanchard from the snowbound farmhouse in Canaan on February 6, 1830. Blanchard was in Chester, New Hampshire, a few miles east of Manchester, and seems to have had little interest in the northern lands. The falls in the Merrimack River at Manchester offered opportunities for industrial investment with far greater possibilities than remote land near Canada. Manchester already had grown to a population of 887 souls, and the old days of its settlement as Derryfield, when the people subsisted on river eels ("Derryfield beef") were gone forever. By contrast, the world of business and industry—the new railroads, for instance—never flourished in the far north of the state.

The spring of 1830 brought the approach of the June session of the legislature. John Haynes went about the settlement taking the depositions of men who remembered the old days fifteen or twenty years before. Samuel Orsborn, whose land purchase from Captain James Ladd went back to 1804, stated that at the time the four families in the territory had all been united under the Bedel title, namely, Nathaniel Wales, his brother, Captain Ladd, and a man named Herman. Settlers who later moved in did so under the Bedel title. Orsborn remembered that six or seven years after he had arrived, Moody Bedel came to the territory and went to great expense in cutting roads. To Orsborn's knowledge, no settlers had held land under any title but that of the Bedel Company until Eastman and Cogswell arrived and got some of them to sign under their claim.

William Hyland had arrived in the territory with his father, Abner Hyland, in March 1816. His deposition stated essentially the same facts about titles that Orsborn's had. Abner Hyland, no longer living, had considered himself a Bedel settler during his entire residence at the former David Tyler farm, although the state had "ejected" him from it. The implication is that he returned, probably after the state granted him two hundred acres in 1824, for he died there and left the property to William.

John Haynes also called on his old acquaintance Ebenezer Fletcher, the second defendant in the squatter cases. Cautiously Fletcher considered John's request for a deposition about his early contract with Moody Bedel. He also pondered his obligations to his old neighbor, and his own complicated position as a holder of a deed to five hundred acres from the Bedel Company, the recipient of a vote of five hundred acres from the Eastman Company, and the grantee of two hundred acres by the state of New Hampshire. At last he agreed to a nonpartisan deposition, in which he stated the simple facts of his contract with Bedel for the sawmill and gristmill in 1811, his moving to the mill privilege that winter, and his building of the mills to the approval of the proprietors, who then gave him a deed to his five hundred acres. John Haynes and David Rogers witnessed the paper. Doubtless Ebenezer went back to work, which to him was the great thing in life.

In his own deposition, John Haynes wrote more detail. He intended to leave no doubt in the minds of legislators that the Eastman Company and its agents, Jonathan Eastman and Pearson Cogswell, had been troublemakers in a peaceful, united settlement. Haynes stated that Moody Bedel had been the only constructive leader in the settlement from the beginning. He suggested verification by William Quimby, the representative from Franconia.

John Haynes's intention to bolster the petition of the previous year—still before the Committee on Public Lands and, unfortunately, attached to the problem of the Eastman petition—must have miscarried. Fletcher's deposition found its way into the papers of the Eastman Company, as they now exist. Perhaps the depositions never reached the Committee on Public Lands, although both John Haynes and Luther Parker were men to deliver them in person. Perhaps Haynes gave them to his old friend, Moody Bedel, for whom they would have been a powerful lever in negotiating with the Eastman Company. Whatever the use to which they were put, they did not help settle the land problems of Indian Stream.

On June 10, 1830, Moody Bedel merged his claim and title with that of the Eastman Company. Of twenty-five shares in this reorganized company, Bedel received—or his company received—twelve, the Eastman Company thirteen. Each share represented twelve hundred acres. This new group of men, united at last and assisted by Bedel's early, long, and forceful association with the territory, as well as his military reputation as a veteran and hero (he received a letter of praise and wonder from a man who visited the site of Fort Erie), should easily press their petition through the legislature.

To their disappointment and dismay, they could not. After careful consideration by the Committee on Public Lands and by the House, including reconsideration of the Parker petition, the House again postponed the problem to the next session. This did not have any enduring effect on the policy of the Eastman Company, for its members regained their confidence, but it took the heart out of the petitioners at Indian Stream.

The Committee of Safety faced a disastrous defeat and a loss of prestige. They began to think in terms of their own inner resources and capabilities, and of those of their adherents. The future of the settlement, if it were to maintain the identity and coherence its people had developed despite the neglect of the men at Concord—and yes, neglect by Bedel, too, since he had moved away—depended on closer action taken on the foundation of the annual meetings. Why should the men of the land company profit from the efforts of the settlers themselves? The inhabitants, using common sense and their past experience in town administration, could deal with their own community problems. Then why not their own land problems? A step toward this would be the recording of actual deeds in the possession of the settlers. John Haynes had experience with deeds from the old Bedel Company.

Luther Parker was occupied with family problems during that summer of 1830. His disappointment once again at the rejection of his petition lost significance in the shadow of the death of his younger brother, who was only twenty-three years old when he died in July. Edwin had been the mainstay at the home farm in Temple, and had made probable young Asa's joining Luther at the Lake Settlement. Turmoil at the settlement came at a time when Alletta Parker's pregnancy was nearing its end. The tragedy of Edwin's death had scarcely eased when, in August, Alletta gave birth to a baby girl. This was Persis Euseba Parker, three years younger than her brother, Charles.

Edwin's death left the farm in Temple shorthanded, especially if Asa, now twenty, should follow his inclination to join Luther in the north. Joshua could return home with the blessings of his brothers and parents. He could please himself also, for he had become discouraged with his life at the Lake Settlement, where he led a bachelor existence in a harsh, cold country. A September snowstorm recently had flattened and ruined a crop of ripe oats over which he had labored. On December 20, 1830, he sold his ninety-seven acres at Lake Settlement to Zebedee Thayer from Bethlehem for the trifling sum of $50 and returned to Temple.

The previous month, taking notice of the strange legal situation of the territory, Phineas Willard and Justice R. Davis described their position in an agreement they made on a land sale, beginning: "Whereas there is no law in this place for the collection of debts except as we are a law to ourselves." Davis agreed to allow confiscation of his property peaceably if he failed to pay his promissory notes.

The snows deepened while the slow days following the winter solstice crept into the new year. There was the old adage, "When the days begin to lengthen, then the cold begins to strengthen." But would they ever lengthen? A settler could hardly believe that they would. The short days of cheerless sun, low in the south, followed storms that muffled the clearings and cabins. The sun rose at seven o'clock, or thereabouts, and set shortly after four. Between mid-December and early January, the nine hours of daylight hardly changed and seemed to deny the promise that, by June solstice, daylight would last for fifteen hours. But at last the days did begin to lengthen perceptibly. The deepening cold held the snow particles in a frosty matrix that crunched under boots. Bright sun and brittle cold shaped the crystal days between storms.

Sometime after February 1831, news came that the international boundary had been settled. The king of the Netherlands had awarded the territory to Great Britain. Luther Parker, John Haynes, and the other members of the Committee of Safety, as well as their opponents, Zebulon Flanders and Reuben Sawyer—in fact, all the inhabitants from Indian Stream to Lake Connecticut—suddenly learned that they were Canadians, or very nearly so. The award by the king struck fire again to the factions in the territory. It gratified men with Canadian backgrounds, property, or inclinations. It graveled the New Hampshire men. It caused searching speculation among those who wanted political unity in the settlement itself. It brought to everyone one big question: What would Canadian authorities do about their land claims, rights, titles, and deeds?

It also caused the customs collectors at Stewartstown and Canaan, Lewis Loomis and Theophilous Grout, to levy United States' duties on produce brought into the country from that foreign land, Indian Stream.

CHAPTER 25

JOHN HAYNES: REGISTER OF DEEDS, 1831

After the award by the king of the Netherlands, complications unfolded slowly for more than a year. News of the award reached the United States in February 1831. By the end of March, it had shocked or pleased the men of Indian Stream and their wives and families. Almost at once, various men assumed that the king's decision had made them Canadians, whereas others knew that Congress had to ratify the award. Communications were so slow that for months no official decision on this apparently simple problem clarified the citizenship of Indian Stream residents.

Perhaps news of the award arrived through the outcry of farmers and lumbermen in the State of Maine. They complained mightily, although Maine had been allotted two-thirds of the area it disputed with New Brunswick, which caused a wail from that province. Vermont was to lose territory by abandonment of the Vallentine-Collins Line in favor of the corrected Forty-fifth Parallel. By a jog in the proposed boundary, New York would retain Rouse's Point and the fort on the old invasion corridor north of Lake Champlain. New Hampshire was to lose all the disputed land north of the Connecticut River.

Great Britain accepted the decision of the king of the Netherlands. The United States Senate balked until it finally rejected his arbitration in June 1832, a year and a half after he announced the awards.

At the time of the king's award, the men of Indian Stream had been governing themselves, after the fashion of New Hampshire towns, for nine years. For at least part of the period, such government blended with the affairs of the Bedel Company. John Haynes had been company clerk year after year. In 1827 and 1828, David Mitchell took over, either through appointment or election, and signed himself "Clerk of Bedel Proprietors" when he recorded deeds or dates of pitching. In March 1828 he recorded that Seth and Burleigh Blood had pitched on the so-called meadow lot a mile north of the inlet of Lake Connecticut on July 31, 1823.

John Haynes began again to record deeds in the spring of 1831, as though he were attempting to carry on the tradition of official transactions, hoping to preserve some order and continuity of property rights. He doubtless was encouraged to do so by the annual meeting of the settlers and by the confusion caused by the king's award, by the merger of Bedel and Eastman, and by the troubled future that seemed to be shaping for the territory. His work appears to be distinct from similar recordings he made for the Bedel Company. When the old deeds that he copied specified location in "Bedel's and associates' Grant," he signed himself "Clerk of said Grant" instead of "Proprietors' Clerk." He had begun to think of the settlement as a separate entity in territory of its own.

John Haynes made his first entry in the leather-bound account book on April 1, 1831. It was a deed from Anna and Cyrus Eames, dated May 19, 1824. They were administrators of the estate of the late Jeremiah Eames of Stewartstown. For the sum of $4,000, they deeded to Ira Ladd of Dunstable twenty-five hundred acres of common and undivided land, part of Bedel's and associates' grant, situate and lying in the United States of America, bounded south on the Connecticut River, east by the State of "Main," and north and west by the Canada Line. John Haynes copied it in his careful handwriting and signed himself "Clerk of said Grant."

He continued during the next few days to record other deeds. On April 5, he copied his own deed for land bought from David Gibbs in September 1817 for $1,000. It conveyed to him a thousand acres of the common and undivided land in Bedel's and associates' grant, situate north of latitude 45 in the United States of America.

John Haynes kept adding to his records until February of the following year, 1832. The twenty pages of legible, deliberate penmanship included the deed of Joshua Parker to Zebedee Thayer the previous December, and recorded a total of eighteen documents. Men brought some of them from old chests or tin boxes preserved from the early days. Such was Nathan Judd's. By the terms of Judd's deed, John Rowe of Prospect, Canada, tenant in common with General Moody Bedel and others, conveyed to Nathan Judd of Concord, New Hampshire, one hundred acres for $100, current money of the United States of America, on October 1, 1811. (This "Concord" was probably present-day Lisbon, former home of John Haynes.)

Nathan also acquired two hundred acres for pitching and doing settler's duty, agreeable to the proprietors' rules and regulations. This deed had become a relic by the time of recording, for the state had in 1824 secured to Nathan the two hundred acres due him through the Resolve. No doubt he still hoped to obtain legal title to the other hundred acres, although his name on Luther Parker's list showed a total claim of only two hundred acres. His farm was west of the mouth of Indian Stream, below that of Nathaniel Perkins.

The deed given to Nathan by John Rowe for the sale outright of one hundred acres in the common and undivided land contained clauses usually in the proprietors' deeds. It specified that Judd, as settler, could not choose his pitch if he waited until the last division of the land among the proprietors. The condition brings up a picture of settlers crowding into the territory as they did into some new western lands many years later. If Judd waited till the final day of division, he must take the acreage allotted to him. Another clause allowed his assigns to make the pitch. His chosen spot must not "impinge" on any settlement or pitch already made, or that "may be hereafter pitched before the said Judd or his assigns shall have pitched." The phrases foreshadow later land controversies.

These early land deeds, with their vague, spacious bounds, gradually gave way in the 1820s to more definite terms. By 1824, Rufus Brockway, husbandman, of Indian Stream Territory, supposed to be within the bounds of the United States of America, sold to David and Amos Tyler, yeomen, of Waterford, Vermont, for $350, land beginning at the southeast corner of the lot of land that Jeremiah Tabor lately had purchased from David W. Wells, thence due west to the land of John Haynes, Esq., thence south on Haynes's line to the Connecticut River, thence up said river to Moody Bedel's line, thence following said line due north to the first bound, "meaning the place I lately purchased of Richard Quimby." It was signed by Rufus Brockway, October 25, 1824, and witnessed by Nathan Perkins and Benjamin Coon. There was no acknowledgment before a justice of the peace. Some of the earlier deeds had been acknowledged before Micaja Ingham at Canaan. It did include the elusive "more or less," which was sometimes spelled "moar or less," as, for example: "to contain 100 acres or moar, be the same moar or less." "Moar" forecasts of land disputes.

The pattern of the deeds by 1830 reflected the trading, dickering, and jockeying caused by the conflicting bounds and claims. The irregular legal position of the territory showed in the deeds, as in the agreement between Willard and Davis made on November 18, 1830. Justice B. Davis promised to pay Phineas Willard "for the farm I this day bought of said Willard," in neat stock and grain, $25 a year with interest, for five years. Recognizing the lack of legal machinery for the collection of debts, he further promised that if he neglected or refused to pay the notes, Willard (or the bearer of the agreement) could take any property belonging to him (Davis). Willard then could have it appraised by the judges appointed by the inhabitants of Indian Stream or, should there be none that year, by two "indifferent" men. Davis would abide by the value set. If there should be no property to take, Davis would give up the farm peaceably.

Apparently Davis made good on the first note, then decided to get out while he was ahead. Perhaps he didn't like the classification as Canadian, which by then hung over the territory. A year and three months after he bought the farm, he sold it back to Willard for $150, along with a small parcel of land that Nathan Judd had quitclaimed to him without charge. Davis charged Willard $10 for this land, "laying easterly of the Haynes lot so-called on which Tim. N. Haynes now lives and adjoining Back Lake Brook, being the same lot on which Zacheus Clough cleared about 2 acres in 1825." In theory Davis made $35, less his interest. The suspicion remains, as it does in appraising many of the deeds, that no cash changed hands, and that the deeds, whether based on promissory notes or mortgage agreements, were fundamentally records of debts that the creditors hoped to collect in the neat stock or grain sometimes specified, or in labor on land that might return by default.

Justice Davis left no further record at Indian Stream, having sold his farm (originally pitched by Jedediah Buttens, who sold to Ebenezer Fletcher, who sold to Phineas Willard, who sold to Justice B. Davis) on February 17 and 22, 1832—the latter date being Washington's birthday, only thirty-three years after the first president's death.

Some of the deeds that John Haynes recorded had their origins in motive of quick speculation for gain. Samuel Danforth, 2nd, engaged in such a transaction, perhaps even for cash, for the money involved was not excessive. He began with land he bought on July 19, 1831, from Southwood Sibley for $20. It was an area with river frontage, about eighty-three acres, which might be valuable. The bounds began at William Sibley's southeast corner, and ran due south to a fir tree on the bank of the Connecticut, thence up the river 100 rods to an elm stake, northerly 160 rods to a cedar post, and west back to the first bound. Danforth kept the lot two months, added a little gore of land near the line-fence he built with Sibley between their two houses, about twelve acres, and sold it all to David Rowell for $75.

In contrast to the early deeds, some of the later ones accurately specified the surveyed bounds. Jeremiah Tabor sold one hundred acres to young Orsman Carr for $100, all surveyed in rods, bearings, and witness trees: south 75 degrees east, 160 rods, and so on, between two spruces, a cedar, and a white birch tree spotted and marked on four sides.

Other deeds specified land divisions from Ladd's surveys for the early Bedel Company and attempted to define the bounds, sometimes gathering together smaller parcels of land. These deeds embodied the express purpose of straightening property lines. David Eaton sold to Moses Thurston fifty acres for $12.50, beginning near Thurston's buildings. Eaton reserved the right to cedar timber in the east part of the lot. On the same day, February 4, 1830, Moses Thurston sold to Sampson Thurston land that began at the corner of the lot he had just bought from Eaton, extending along Gage Brook between a ledge and a small orchard near his house.

In these various ways, John Haynes devoted himself to the office of register of deeds in the territory. He kept the post for a year, and signed his records with the designation of the place as Indian Stream Territory and himself as "John Haynes, Clerk of said Territory." Once or twice, in a sadly humorous mistake, he added "Alas Bedel's Grant" instead of "Alias Bedel's Grant."

In March 1832, John Mitchell took over as register of deeds. His first recording was of an old deed, dated 1824, between Richard Quimby and Rufus Brockway. Quimby sold for $200 land between John Haynes's and Moody Bedel's along the Connecticut River. Two days later, Brockway sold it (in an unlikely deal he caught two Vermonters, apparently) for $350, but that deed already had been recorded by Haynes, with all its detailed bounds, on page 230 of his leather-bound account book. Mitchell's entries began on page 240. The recording would continue for another 100 pages—115 in all (John Haynes had not started at the beginning of the book), till Alanson Cummings would record the last deed in July 1835. By then the government, whose constitution had been recorded in the same book, would be disintegrating in the face of inner and outer pressures, but descendants of these men would use their records in the courts of Coos County.

In 1831, at the same time John Haynes was keeping his records, Moody Bedel down in Bath (where spring arrived almost a month sooner than in Indian Stream) was recovering from a winter of sickness and poverty. His friends had helped. A loan came from as far away as Washington, D.C. During February, L. D. Wheeler, learning of Bedel's illness, sent him $5, to be repaid without interest when he could. In March, a visit from his daughter, Mary Quimby, had to be postponed when whooping cough broke out in

Bath. Writing from Barnet, Vermont, Mary said that she knew a man who would pay her father $500 for his place at Indian Stream. Moody Bedel did not give up the land, despite his need.

During this year the customs collectors would have designated produce from his northern lands—had he been in Indian Stream—as "imports." Carts or sleds driven into New Hampshire and Vermont were coming from "Canada," the reins of the horses held by "Canadians." Lewis Loomis and Theophilous Grout interpreted most literally the award by the king of the Netherlands, to the outrage of Luther Parker, John Haynes, and others who knew the award was not valid without ratification by Congress.

Canadian authorities also assumed that the award gave them authority over the territory. Officers in charge of the Canadian militia ruled that the young men of Indian Stream must now take part in the summer training. To facilitate jurisdiction over the territory, the Canadians laid out a road from Hall's Stream over the ridge eastward into the valley of Indian Stream, near Nathaniel Perkins's farm.

The New Hampshire legislature again postponed the Eastman Company bill for a land grant. It could do little else; the land had been awarded to Great Britain.

At last in the fall came an incident that relieved the tension, a controversy of the gossip-creating type that did not soothe the participants but amused the neighbors. Melissa Thurston went to Colebrook and hired Ira Young, the lawyer from Bath. Young instituted a proceeding in October against Moody Haynes. Melissa charged he was the father of a child with which she was pregnant, having begotten same in April at Indian Stream.

A sheriff from Coos County went to the territory and arrested Moody Haynes, no doubt with Haynes protesting loudly, but without the physical furor that has left other arrests permanently in the records. Moody Haynes was bound over to appear at the Court of Common Pleas in Coos County the following September. By then the result of the complaint would have reached the age of about seven months, depending on the date of birth. Moody Haynes did not languish in jail and must have provided bond, probably through a solid citizen who appears to have been his father, John Haynes. During that year of waiting for his case to come to court, he or his lawyer thought up a defense both ingenious and of historical interest, for it impaled desire on a point of law, involved the international boundary, the deliberations of the United States Congress, the arbitration of the king of the Netherlands, and the claims of Great Britain. Moody Haynes maintained that the court had no jurisdiction, as the cause of the complaint accrued to Melissa at Indian Stream.

CHAPTER 26

LUTHER PARKER WRITES TO THE SECRETARY OF THE TREASURY, 1832

The talk in the settlement about Melissa Thurston and Moody Haynes had scarcely died down (the gossips still waited for the case to come up in the Coos Court) when a new incident, this one at the customs office in Vermont, outraged the men who had been protesting collection of duty on their produce.

The duties had been imposed earlier in the year. Most of the arguments had taken place at the New Hampshire collection point in Stewartstown. By December 1831, Lewis Loomis remained unconvinced of the error of his position and continued requiring duty. Loomis, the wrestler and sheriff who had overcome the murderer from the Magalloway, was a difficult man to influence when he saw his position and stood firm on it. He did consent to take bonds, or promissory notes, instead of cash. This was all he would concede; a New Hampshire man sympathetic to anyone from Indian Stream with New Hampshire sentiments, he yet did his job as he saw it after the king of the Netherlands awarded Indian Stream to Great Britain.

Uselessly the drovers, traders, and farmers argued, but argue they did: the United States Senate had not yet accepted the award, and Loomis had no directive from Washington to collect duty. Where was his paper showing that the Senate had voted for ratification? Where was his letter from the Treasury Department instructing him to collect on Indian Stream produce? They wanted to see the signature of Secretary Louis McLane.

Loomis continued to insist on their posting bonds for the duties. If the award were rejected by the Senate, he would return the bonds, and no harm done. If the award were accepted, the settlers must make good on their notes in cash. The settlers grumbled and cursed and signed the bonds and went on their way through Stewartstown to Colebrook with their wagons and teams. As the season changed to winter, the teams drew sleds.

The men talked and speculated. There was another route south by way of Vermont. At Canaan, Theophilous Grout guarded the border as customs officer. He interpreted the king's award as did Loomis: the inhabitants of Indian Stream were Canadians and must pay import duties, or at least post bonds as they did when taking goods into New Hampshire. To the settlers, however, Canaan offered possibilities involving the various roads that passed through the town toward Hereford, Canada, and back into Vermont, little-used tracks similar to the one laid out that summer by Canadian authorities over the ridge from Hereford to Indian Stream. Some dark night, with snow blowing thick down the valley of Hall's Stream, shrouding the road over the mountain to Leach's Stream, and back to the river road south beyond the customs station . . . Theophilous Grout had no right, no authority . . .

Grout caught them. He seized three loads of goods driven by Indian Stream men. Angered by their slipping past his office, he refused to take bonds. Instead, he held the loads until the Indian Stream men produced cash money, which they did at last, protesting and threatening all the while.

This situation aroused the settlement in three ways. The New Hampshire men were outraged; they organized meetings among themselves to discuss ways of stopping Loomis and Grout in their illegal and high-handed collections. Canadian sympathizers shrugged and laughed, but felt drawn together; Canadian authorities would never collect duties—they never had and wouldn't start now. A third group saw ahead the probability that the Senate would reject the award and that the nebulous position of the territory would continue. Thus a closer political unit must be devised to act effectively against outside injustices such as the collection of duties.

So thought John Haynes, and so, with reservations, thought Luther Parker. Haynes represented the men who wanted to be left alone in northern peace. Parker, more and more, represented New Hampshire men determined that the territory should become part of the state. But a coalition of the two was possible in dealing with the collection of duties. It might bring attention in Washington.

As the annual meeting approached, "warned" for March 5, 1832, discussion and arguments broke out repeatedly between men who met by chance at the mills, at the store Luther Parker had started in one room of his house, or along the roads, where they whoa'ed their oxen and stopped to talk.

At the meeting, the usual airing of grievances, of long-winded harangues between feuding factions, cleared at last before the undeniable importance of unity against outside threats. There in the Center Schoolhouse, near where Gage Brook ran through the little hollow below the cemetery, the men settled down to listen to John Haynes. Outside, crusted snow piled high about the windows. The room was light and dark, the bright sun shining in contrasting with the dark shadows around the stove, which glowed at the draft door from the burning chunks of maple and birch. Above the schoolhouse, snow lay on the wooded slope and on the gravestones in the cemetery. It hid completely many of them, for a sad proportion were the small stones of babies: an infant son of Ebenezer and Sally Gitchell died February 20, 1825; a son, fourteen months old, of Richard and Sally Blanchard died May 10, 1825. Other little stones lay under the snow. There would be more over the years, some soon. Twin babies born to a Haynes family the previous May would die within the next month and be buried under a small, home-carved stone.

The fathers of these children gathered at the school on March 5, 1832, "agreeable to notice." John Haynes read the warrant. The men chose David Mitchell for moderator. They reelected John Haynes as clerk, but he asked to be excused from the duty. They chose John A. Mitchell in his stead. They then continued the definition of the territory that had been used in former years, by which inhabitants who lived on the west bank of Indian Stream should be considered legal voters, until other authority or regulation was established.

After a brief controversy over the election of judges, the men chose three: Abner Hyland, Jr., Burleigh Blood, and Clark J. Haynes. They next chose Herman Bachelder for sheriff, and seven men to superintend at funerals and act as sextons, one in each highway district, as well as three fence viewers to investigate complaints about property lines. John A. Mitchell was to record deeds. They then chose a committee—Luther Parker, Clark J. Haynes, and Nathan Judd—to do something about the customs collection. The next vote, to raise taxes in the usual way, gave Luther Parker another job, that of tax assessor, along with John A. Mitchell and Ross Haynes.

Following a spirited debate, the men voted to choose a committee of six to adopt some measure to prevent people from cheating, lying, and swindling other people out of their property. The elected members of the committee could not agree. Sampson Rowell, Elija C. Sawyer, John Haynes, Jonathan Hartwell, and Reuben Sawyer (who had given up on the Eastman Company) concluded that indeed something should be done but that they didn't have the authority to do it. They so informed the meeting and referred the problems of cheating, lying, and swindling to the judges.

At this time, Luther Parker's committee on customs collection presented its report. It proposed a letter of protest to the Treasury Department. But more than this, it recommended forming a "society" that could provide the unity necessary to deal with illegal customs collections, with conflicting land claims, and with the administration of justice within the territory. The men of Indian Stream, who for the most part had been unaware that they were ready for such a move, found that they were, and voted to accept the report.

They then turned to more practical arrangements: "Voted that a person wishing to be married can be published by the clerk and married by any ordained minister; Voted that judges have power to administer oaths to witnesses; Voted to dissolve this meeting."

Luther Parker set to work at once writing a complaint to the Treasury Department. He finished it within a week, including a short history of the territory. To the Honorable Louis McLane, Secretary of the Treasury of the United States, he presented the appeal of a committee appointed by the "United Inhabitants of Indian Stream," and he described the very difficult and embarrassing state in which they had been placed because of the opinion adopted by Lewis Loomis and Theophilous Grout, Deputy Collectors in New Hampshire and Vermont, that Indian Stream was outside the United States and its inhabitants were liable to pay duties.

Luther proceeded to review the geography, the background of claims and surveys, and the jurisdiction by New Hampshire, beginning with the survey of 1789 made by Jeremiah Eames along the supposed international boundary. The inhabitants, Luther wrote, of which there were three or four hundred, feared being caught between the jurisdiction of two governments. A lawsuit settled in New Hampshire might result in a countersuit by Canadian authorities against the New Hampshire sheriff who performed his duty in trying to enforce the New Hampshire court ruling. (This came to be the final cause of open hostilities in 1835.) Consequently, the inhabitants felt that their duty and interest lay in avoiding acts that would bring the law of either the United States or Canada into the territory. The different authorities might easily come into collision, with international repercussions. Therefore the inhabitants had found a way to settle their own problems and had preserved peace and order in society by the virtue and intelligence of the people, which induced them to submit to things necessary for the public good. In this way, they believed, they might avoid difficulties such as those that had arisen from a different course pursued by the inhabitants of Maine's disputed territory.

In this same spirit, they had submitted to military service in Canada, although they considered it a violation of the agreement that they understood existed between the United States and Great Britain, according to which neither should exercise exclusive jurisdiction in the territory. They thought it better to submit, hoping that before another training session, the Canadian authorities might be convinced of their error.

As for the collection of duties, taking bonds was one thing; seizing and holding loads of goods for cash was another. Luther admitted that several inhabitants had "passed by the collector's office," for they were convinced the collector acted without authority and contrary to the wishes of the United States Government. The money extorted from three of the inhabitants, by holding the loads of goods, had aroused against Grout the just indignation of them all. Continued collection must certainly convince people that the government sanctioned it. Canadian authorities might step in, assuming that the United States had relinquished its claim to the territory.

The inhabitants, continued Luther, having been born and educated as citizens of the United States, and believing they still inhabited territory of the United States, could not willingly submit to foreign jurisdiction. The inhabitants held the strong impression that the United States Senate would not ratify the award by the king of the Netherlands. The territory must in all likelihood continue in dispute for several years. If duties continued to be levied, the inhabitants must find another market, the import charge being so high, or they must stop raising produce.

In short, asked Luther Parker and his committee, are we liable or not to pay duties?

The men of Indian Stream on March 13, 1832, held a meeting to hear the report of Luther's committee. They voted that their acting committee sign Luther's letter and send it to McLane in Washington. John Haynes signed first, then Elija C. Sawyer (like Reuben Sawyer, he had given up trying to work through the Eastman Company), and then Ephraim C. Aldrich, a man who would take center stage in three years with a cavalry saber in his hand and, one or two spectators claimed, considerable rum in his veins. The three signatures at this time represented the new unity that was forming within the framework of the annual meetings, road appropriations, and an embryonic legal code. The three men had diverse backgrounds and sympathies, but managed to submerge them for the sake of an organized community.

The voters went home to await word from the secretary of the treasury. In the following weeks they (except those favoring Canada) continued to debate ways and means of preserving their property, and their place in the

United States. Eventually the talk always turned toward the notion of a "society" as proposed by Luther's committee—to independence, no less.

Previous to the meeting, three months back in January, Deputy Collector Grout had become worried. After the Indian Stream men tried to slip by his office, he began to think they might have right on their side, although not in the sense of it being right to act like smugglers. In a letter to his superior, General Cahoun, on January 25, 1832, he asked whether he should collect duties from men of the disputed territory, for some Customs House officers thought they should and some thought not, which was causing much difficulty in the vicinity. This letter reached the State Department in Washington, where it was passed along to John W. Weeks of Lancaster, then representing Coos County in Congress. Weeks, in turn, sent the problem to another New Hampshire man in Washington, Levi Woodbury, the secretary of the Navy. Woodbury might not have the personal knowledge of the area that Weeks did, but he certainly had the legal background, for he had acted as counsel for the Eastman Company in the Hyland-Fletcher cases in 1824, only eight years before. Also, he continued his association with the region through his law office. His most recent legal stand had been that the territory belonged to New Hampshire, as it must if the legislature were to grant it to the Eastman Company. Quite naturally, therefore, he wrote the same opinion to Weeks; the people of Indian Stream were, as concerned duties, on the same ground as the people in the rest of the state.

This cannot be called a direct cause of the action taken by the Treasury Department, yet it could scarcely be a coincidence either. Two days later, on March 1, 1852, the comptroller of the Treasury Department wrote to Weeks. He enclosed a copy of the order directing collectors to stop collections on Indian Stream products.

News of this order did not arrive at Indian Stream within the next two weeks, so Luther and his committee composed the letter to McClane, the acting committee signed it, and away it went to Washington, perhaps starting its journey in the pack of a man on snowshoes headed for Colebrook over the hills of Clarksville south of the settlement, toward springtime and the nation's capital.

Winter, for all practical purposes, continued at Indian Stream into April. The ice still held the lakes motionless. Snow lay in the woods beyond the bare fields. The white northern hares, not yet changed to their brown fur for summer, looked like animated paper cutouts against the dead grass of the clearings, where they sometimes came to play and leap about in their mad mating season. The birds were returning. In the maple woods, the sap-run was over. While men took in the wooden sap buckets, their wives boiled the syrup down to sugar, carefully tending the fire, nursing it to the right flame, stirring the syrup constantly lest the molten sweetness catch on the iron kettle and scorch at the last moment.

Secretary McLane's reply arrived in April. Luther Parker was told of it by the three members of the acting committee. McLane had ordered the collectors of New Hampshire and Vermont to give up the bonds they had taken, to restore the money taken, and to stop further collections.

The credit for McLane's order, deserved by Grout and his letter, was doubtless claimed by the men of Indian Stream through their appeal to McLane, the arrival of which after the decision had been made may not have been known to the committee. From either perspective, the victory went to Indian Stream. It gave the men a sense of common cause and a feeling of effectiveness as a group, which they now regarded as a "society." The next step might be effective control of their own territory, at least while the United States and Great Britain argued about the boundary.

April moved along slowly. It could not be said to blossom, for there were no blossoms in April at Indian Stream, save those of the swamp maples whose red tassels appeared late in the month. April did at last turn into May. The little brooks along the edges of the clearings, and the pools in the woods, no longer froze to silence and sheets of glass at night. Ephraim C. Aldrich, being a former Vermonter from Bradford, took particular care of his sap pails and sugaring equipment in the large maple orchard he was opening up from the wild woods, trimming out roads and paths from tree to tree and burning the underbrush. Luther Parker, busy with spring work on his twelve acres of farmland—six acres mowing, five acres pasture, one acre tillage—had a horse now. He had given up the slow oxen, for he planned little heavy farming or logging. He kept three cows and some young stock. His real interest lay in the store.

At this season he packed furs and wool and hides of deer. The deer population had increased greatly in recent years, and men still hunted them for the purpose of extermination, still in hopes of thus driving the wolves from the territory. There were wolf pelts, too, and moose hides from hunters from the upper river and lakes. Luther was secure now in the assurance that the furs and hides would go down to Colebrook free of duty, along with kegs of potash, bags of wheat and grass seed and corn, bundles of shingles, kegs of salt beef and salt moose meat, ham, bacon and salt pork (butter, cheese, and potatoes were out of season)—all articles he had taken in trade.

This year, 1832, he planned to enlarge the value of his stock to several hundred dollars: axes, harness, molasses, salt, whiskey from the potato stills in Colebrook. In all probability he disapproved of whiskey, or tolerated it as one of the unavoidable facts of existence. Nobody could approve who saw it drag down the poor families that didn't even own a cow. Many folks claimed it was a restorative, a salutary drink from which the drunkenness was no more than a period of joyful elation, quite all right to indulge in several times a day without harm. A family might use almost a gallon a day, bartering as much as three bushels of potatoes for it. It was a "common and frequent beverage," and Luther Parker had to stock it.

The contents of his backwoods store answered the needs of the frontier: knives, hammers, hatchets, fish lines, hooks, steel traps, scythes, whetstones, awls, needles, tin pans, kettles, spoons, gunpowder, flints, lead for casting bullets, birdshot to use in fowling pieces when the ice melted and the geese came, twine to make nets for trapping the pigeons that would arrive in thousands, and some ribbons and lace foolishness for the women. Already his stock-in-trade was assessed at $400. With this and his farm animals and cleared land, and with his own poll tax, he had to pay a total tax of $5.41.

Planting time arrived late in May. The men of Indian Stream went about their farm work. Their feeling in favor of a society grew as the legal status of the territory continued in a muddle, drifting into a worse one. They wouldn't drift.

They called a meeting for June 11, 1832. Again they chose David Mitchell for moderator. They voted for a committee to draft a constitution and laws for the preservation of order and peace in society until the boundary was settled. As members they chose David Mitchell, Luther Parker, Phineas Willard, Herman Bachelder, and Nathan Judd. They gave the clerk, John A. Mitchell, authority to call a meeting, when the committee "thought expedient," to consider the constitution. Then they adjourned and went back to planting crops and fighting blackflies.

The Eastman Company, that June, withdrew its petition for a grant of land from the New Hampshire House of Representatives. The status of the area made it political dynamite until, that same month, the United States Senate turned down the boundary decision by the king of the Netherlands. The vote was close, twenty-three to twenty-two.

In this decision, President Jackson, for all his friendliness toward Great Britain, did not oppose Maine's contention that her agreement was necessary before a treaty could take territory away from her. According to the New Hampshire view, the king's award showed a completely inadequate grasp of geography. The northwesternmost head of the Connecticut obviously lay at the source of Hall's Stream. In the Senate debate, the king's legal qualifications were questioned. He was no longer king in the sense that he had been when appointed arbitrator. The Belgians had revolted successfully, so he was king only of Holland. Finally, the Senate rejected his decision, although he gave to the United States more territory than it obtained by Daniel Webster ten years later.

Canadians in the vicinity of Indian Stream wished that the Senate had not thought up such a specious excuse for rejecting the award, and that New Hampshire would stop harping about Hall's Stream. Did the United States still think they would get any or all of Canada after the trouncing they took in the War of 1812? A few settlers wondered the same thing, not always secretly. Certainty and security—even belonging to Canada—appeared to them better than this nonexistence and nonownership.

After forty-nine years, the boundary dispute resumed its course toward some future solution.

The committee delegated to draft a constitution for Indian Stream began to hold meetings. David Mitchell and Luther Parker talked of forms of government. New Hampshire men were familiar with their state's constitution, or with the form it took—the General Court or Legislature, with its House and Senate, the Council, and the governor. In its original form, the Declaration of Rights, and Plan of Government for the State of New Hampshire had been adopted in 1783, then revised a decade later. Copies of the state constitution could be seen in Concord. In a more definite way, David Mitchell, Luther Parker, Phineas Willard, Herman Bachelder, and Nathan Judd discussed wordings that would shape a government not so confining as to be turned down by the men of Indian Stream. They discussed the methods of organizing a general assembly. More and more, the actual writing fell to Luther Parker and David Mitchell.

CHAPTER 27

A CONSTITUTION FOR INDIAN STREAM, 1832

July brought an event that never before or after was part of haying time. Notices for a meeting to vote on the constitution appeared at the mills of Ebenezer Fletcher and Peter Barnes.

In the first week of July, provident husbandmen were going into the meadows day after day before sunrise to sweep down the tall grass while the dew eased the scythe blades. On good days, if the sun stayed hot and bright, the hay dried by afternoon, ready for raking and tumbling into piles for loading on the wagon or drag or sledge, to be stored in the barn or in outside stacks. On those days, the grass dried green and pungent and sweet. Other times a shower came over the ridges to the north and west, soaking the hay as it lay almost ready to take in. Spread out to dry again, it was never the same; it lost the fresh green of the first curing and eventually, after repeated soakings, became yellow and straw-like, with the tenderest blades broken and fallen away.

On July 9, 1832, sixty men crowded into the Center Schoolhouse. They wore their work clothes: homespun shirts of flax and of wool raised on their farms, pants of the same, homemade boots, moosehide moccasins, hand-knit wool socks, leather breeches, hats (of cloth, skin, or felt, one or two old cocked hats worn for the occasion), and a few threadbare broadcloth coats, soon shed and left with the women at the wagons, where the horses had been hitched in the shade while children played by the brook trickling down the hollow toward the Connecticut River.

At the hour posted, or near it, the clerk of the territory, John A. Mitchell, stood up in the schoolhouse and read the warrant. It had to do with the formation of a government and the adoption of a constitution, specifically, to see whether the legal voters of Indian Stream—legal only to themselves, in actual fact—would adopt such a constitution.

The men wanted to discuss the issue freely. They voted to adjourn for thirty minutes. There may have been a gathering at the wagons of those who had thought to bring along a jug of potato whiskey. There also may have been a flask or two of West India rum or of French brandy, the occasion being worthy.

The meeting resumed after the adjournment, and the men chose David Mitchell for moderator. Although he was on the committee to draft the constitution, as moderator he could take no active part in the committee's report. The other members of the committee were Luther Parker, Phineas Willard, Herman Bachelder, and Nathan Judd. The reading of the constitution and the explanation of it fell to Luther Parker and the other members.

The proposed constitution began with a preamble describing the geographical and international location of Indian Stream: "Whereas we the inhabitants of the tract of land situated between Hall's Stream and the stream issuing from Lake Connecticut, being the disputed tract of country near the head of Connecticut River which is claimed by the United States and Great Britain . . ."

The document then went on to explain why a formal establishment of authority was necessary. The inhabitants, it stated, had met from time to time and passed votes and laws for their own regulation, with no penalties or machinery to enforce them. Now, as the population and improvements had considerably increased, they wished to adopt and enforce laws on a more permanent basis, and to provide for supporting schools, all for the benefit of the rising generation. The time had come to make and enforce laws for the protection of citizens who otherwise would be a law unto themselves. This need had become especially evident, "considering the power of self-love in prejudicing the mind where the individuals are interested and act under the impulse of passion." Anarchy lay in that direction.

Neither the United States nor Great Britain had exercised jurisdiction. Therefore, the citizens must do so. The proposed constitution would remain in force at least until the United States and Great Britain settled the boundary controversy.

The spirit of the constitution was set forth in a bill of rights, which included the following:

1. The right to originate their own government.
2. The right to religious freedom.
3. The right to life, liberty, property, happiness. "Hence arises the right

of controlling the vicious members of society who invade the rights of others."

4. Men entering society surrender some natural rights for the protection of other rights.

5. Every member has an equal right to be protected and is equally bound to contribute his share in the expense of such protection and to yield his personal service when necessary.

6. The right of "every subject of the government" to the protection of law in defense of injuries to his person, property, or character; the right to justice without delay, conformable to the law.

7. "No subject shall be held to answer" without a description of the crime, and has the right to produce all evidence in his favor, to meet the witnesses against him, and to have judgment by his peers and by the law of the land.

8. "No subject" shall be tried, after an acquittal, for the same crime; no law shall enforce corporal punishment without trial by jury, except in the militia in time of service.

9. No excessive, cruel, or unnatural punishments should be inflicted, "the true design of punishment being to reform and not to exterminate mankind."

10. No unreasonable seizures or searches should be held; an officer must have a warrant confirmed by oath and describing specific charges.

11. Every inhabitant, having the proper qualifications, shall have the right to elect and be elected, to enjoy freedom of speech, and of debate.

12. All officers shall be agents of the people.

13. All societies of men without government have the right to form a government; where a majority unites to do this, the minority "ought to submit to the majority and be controlled by them."

These rights, provisions, and theories having been set forth, the constitution moved on to the exact form of government.

The people inhabiting the territory formerly called Indian Stream Territory do hereby solemnly and mutually agree with each other to form themselves into a body politic by the name of *Indian Stream* and in that capacity to exercise all the powers of a free, sovereign, and independent state so far as it relates to our own internal Government till such time as we can ascertain to what government we properly belong.

The supreme legislative power within this place, the constitution decreed, shall be in a council and assembly, to meet each year on the second Monday in March, and when called by the council. The assembly shall be known as the General Assembly. It shall consist of every male over twenty-one with three months' residence who shall take the loyalty oath for members of the assembly.

The General Assembly shall have the power to set up courts and make wholesome and reasonable laws and regulations with or without penalties.

No bills, acts, or resolves shall originate in the General Assembly, but it may propose amendments to those of the council, which may reject the amendments. The assembly, however, can pass over the objections of the council by a two-thirds vote, in which case the council need not sign.

The assembly shall have the power to regulate its sessions, to elect civil officers, and to adjourn from time to time, but not exceeding three days without the consent of the council.

The council shall consist of five members chosen by the assembly, who shall take the loyalty oath for officers and have the following powers:

1. To meet as often as they deem necessary.
2. To watch over the general peace and safety of the inhabitants.
3. To draft and present all bills, acts, and resolves for making laws and regulations as they consider necessary for the public good.
4. To commission militia officers.
5. To cause complaint to be made and to prosecute to final judgment before any court all persons subject to indictment for any criminal offense against the peace and dignity of the people.
6. To command the militia.
7. To assemble and conduct the militia.
8. To encounter, repulse, resist, and pursue by force of arms within the limits of this place, and "also to Kill, slay and destroy if necessary and conquer and compel to obedience to the laws" hostile persons attempting the destruction or annoyance of the inhabitants of Indian Stream, or rising in insurrection.
9. To pardon.
10. To call special sessions of the assembly.

The constitution provided also the parliamentary machinery used in adopting it, in establishing the assembly, in electing the speaker and the clerk, and in choosing the council. It included a provision for altering itself, by giving the speaker the power to ask at each annual meeting, "Is it necessary to alter or amend the constitution?" If so, the assembly was to choose a committee and vote on its proposals.

The constitution ended with another geographical comment—a limitation to the westward, where lay the Canadian town of Hereford, somewhere beyond the ridge of Nathaniel Perkins's back pasture, and beyond the cedar post on the bank of the Connecticut River: "Provided that nothing contained in this constitution shall be so construed as to extend the Jurisdiction of this government over any inhabitants settled on the east side of Hall's Stream, if any there are who are included within the chartered limits of Hereford."

At the conclusion of the report, the men voted another adjournment, this time for fifteen minutes. When the meeting reopened, the period of debate passed quickly. The majority of the men favored the constitution. In a short time David Mitchell put the question: "Is this constitution approved and shall it be adopted?" He then began to call out the names from the roll of voters handed him by John Mitchell. As he read the names, each man answered "yea" or "nay." John wrote down the results of the vote. "Yea" resounded again and again.

John handed the list of votes to David, following the procedure laid down by the committee. David cast up the votes.

Whole number	59
Yea	56
Nay	3

He declared the constitution adopted and began the organization of the assembly, to which every legal voter was eligible. From the roll, he again began calling out the names of the voters. Forty-four men answered that they wanted to become members of the assembly. The three men voting against the constitution legally could have joined, but probably did not. Eight men who were in favor of the constitution did not want to go further and be in the assembly. Their names were crossed from the list.

Of these men rejecting membership in the assembly, some were old-timers. David Eaton had settled in 1819. Perhaps he still hoped for some vague accomplishment in the territory by the Eastman Company. Ebenezer Gitchell had made his pitch in 1823, Jeremy George in 1820. Neither of them had any land secured to him by the state, nor were they Eastman men. They appear to have been nonparticipants beyond their vote for the constitution. David Tyler had sold his farm to Abner Hyland in 1816 and had made various moves to other property, never taking any active interest in the politics of the settlement.

Other men who rejected membership in the assembly were newcomers. Nathaniel French had arrived in 1828, Jonathan Lamb sometime after 1829.

They had not a long experience of annual meetings and the territory's problems.

None of these men who rejected membership would have a part in the new government. Members of the assembly alone had the vote, curtailed to some extent by the council. Therefore, the men actively involved in the new government numbered forty-four, about two-thirds of the men in the settlement.

These included the two mill owners, Ebenezer Fletcher and Peter Barnes. Most of the old-timers joined the assembly: Zacheus Clough, Benjamin Coon, Burleigh Blood, John Haynes, Jonathan Hartwell, Samuel Orsborn, Daniel Rogers, Clark J. Haynes, Nathaniel Perkins, Reuben Sawyer, Jeremiah Tabor, Alanson Cummings, Sampson Thurston (not Moses), Phineas Willard, Richard I. Blanchard, Nathan Judd, Luther Parker, Elija C. Sawyer, Emor Applebee, John H. Perry, and David Mitchell.

The more recent arrivals included John A. Mitchell, William Fessenden, John Robie, and John H. Tyler, this last man in due time to be the cause of riot and insurrection. The younger generation was represented by Rufus Hartwell, son of Jonathan, and by John Langdon Haynes, twenty-eight, and Ross Haynes, twenty-one. Their brother Clark, at thirty-three, was nearer the age of the older men. Timothy N. Haynes, twenty-three, joined. Thus the Haynes family, including the patriarch, John, could rally five votes among father and sons.

Certain men were conspicuous by their absence: Zebulon Flanders and Ephraim C. Aldrich. Flanders held definite Canadian sympathies. The absence of Ephraim C. Aldrich cannot be so easily explained. He had been appointed to a committee in March and had signed the letter to Secretary McLane. A man of quick action and temper, he could not have fitted easily into the parliamentary procedure of town meetings, nor into the judicious weighing of conflicting suits. Yet he came to support New Hampshire's claim to the territory—provided it left him alone.

So the men stood waiting while the eight nonparticipants went out of the schoolhouse to join the three Nay voters and others—a total of sixteen—who were against, neutral, uninterested, or ineligible. The forty-four members of the assembly proceeded with the business of governing themselves.

David Mitchell brought the meeting to order, and John Mitchell administered to the members of the assembly the oath of loyalty: "I solemnly swear that to the best of my power and ability I will support inviolate the constitution and laws of Indian Stream, so help me God."

John Mitchell wrote at the bottom of the list his certification that the men had been duly qualified and admitted as members of the assembly, agreeable to the constitution. He signed his name and title, Clerk of Indian Stream. Below this he wrote the customary "Indian Stream Territory" and date, July 9, 1832. Then he realized that the official name of the country was now only "Indian Stream," and crossed out the word "Territory."

David Mitchell called upon the assembly to perform its first official act, that of voting for officers. He soon found himself speaker instead of moderator, with John Mitchell the new clerk, or continuing clerk. David administered the oath to John, then John to David: "I do solemnly and sincerely swear and affirm that I will faithfully and impartially discharge and perform all the duties incumbent on me as Speaker of the Assembly (Clerk of the Assembly) according to the best of my abilities, agreeable to the Constitution and Laws of Indian Stream, so help me God."

David, as speaker of the new assembly, declared the old meeting dissolved and went on to the business of the General Assembly of Indian Stream at its first annual session.

To perpetuate successful methods used in the past, the assembly first adopted from the earlier meetings all the former rules and regulations for operating itself, at least until others were made. It elected the five-man council provided for by the constitution—Phineas Willard, Luther Parker, David Mitchell, Nathaniel Perkins, and John Haynes. Then it chose three justices of the peace—Nathan Judd, Clark J. Haynes, and Burleigh Blood.

The council, headed by Parker and Mitchell, proposed—by the constitutional authority vested in it—laws that the assembly could not originate but could only approve or amend. During this first day it approved of eight acts bolstering the new government:

* It voted that the council draft rules for the government of the "house" (i.e., the assembly).
* It established a court of justice by empowering the justices to try all actions, pleas, and controversies, and to render judgment for debt, damage, and costs.
* It established a jury system.
* It empowered the court to authorize the sheriff to attach and sell at auction goods sufficient to pay judgments.
* It regulated the sheriff's fees at 4 cents a mile, 25 cents for serving a writ, 50 cents for arrest by warrant, and 12 1/2 cents for summoning each juror.
* It established the sheriff's duty to execute orders of the court, and to "obey the instructions of the plaintiff in attaching and selling property on writ or execution, provided he shall receive good and sufficient bonds to in-

demnify him in case the property does not belong to the person whose property he was ordered to attach."

* It also provided for jurors' fees: 4 cents a mile for travel, 33 cents for a half-day's attendance, 33 cents for time over six hours, the fees to be paid by the person requiring a jury. The fine of $5 was imposed for failure of a juror to obey his summons, unless disabled by the hand of Providence.

* It voted that no liquor be allowed within a quarter of a mile of the assembly rooms, on pain of forfeiting all said liquors to the sheriff, by order of any justice. The sheriff was to sell said liquor—including the vessel or cask—within four days and lodge the proceeds with the treasurer (after deducting his fees) for the use of the inhabitants of Indian Stream.

The assembly voted to repeal former rules and exempted certain property from attachment. Each inhabitant should be secure in the necessities of life, namely:

1 cow
1 hog
1 swine not over six months old
The meat of 1 hog
7 sheep
The wool of 7 sheep
3 tons of hay
1 bed and bedding for every two persons
All wearing apparel
All their books
$20-worth of tools for a farmer or mechanic
1 gun and equipment
$20-worth of household furniture
1 bushel of grain, meal, or "flower" to each person
5 bushels of potatoes
2 bushels of salt

The assembly then voted in favor of a militia consisting of every able-bodied man between the ages of eighteen and fifty. They were to meet after the assembly adjourned to choose their captain, lieutenant, ensign, and first, second, third, and fourth sergeants. They were to gather annually in the future on the second of June for military duty, inspection, and instruction in tactics, with such arms and equipment as they might possess, and were to offer strict obedience when the captain ordered actual service. Then each citizen must rendezvous as ordered, armed with a "good musket, two spare flints, and twenty-four cartridges with ball suited to the bore of his musket, and powder sufficient to discharge the same, and knapsack with one day's provision."

After that vote the assembly adjourned and went home to feed the cattle and hogs, to drive in the sheep for the night, and to eat the cold porridge that was all the womenfolk had provided, having been with their men or, if left at home, having no enthusiasm for preparing a big meal at an indefinite hour.

And so, in an area of uncertain boundaries, the men of Indian Stream set up their new government on that ninth day of July. The doubts that were felt—and probably voiced—by opponents of the constitution and by those who refused to join the assembly might very well have been aroused at the powers wielded by the council. Oligarchy did not appeal to true northern independents. Although the council would consist of neighbors and even friends, it represented solid, well-to-do citizens who had power over other men's lives.

Forty-five years before, James Madison had dealt with the problems of small governments in one of his *Federalist* papers. Having described the effects of faction in destroying democratic governments, which he called popular governments, he traced the chief source of dissension to the diversity in the faculties of men, from which the rights of property originate, as well as the diversity in the amount of property itself:

Those who hold and those who are without property have ever formed distinct interests in society. Those who are creditors and those who are debtors fall under a like discrimination . . .

From this view of the subject, it may be concluded that a pure democracy, by which I mean a society consisting of a small number of citizens, who assemble and administer the government in person, can admit of no cure for the mischiefs of faction. A common passion or interest will, in almost every case, be felt by a majority of the whole; a communication and concert results from the form of government itself; and there is nothing to check the inducements to sacrifice the weaker party or an obnoxious individual. Hence it is that such democracies have ever been spectacles of turbulence and contention; have ever been found incompatible with personal security, or the rights of property, and have in general been as short in their lives as they have been violent in their deaths.

CHAPTER 28

A BRIEF GOLDEN AGE, 1832–1834

The constitution placed most of the power in the hands of the council and set up a formal means of collecting debts. The assumption seems fair that the council, whose members more nearly approached the role of creditors than did various other citizens, tried to use the new machinery. In years past, except for rare invasions by a few rugged sheriffs, the territory had been beyond reach of legal process from New Hampshire. Canada had never attempted jurisdiction, until the previous year when it made some of the young men take militia training. Therefore old debts and obligations had accumulated. There were land agreements never fulfilled, promissory notes neglected, taxes to the settlement unpaid, and debts for grain bought during hard times put off long after the grain itself had been ground into meal, baked into bread or boiled into porridge, and eaten.

For years, as men tried to set themselves up in the wild land of New Hampshire, they incurred debts, or left debts behind them. Some managed to prosper. At Indian Stream, these were such men as Ebenezer Fletcher, Nathan Judd, Luther Parker, and John Haynes. Many more did not prosper. Their debts exceeded their income from their farms, mills, trap lines, and potash boilers. Perhaps they had started with less in the new settlement. Perhaps they lacked strength, judgment, or luck. Whatever the cause, they made a bare living and could never make repayment. Then, by New Hampshire law, the attachment of their scanty property and its sale at public auction, usually for a fraction of its value, kept them on the belt-tight edge of want.

In the early days of the Indian Stream settlement, debts could be discharged by labor, furs, grain, or cattle exchanged between individuals who would join forces to repel any outside collector. As the bare subsistence days passed, the backlog of local debts mounted, and new opportunities for debt developed within the settlement. Luther Parker could hardly operate his store in such a community without extending credit till the crop was in, the cattle sold, the lumber sawed, or the marten trapped. Previously, Ebenezer Fletcher's sawing and grinding never caused such temptation to slip into debt. The miller ground corn or wheat and kept back in meal the charge for grinding; he sawed logs into boards and took payment in lumber. If he helped his poorer neighbors with credit, he never pressed them for payment.

In the constitution, the wordings of the acts indicate a strong inclination on the part of someone, or of some group, to collect debts, to stop various forms of "self-interest," and to control the vicious members of society. The wording has an overall tone of righteousness suggestive of the stern schoolmaster, or of the Yankee patriarch, and of discipline for boys, paupers, or petty criminals. The constitution, viewed in this cynical light, appears to be the instrument for serving the interests of the well-to-do men who framed it and became members of the council. In the events three years later, this sharp cleavage ceased to be apparent between solid citizens and those less inclined to social order because they had less at stake, for in the tangled relationships of those times, support of New Hampshire or Canada became the opposite poles. Yet the community had long been divided. In the end, confusion of faction led to the imprisonment of Emor Applebee and the arrest of Nathan Judd for rebellion against New Hampshire.

Factions were inherent in the democracy of Indian Stream. Time would bring out the violence. Meanwhile, the gods smiled on this frail example of men's arrangements in a disorderly universe. Society prospered. Tranquility, or a near approach to it, reigned in this two-year golden age of Indian Stream under the constitution. Land sales increased, as though the semblance of authority exhibited by the government brought to its citizens a sense of security under which new projects could be started.

Elija Sawyer bought a sawmill, its equipment, and water privileges near the mouth of Back Lake Brook, at the Connecticut River, in August 1832. Lacking cash for the entire price of $350, he agreed to saw one hundred and forty thousand feet of boards of merchantable thickness for the previous owners, John Haynes and his son Clark, who were to provide the logs. Because the service of sawing was valued at $2 per thousand feet of boards, Sawyer appears to have made a down payment of $70.

In his turn, the same day, Sawyer sold his old mill, a less valuable dam and location, including in the sale the saw, crank, and "irons," as was customary. The crank transformed the circular power of the waterwheel to the vertical power required by the up-and-down saw. Zacheus Clough bought this mill for $250. Clough, having no money at all, agreed to saw one hundred and twenty-five thousand feet of boards from logs Sawyer would provide. He did, too, as Sawyer attested before Clerk John A. Mitchell, who wrote "discharged" on the copied record of the mortgage.

In September, Southwood Sibley, who lived near the farms of Captain McConnell and David Eaton, up the river toward Lake Settlement, sold his hundred-acre farm to Clark Haynes.

That November, Zebulon Flanders and John Haynes surveyed two hundred acres on the northwest bank of Back Lake Brook, north of Flanders's land and east of Sam Orsborn's back lot. It was to be a farm for John's son, Timothy, who would be twenty-four on December 15.

In February of the next year, 1833, John Haynes bought back from Archelaus Cummings one hundred acres of his old farm near Gage Brook, where he had first pitched in 1811.

The same month, Sampson Rowell deeded his farm to David and William Rowell, on the agreement that he would live in the west half of the house, have the south half of the shed, and have a privilege in the cellar. The agreement also stated that David and William must support a cow for him, allow him the use of half of the garden, and let him cut his firewood on the land. They also gave him promissory notes for yearly payments of $50 until 1842. This arrangement turned out to be more optimistic than practical, and in July, Rowell bought for $350 sixteen acres on the road to Lake Connecticut, adjoining some land that Nathan Judd owned, and five acres opposite, with a house, barn, and woodhouse, presumably to live again with complete independence.

Deeds to land this year reflected a renewed uncertainty. Men listed themselves as living at "Indian Stream in the County of Coos and State of New Hampshire, otherwise of Indian Stream in the Province of Lower Canada." Unfortunately, instead of being a bulwark against this uncertainty and providing a sturdy provisional security, the new government encountered its first dissension.

The assembly, meeting on March 11, 1833, did not reelect Luther Parker to the council. The other four members were returned to office: Phineas Willard, Nathaniel Perkins, David Mitchell, and John Haynes. Phineas Willard, however, declined to accept. Replacing him and Luther Parker, the assembly chose Elisha P. Tabor and Nathan Judd. No reason appeared in

Clerk John Mitchell's minutes of the meeting; no undercurrent of antagonism showed on the record.

But the reason came out two and a half years later in depositions by Luther's eventual enemies, who testified in Canada that he "lost the confidence of the people," and that he "threatened to do all in his power to injure the inhabitants and to destroy the constitution." For this—after he had sponsored and helped write the constitution, after he had taken the oath of loyalty and served on the council—Alanson Cummings, Reuben Sawyer, and John H. Tyler could never forgive him. They were carried away by the emotions of 1835 into exaggerating to falsehood a dispute of 1833, later continued by Luther's determined support of New Hampshire's right to the territory.

Thus the exact initial cause remains hidden; certain, nevertheless, was the change in Luther Parker. He became an impassioned advocate of jurisdiction by New Hampshire, rather than a detached, thoughtful, yet energetic exponent of an independent provisional government. He traveled to the south as a trader and made friends along the way. Across the river in Clarksville were other men of his sentiments.

Clarksville took shape from the Dartmouth College Grants. In 1820 two or three Dartmouth students, including Benjamin Clark, had bought ten thousand acres from the college and had settled on the land. Men such as Miles Hurlburt joined them. Hurlburt knew the territory. He had signed as an Eastman settler in 1820. Luther became friendly with him. Other men, liking the looks of the land south of the river, settled on the valley interval and first hillsides that led to the steep ridges and valleys of the interior of the town. These men came to favor expansion by New Hampshire, or the New Hampshire claim, north of the river at Indian Stream.

In Stewartstown and in Colebrook, Luther found men to support his dedication to the idea of New Hampshire jurisdiction in the northern territory. These included Lewis Loomis, with whom his sentiments on the collection of customs failed to upset a mutual respect; Ephraim Mahurin, a prominent citizen of Colebrook and Columbia, who had commanded the fort at Stewartstown in 1812; James Minor Hilliard, a hunter, trapper, and carpenter; and Hiram Fletcher, son of Ebenezer, a lawyer at Colebrook. Luther became known to these as a militant New Hampshire man in a settlement largely composed of independents and pro-British, pro-Canadian men. This did not make his life easy in the territory, but it brought him valuable help at the last crisis.

The assembly of March 11, 1833, suffered no obvious upset through its ostracism of Luther Parker. Its coherence and effectiveness remained intact. It seated three new members whom John Mitchell had examined and sworn in: Elisha Tabor, Nathaniel Perkins, Jr., and John Robie, Jr. For justices of the peace, the assembly chose Nathaniel Perkins, Richard I. Blanchard, and Burleigh Blood. The vote for sheriff went to Reuben Sawyer. Taxation, a problem neglected by the meeting of the previous year, occupied the assembly in discussion, and it passed three acts that detailed and implemented the tax program proposed by the council. The acts had to do with poll taxes, with taxation on livestock and land, and with the method of collection.

In the case of poll taxes, they decreed: "Be it enacted by the inhabitants of Indian Stream in General Assembly convened that hereafter all publick taxes shall be assessed on the polls and rateable estate in the manner following, namely: Each male poll from twenty-one years to seventy, Except ordained Ministers, paupers, and Idiots, to be valued at one dollar and thirty cents."

Livestock was to be taxed in accordance with a scale based mainly on value from youth to maturity:

Stallions and studhorses	wintered	3	winters	$2.00
Other horses and mares	"	5	"	.70
" " " "	"	4	"	.50
" " " "	"	3	"	.30
" " " "	"	2	"	.10
Oxen — — —	"	5	"	.40
" — — —	"	4	"	.30
Cows — — —	"	4	"	.20
Neat stock — —	"	3	"	.10
" " — —	"	2	"	.05

The term "wintered," by vote of the assembly, meant the keeping of livestock from December 1 to March 31.

The assembly divided taxable land into three categories: arable land, mowing land, and pastureland. On arable land, which would produce twenty-five bushels of Indian corn or other grain, the tax was to be 20 cents; on mowing land, which would produce one ton of English hay (or other hay), the tax was to be 20 cents. Pastureland presented a problem of measurement, because the cattle ran at large in the open woods and in the tangled choppings of new clearings. The assembly agreed to treat as an acre of pasture such land as would keep a cow for a year, to be taxed 5 cents.

Mills, distilleries, and other buildings were to be taxed at 0.005 percent of their real value.

To implement the tax bill, the assembly voted to choose three selectmen and a tax collector, the latter to have the power of attaching property and selling it at public auction, "sufficient to pay the tax and cost" of collection. The tax money was for "laying out, making, and repairing highways and Bridges and for the support of schools and other public purposes."

The assembly clarified the authority of the sheriff to attach and sell property for collection of debts, damages, and fines.

Evidently the previous year had uncovered difficulties in administration and judgment, although the records describe no actual cases. The elaborate machinery of collection most certainly ran into various rugged individualists. There is no account in which actual collection was attempted or completed. Taxes, beyond that of labor on the roads, seem to have constituted a mythical sum, as far as the less solvent inhabitants were concerned. But the government was working and the territory prospered.

A few days after the meeting of the assembly in March 1833, Luther Parker's family increased to three children when Alletta bore a girl baby whom they named Ellen Augusta. The boy, Charles, was going on six years old, Persis Euseba three.

That summer—in June—a visitor to New Hampshire, nicknamed Old Hickory, arrived from the south. President Jackson spent the weekend of June 28 at the Eagle Hotel in Concord, reviewed the militia, and made many Democrats happy.

At Indian Stream, Luther Parker's business prospered in spite of his difficulties with the assembly and council. He began to think of investing in a sawmill. His younger brother, Asa, was living with him when he finally made the decision to buy Elija Sawyer's mill and house on Back Lake Brook. This would put him near the more prosperous center of the settlement, about a long mile east of Fletcher's Mills, and seven miles from his farm at Lake Settlement.

Luther intended to keep his property at the lake, if it can be called "his" in view of the dubious title. He even added to it, in a complicated series of land deals that illustrate the speculation, trading, dickering, and stretching of credit in land exchanges between men of Indian Stream.

In January 1834, Luther's neighbor in the district, Zebedee Thayer, who had bought his brother Joshua's adjoining farm, bought another forty acres near Abial Holt's farm from Nathaniel Snow for $30. Zebedee then sold the land to Luther for $15. Did Zebedee owe Luther $15? Would Nathaniel sell only to Zebedee, because of bad blood between him and Luther? Asa was a witness, so the men could not have been at odds. Zebedee appears in the role of a dealer, perhaps: he had sold Joshua's farm—on the same day he bought it—to Levi Thayer of Franconia. Unclear motives hid beneath the steady penmanship of John Mitchell as he copied deeds, but whatever the incentives for the land deals, January brought Luther his mill.

Elija Sawyer's agreement with John and Clark Haynes, to buy the mill through the labor of sawing boards for them, had somehow ended with the mill reverting to them. They also now owned the half acre and house where Elija lived. Perhaps he had been unable to saw out the boards before the mill had been damaged by a freshet. In that event, he had agreed to pay $2 for each thousand feet not sawed, paying in lumber, neat stock, or grain in the following year, with interest, unless the Hayneses had failed to provide the saw logs. But Elija was able to buy back his old mill from Zacheus Clough (this was the mill Clough had bought from him in August 1832).

The implication might be that old John Haynes and Clark set up Elija in business again so he could keep sawing boards for them, at the same time taking the purchase price of $400 from Luther and Asa Parker, "traders," because they had it in cash. This deal took place on January 24, 1834. The sheriff of Indian Stream, Reuben Sawyer, was a witness. A year and a half later, Reuben arrested Luther on a Canadian warrant charging him with assisting Sampson Thurston to threaten destruction and death to Jonathan C. L. Knight.

The immediate effect of buying the mill was to bring Luther's family out of the woods. Alletta and the children moved from the Lake Settlement, which must always have seemed to her remote and on the edge of nowhere. Instead of the bleak, snowy woods and a frozen lake, she now could look out on farms and valley fields and neighbors' houses, with sleds and horses moving past on the road to Fletcher's Mills, or to her husband's mill.

To Luther and Asa, the purchase of the new property brought not only the mill business but a better location for the store, which they set up in the front room of the house. When trade was slack, they could saw lumber, provided the water in the millpond was adequate, for it fluctuated with the seasons. On the farm at Lake Settlement, they would raise grain and cattle. They could cut logs there, or hire it done, and then at the mill saw the logs into boards of "merchantable thickness." Their charge to saw other men's logs would be the going rate of $2 per thousand feet, deductible from the finished product before the owner hauled it away. There might be a chance to collect on store debts by holding back more of the boards, or by taking logs in trade.

But those problems were in the future; the chances for prosperity in January 1834, seemed weighted in Luther's favor. The mill stood near the road leading from Zebulon Flanders's place, farther up Back Lake Brook, and from the clearings and farms over near Back Lake. It joined the River Road that came up the valley from Fletcher's Mills and led east toward Lake Settlement. Most of the farmers, trappers, settlers, and choppers in that area would come past the store and mill, either going east toward the upper farms and wilderness, or going west past Fletcher's Mills to Canaan and Stewartstown, where they could turn north to Canada and Hereford, or south to Colebrook and Lancaster. Across the bridge at Fletcher's Mills, a road climbed up a steep hill through Clarksville toward Colebrook. The road was only a rutted cart track, but in years to come it would be a shortcut to the larger town.

The settlement was still growing. John Haynes found another investor in Columbia, south of Colebrook. On February 6, 1834, Noah Lyman bought a thousand acres from John for $1,000, part of the common and undivided land of Bedel and Associates' grant north of latitude forty-five in the territory of Indian Stream. John's wife, Dolly, relinquished her rights of dower. Moody B. Haynes and Calvin Tyler witnessed the document, and John Mitchell recorded it. Lyman's rights included that of subdividing by allowing each actual settler two hundred acres for moving onto the land and clearing it. This was the last of the large sales to investors or speculators recorded by the clerks of Indian Stream. The local trading, buying, selling, and mortgaging of smaller parcels of land went on unabated.

In the following month, March 1834, Ebenezer Fletcher recognized a son's interest in farming, which contrasted with brother Hiram's lawyering, and sold him land along the Connecticut River downstream from the mill. Kimball, married the previous September to Archelaus Cummings's daughter, Sarah, bought 235 acres from his father for $240. The land extended more than two thousand feet below the bridge that spanned the Connecticut west of the mill, to the land of Simon Willard. His mother, Pedda, relinquished her rights to this western portion of her husband's land. To ensure legality perhaps, Ebenezer acknowledged the deed to be a voluntary act before Benjamin Drew of Stewartstown, thereby placing on it the signature of a justice of New Hampshire; but he gave it to John Mitchell for recording at Indian Stream.

Ebenezer also sold to Kimball for $60 the north third of his large barn, and the land on which it stood, reserving the right to pass through with teams. The term "large" was inadequate to describe the barn. Ebenezer had framed it of great hardwood timbers, pinned together through the carefully fitted mortise and tenon joints. He had constructed the strongest building in the north country. It resisted the tornado of July 30, 1868, but finally gave up its roof. A few beams came to rest twelve hundred feet away. The wind smashed the nearby house and carried the pieces into oblivion. The only casualty in the village was a man named Campbell whose leg was broken by a timber.

Ebenezer and Pedda Fletcher could be proud of their son Kimball. A young man of varied talents, he could kill a bear or wolf, handle oxen or horses, hold plow or axe; but he was more than a woodsman and farmer. He enjoyed the community gatherings and could write verse on occasion, as he did for the house-raising for Parker Tabor, before Parker was married.

The citizens of Indian Stream met in General Assembly on March 10, 1834. They waited while Clerk John Mitchell checked the qualifications of men who wanted to join. He gave the oath to eleven. Among these was William White, soon to become a member of the council, a man with strong Canadian leanings. Rufus Brockway joined. Colonel Samuel Huggins, of Lake Settlement; James Abbott, a neighbor; and Simon Danforth decided to support the new government. Enos Rowell joined. His arrest the next year by the Coos County deputy sheriff, William Smith, raised a controversy over New Hampshire's violation of Indian Stream sovereignty and was the real beginning of the government's external troubles.

When the new members were all admitted to the assembly, the men of Indian Stream reelected David Mitchell as speaker and John Mitchell as clerk and treasurer. The assembly rejected the old council entirely. It chose, instead, Jeremiah Tabor, Phineas Willard, Abner Hyland, Jr., William White, and James Abbot. The men were oddly assorted. Jeremiah Tabor operated a big farm in the valley of Indian Stream. James Abbot was one of the rugged Abbots from Lake Settlement. Abner Hyland, Jr., whose father had been found guilty of trespass by New Hampshire, had no fondness for state interference. William White had lived in the settlement scarcely a year, and favored Canada. Phineas Willard appears to have been again reluctant to serve, or sick, because his post was later taken over by Richard I. Blanchard.

For justices of the peace, the assembly chose Elisha P. Tabor and Alanson Cummings to replace Nathaniel Perkins, Jr., and Richard I. Blanchard, but reelected Burleigh Blood. Burleigh lived at the most remote clearing along Lake Connecticut. He was thirty-five, four years older than Cummings.

In its last elective action for the year, the assembly relied again on Reuben Sawyer for sheriff. This represented a continued and growing opposition to New Hampshire. Reuben had firm beliefs against the rights of the state, and particularly against the rights of its deputies who invaded the territory—he thought they had no rights at all.

The ensuing votes on legislation were negative. The assembly placed on

TABLE 2
Council Members by Election Year

	1832	1833	1834	1835
David Mitchell	✓	✓		
Luther Parker	✓			
Phineas Willard	✓	✓(R)	✓(R)	
Nathaniel Perkins	✓	✓		
John Haynes	✓	✓		
Nathan Judd		✓		
Elisha Tabor		✓		
Jeremiah Tabor			✓	✓
Abner Hyland			✓	
William White			✓	✓
James Abbot			✓	
Richard Blanchard			✓	✓
Burleigh Blood				✓

(R) = resigned

the table or returned for amendment six acts proposed by the council. These acts, reported by the old council (the new council had not met), found insufficient support at the time and failed because of the opposition to the 1833 council. In a continuation of the meeting five days later, after revision under the new council, most of the legislation passed.

The assembly had one constructive request of the council before it adjourned until the following Saturday, at "ten o'clock AM." It wanted the council to report a bill for a committee to lay out a road to the State of Maine, "and to pay them for it." This side-door to the territory had the appeal of a third exit, as when Pearson Cogswell proposed one in 1822. Such a route would be unhampered by either New Hampshire or Canada.

When the meeting continued on Saturday, the mood was more businesslike. Two new members were admitted to the assembly, Samuel Danforth and Moses Thurston. The assembly chose eight men for highway surveyors, one in each district, according to the custom established before the constitution had been written. Young Kimball Fletcher had the district around the mills. In the previous year, the assembly had voted to choose, and had chosen, selectmen and a committee to lay out new roads. This year, Luther Parker was elected to both offices. As selectman he worked with Elisha P. Tabor and David Mitchell, as well as on the road committee with Richard I. Blanchard, a member in 1833, and Jeremiah Tabor.

The assembly selected Simon Danforth and Burleigh Blood "to look out the Eastern road," and to "attend to their duty as soon as convenient." Blood was a logical choice, for the road would probably leave his clearings, and he was a surveyor. The assembly listened to an encouraging letter from

Dr. Josiah Prescott of Farmington, Maine, describing the advantages of a road to the Maine markets. Danforth and Blood were instructed to ascertain the distance over "the best course" to the first good road over the line in Maine. (If they did, their exploration has escaped the records; the Maine road remained a dream.)

The legislation that was passed by the assembly in 1834 dealt with some of the problems faced by the border democracy, both in controlling the community and in buttressing the government. To paraphrase and summarize, the seven new acts included:

1. An act to prevent vexatious suits at law. No creditor shall for any contract recover before any court in Indian Stream more cost of suit than debt or damage shall amount to, when the debt is less than $2. (The justices appear to have been overwhelmed by claims in the range of 50 cents or $1.)

2. An act for the punishment of assault and battery and murder. Assault and battery: six months and a fine not over $10, and costs. "Wilfull murder": death.

3. An act to provide for laying out and discontinuing public roads and highways. A committee of three shall determine which roads are to be considered public ways, and which shall be classed as discontinued. A petition by ten citizens for continuance, discontinuance, or new routes shall bring a ruling from the committee, as well as necessary surveys and damage awards. The committee shall also have authority to close roads by means of gates, between May 1 and November 1. Any person leaving open a lawful gate shall be liable to an action of trespass, as though he had broken open a private close.

4. An act to raise and assess a tax for making and repairing highways and bridges. The $300 needed shall be paid for in labor in the various districts, allowing "to each able-bodied man finding his diet and tools (leaving it discretionary with the surveyors to allow for extra tools as they think right) one dollar per day for labor done previous to the middle of September, and after that time seventy-five cents a day and oxen the same."

5. An act to raise a tax for support of government and to defray necessary expenses. The selectmen shall assess a tax of $75, to be paid into the treasury by February 1, 1835, in wheat, grass seed, oats, rye, or cash. (Still hopeful of hard money, the council specified, and the assembly optimistically voted, that after February, all remaining taxes were to be paid in cash.)

6. An act making provision for confinement of criminals. "Whereas, there is no gaol within the bounds of Indian Stream, and whereas there has been and may be criminal offenses committed against the peace and dignity of the inhabitants of Indian Stream by persons who after convicted thereof

refuse or neglect to perform the sentence of the court before whom the respondent was convicted, and bid defiance to the law of the land: Therefore to remedy the evils aforesaid and others which may arise," the sheriff shall have as one of his duties the confinement of criminals in his own house, outhouse, or any other building he may provide. If a criminal shall be hostile, or attempt to escape, the sheriff may lawfully bind him, doing so without abusing him unnecessarily. The cost of supporting the prisoner shall be paid by the prisoner himself, unless the the prisoner have no property, when the cost must be paid by the inhabitants of Indian Stream. (This act gave the sheriff latitude in the confinement of criminals, which he further construed, legend asserts, to allow use of a huge, iron potash kettle inverted over the prisoner on a ledge, propped up with a stone to let in a little air. The industry of boiling down lye leached from wood ashes had declined; one of the great kettles might easily have been available. Seven feet in diameter, six or seven inches thick at the bottom or, when inverted, at the dome, it formed a jail under which no prisoner would stand up and walk away. The persistence of the legend indicates that at least once Reuben Sawyer did use such a jail, on a ledge in back of his house. The tale may be of dubious authenticity, yet its very originality is its strongest recommendation. The story of the kettle's disappearance among the wilderness ridges of eastern Clarksville seems more unlikely. None of this is to be taken as implying that the sheriff tipped the kettle over his prisoner unaided. The next act passed by the assembly provided for deputies.)

7. An act authorizing the sheriff to appoint deputies who shall serve writs from the justices. The sheriff shall put up a bond to the council for his faithful discharge of his duties. If he fails to turn over the money or property collected to the person to whom it is due, the creditor shall have the right to an action against the sheriff.

One other act deserves mention, for its regulations were important to the independence of the community. Although chronologically its place is uncertain, it perhaps was passed at the March 10 meeting. After its passage by the assembly, marriages could be performed by any ordained elders or ministers of the gospel, and by justices of the peace. The assembly authorized them to solemnize marriage between persons who might lawfully enter into that relation. First, such persons must have the clerk publish their intentions at three public meetings or on three Sabbath days, and they must show the clerk's certificate to this. The fee for a clerk was 25 cents; for a minister or justice, $1.

A small but significant change took place in the meeting of March 15. Because John A. Mitchell had requested a leave of absence, the assembly chose Alanson Cummings as clerk *pro tem*. He continued in the office the next year and witnessed the disintegration of the government, indeed, furthered it through his support of the Canadian faction and through his antagonism to New Hampshire.

In June of that year, the Eastman Company almost pushed their bill for a land grant through the New Hampshire legislature. They succeeded in the House, but failed in the Senate, where their bill was postponed. For eleven years they had tried for a grant of the northern lands; this time they missed by two votes. The failure could have been seen as a victory, for the House favored them whereas previously the heart of the opposition had centered there. Perhaps Moody Bedel's influence helped. A man of seventy now, a military figure of years gone by, long associated with the development of the northern lands, he was also a Jackson man. Andrew Simpson of the Eastman Company in a letter to Bedel outlined succinctly the political scene and the moral excuse for land grabbing:

I think it is now a good time to apply, as we have a good Many old friends, in the house, and but few of the old opposers, except Gove, and I should think Strange if you could not keep him Still as you and him are good Jackson Men. It is vaine for the State to delay acting till the line is Settled with great Briton, for all we ask is for the State to release all their claim above the 45th degree of N. latitude . . . I have no doubt but we can get a settlement with the State.

They would get a settlement, indeed—of some sixty families—and an independent government, if they won.

In the end, the bill was postponed by seven members of the Senate who opposed the four members favoring the Eastman Company. Had two of the opposition joined those in favor, Moody Bedel would have retrieved his slumped finances that year. He didn't, but next year sure . . .

At Indian Stream, the summer passed with this danger a main topic of discussion. August came with thundershowers and the beginning of harvest late in the month. The men asked themselves whether another year would find them harvesting on land granted to the Eastman Company. Soon they faced another threat. Sheriffs from New Hampshire arrived—invaded the territory, many said—to confiscate property for bad debts. The days of peace and tranquility were over. The golden age of Indian Stream, July 9, 1832, to August, 1834, came to an end.

CHAPTER 29

NEW HAMPSHIRE MOVES ON INDIAN STREAM, 1834–1835

By September 1834, events forced the council into action. On the second day of that month, it sent off two letters, one a petition to the secretary of state in Washington, the other a protest to John H. White, the high sheriff of Coos County, whose deputies were again attempting to confiscate the property of settlers who had unpaid debts.

The members of the council knew the temper of the inhabitants. Their neighbors and fellow citizens would certainly resist the New Hampshire sheriffs with fists and clubs, if not with powder and shot. The State of New Hampshire, thought many men of Indian Stream, had no right to invade a territory operating under its own government in peace and tranquility. They clung often to the misunderstanding that the United States and Great Britain had agreed to refrain from governing the territory until the boundary was settled and for this reason believed that New Hampshire had no rights over them. Once the boundary was finally agreed upon, they would be ready to dissolve their government and accept whichever nation they might be assigned to. Meanwhile, they wanted to be left alone; they wanted to avoid entangling the United States and Canada in embarrassing confrontations such as took place on the Maine border; they wanted to avoid forceful resistance to the New Hampshire sheriffs.

In this vein the council petitioned John Forsyth, secretary of state in Washington, for a ruling that New Hampshire had no jurisdiction in Indian Stream.

The council also sent a letter of protest to Colonel John H. White on the same day, September 2, 1834. It pointed out the danger of an "effusion of blood" if he persisted in sending deputies to Indian Stream. The council was taking "every precautionary measure to prevent any outbreak of hostilities." Let Sheriff White stop trying to serve writs until word on jurisdiction came from Secretary of State Forsyth. First to sign the letter was William White, then Richard I. Blanchard, James Abbot, Abner Hyland, Jr., and Jeremiah Tabor. They sent off the letter and prepared to wait watchfully until Forsyth replied.

That well-dressed, well-mannered Georgian, who had come to favor in Jackson's administration because of his part in the president's fight against the bank, now propounded the beginning of a detached, nonintervention policy, which he continued into the more serious events of the next year. He of course refused to recognize the Indian Stream government and wrote to the council that "if you are within the limits of the United States, as has always been maintained by this Government, it is because you are within the limits of the State of New Hampshire." He went on to advise the council to take its pleas to the courts of New Hampshire.

The letter, dated September 23 and addressed to the council, was directed to be left at the post office in Bradford, Vermont. As aid to their cause of independence or federal backing, it was a disappointment, but it did not fall into the hands of their opponents and give comfort to them.

Sheriff White probably did not see Forsyth's opinion that Indian Stream belonged to New Hampshire. He wrote to Chief Justice Richardson of New Hampshire and Governor William Badger. Richardson withheld an opinion on jurisdiction, indicating he would support Governor Badger's policy. Badger consulted Attorney General George Sullivan, the prosecutor of the cases against Ebenezer Fletcher and Abner Hyland, Sr. In forthright and resounding terms, Sullivan stated that the courts must enforce the laws pertaining to the boundaries claimed by the state. He upheld practical politics, states' rights, and territorial claims in the spurious majesty of legal language: "When the Sovereign Power of a State claims a right to any territory, to a particular line, its courts are bound to enforce the laws as far as that State claims Jurisdiction." More specifically, Indian Stream inhabitants should be punished for resisting officers of Coos County, as other men would be punished in other parts of the state.

Governor Badger sent this opinion to Sheriff White. By then, January 1835, winter had come with snow and cold. The season did nothing to deter Sheriff White. He wrote to the council of Indian Stream and sent them Sullivan's letter. He stated his own intentions of enforcing laws as his duty required, without fear or favor.

Through all these tribulations of autumn and early winter, the government had continued to function. Even while negotiations went on, the adjustment of property disputes proceeded, if not quietly at least steadily, toward some distant goal of order. Moses Thurston yielded to the decision of three judges. He agreed to give a quitclaim deed to Sampson Thurston, thereby relinquishing his right to the land on which Sampson's house stood near Gage Brook. This would settle a dispute of two years' standing and would follow the judgment handed down by Zebulon Flanders, Phineas Willard, and Ebenezer Fletcher.

As early as March 1834, John Haynes had been trying to untangle claims to various parcels of land in the area south of Reuben Sawyer's house. He arrived at a series of complicated bounds, which emphasized again the confusion caused by the surveys of 1820, particularly those of Jonathan Eastman. The shuffling and trading in lots continued, as did the borrowing, the promissory notes, and the mortgage deeds. In January 1835, prospects for the territory seemed sound enough to John Haynes; he accepted a promissory note of $1,000 from Ephraim and Jeremiah Aldrich for land on the south side of the Connecticut, where the fertile meadows lay along the quiet section of the river known as deadwater. Money continued scarce. He did not expect payment in cash, but in produce—neat stock and grain.

They entered into this agreement the day after Sheriff White sent Deputy William Smith into the territory with a warrant for the arrest of Enos Rowell. Smith served the writ and took Enos to jail in Lancaster. A Canadian account names Luther Parker as the complainant. True or not, this would be in keeping with Luther's determination to further the jurisdiction of New Hampshire. Also, the complaint (apparently concerning a bad debt), from whatever person, gave Sheriff White the opportunity, three days after he had warned the council of his intentions and of his legal backing, to demonstrate that he would not be bluffed by a provisional government of border farmers and woodsmen.

White's act appeared as a violation of sovereignty to the men who supported the constitution of Indian Stream. To Luther Parker and other enthusiasts for New Hampshire jurisdiction, including those such as Nathaniel Perkins whose partisanship was less keen than their desire for law and order, White's action was a triumph for their cause. Unfortunately for the peace of Indian Stream, it solidified the opposition of their enemies. Canadian sympathizers and independents joined forces. The bitter quarrels that resulted arose from the presence of such enemies in the government itself. Luther Parker was a selectman, Reuben Sawyer the sheriff. Richard I. Blanchard was an acting member of the council, which included the pro-Canadian William White. Burleigh Blood, a justice of the peace, faced Alanson Cummings, also a justice as well as clerk. Cummings's views and actions eventually led him to flee into Canada.

Despite the presence of these "opposed" men in the government, during its last months of existence it managed to maintain for a time the moderate, controlled policy that had been the foundation of the constitution. But now independence and opposition to New Hampshire became entangled with a desire among a large portion of the citizens to throw the territory and themselves under the protection of Canada, of Great Britain.

The assembly met on March 9, 1835. It chose Alanson Cummings, the acting clerk, as clerk in the coming year. The records are scanty, and the office of speaker is not listed. David Mitchell and John Mitchell had sold their property to Ross Haynes on February 19 and took no further part in the drama. Alanson Cummings gave the oath to four new members. He listed their names in his thin handwriting, with its feathery suggestion of letters and its odd shadings, elegant but almost illegible. Two of the new members were Applebees, independents or pro-British, from the Perry Stream district. They were enemies of Luther Parker, as was the head of the family, Emor.

This year, Richard I. Blanchard served as the leader of the council, to which only four men were elected. The others were Jeremiah Tabor, Burleigh Blood, and William White. Except for White, the men had long been in the settlement. Blanchard had come as a young man of twenty from Haverhill to chop a farm from the woods. He lived now, fifteen years later, north of the Center Schoolhouse toward Back Lake. It was a typical small, subsistence farm of two hundred acres. The Resolve of 1824 had secured to him one hundred acres of this. The land supported him and his family. He kept a horse, two oxen, two cows, two head of neat stock, on five acres of mowing, one acre of tillage, and four acres of pasture. Burleigh Blood, of almost the same age, had a similar background, except that his hometown was Temple, and his farm lay farthest from the settlement. In contrast, Jeremiah Tabor had bought a farm in the best valley interval of Indian Stream and was a man of substance and moderation and greater years. William White, the newcomer mistrusted eventually by proponents of New Hampshire, owned a piece of land on the north side of Back Lake near the mouth of Sucker Brook, a holding of little value compared to Tabor's or even Blanchard's, and valued at $50 when he sold it to Elija Sawyer that June.

These then were the men of the council for the last year of the government, 1835. The citizens who had brought the government to reality were no longer with it.

After the meeting, two days of cold March snows and winter weather brought another task to a member of the assembly, William Fessenden. His baby son, three months old, died. In the little cemetery west of Back Lake Brook, and above its junction with the Connecticut, Fessenden and his neighbors shoveled away the snow that had covered the ground since early fall and prevented the earth from freezing deep. They buried the baby boy and marked the grave with a small stone of the slate common in the settlement. A verse had been composed and carved upon it.

Sometime later in March, Sheriff White again asserted his authority. He sent two deputies this time, one the same William Smith, and the other, Milton Harvey. The warrants were for Clark J. Haynes and Reuben Sawyer, unpaid debts the cause.

Clark Haynes had big plans for the year. He was building a house and barn in hopes that he and his wife, Adeline (a daughter of Moody Bedel), might at last live alone on their own land. Father Haynes, as Adeline called old John, knew of their financial troubles but lacked either the cash or the inclination to help with a loan. Clark thought that Moody Bedel might help. Adeline put off writing to him, not at all sure how true might be the rumors Clark had heard that her father would perhaps come into some money. Clark had every intention of paying his just debt, when he could. Meantime, he had *no* intention of being jailed by New Hampshire deputies.

In this Reuben Sawyer joined him. As sheriff for Indian Stream, Reuben objected in principle to interference from New Hampshire, and in particular to being arrested himself. They were not alone in strong feelings about the injustices of the debt law and about abuses in its enforcement. In June of the next year, 1836, Isaac Hill, the new governor, felt called upon to address the legislature on the need for revision so that public sale of property, at absurdly low values, would not ruin a debtor often unjustly served a writ of attachment.

In March 1835, Clark Haynes and Reuben Sawyer defied New Hampshire law. Jointly or individually, they resisted, beat off, beat up, and drove away Deputy Smith and Deputy Harvey. In the process, they left no doubt in the minds of their opponents that Indian Stream was an independent government and that they were members of it.

This fracas prompted Luther Parker to appeal to Governor Badger for protection of lives and property in the territory. He obtained the signatures of Ebenezer Fletcher, Sampson Thurston, John Carr, and William Rowell, as well as of his brother, Asa. To the anger of Reuben Sawyer and Alanson Cummings, he also had the petition signed by men in Stewartstown and Colebrook. Then he sent it off to the governor by Asa.

Backing Haynes and Sawyer, Richard I. Blanchard and the other members of the council at once wrote a petition in behalf of the government at Indian Stream, protesting the serving of writs by New Hampshire sheriffs, and objecting to the attempted jurisdiction. As evidence that it represented the majority of the inhabitants, the council had sixty-four men sign the petition. And as evidence that it represented solid citizenry, the council asked John Haynes to take the petition to Governor Badger, which he did.

The council also sent a delegate into Canada to talk with a provincial authority, Judge John Fletcher of Sherbrooke. Judge Fletcher, in his turn, described the territorial situation in a letter to Lord Aylmer, the governor general, and listed the events of the past few months, as well as the opinion of the majority of the inhabitants that they "ought to be described as living to the north of the frontier," which they took to be the Connecticut River.

Soon after this, on April 6, 1835, Lord Aylmer notified the British Minister in Washington of New Hampshire's actions in territory claimed by Great Britain. He asked Sir Charles Vaughn to request the release of Enos Rowell from the Lancaster jail. Apparently by this time Rowell was out on bail, but his case retained its international implications. Lord Aylmer had used the troops to put down riots in Montreal during the election of 1832; he could be expected to press the charges against New Hampshire, but he left the matter in Vaughn's hands.

On April 18, 1835, while Indian Stream citizens gathered at the schoolhouse to formulate legal resistance to New Hampshire sheriffs, at Washington Sir Charles Vaughn protested to the secretary of state. Secretary Forsyth was well aware of the situation on the border, because of the council's petition the previous fall. He again stayed clear, and sent the British note to Governor Badger.

The governor had learned of the incident of Sawyer-Haynes versus Smith-Harvey through Sheriff White, who had written to the New Hampshire secretary of state. White was convinced that the men of Indian Stream would resist "to the utmost of their ability." They were building a structure they called a jail. He understood it to be more of a fort. They were preparing to resist any force that might be brought against them. Besides, they had enlisted the help of a dozen Indians. Sheriff White did not express the contemptuous view of Indians common then to north country men, probably hoping the secretary would be impressed by his need for support.

Up at the Center Schoolhouse, the men of the assembly, in a special meeting held April 18, 1835, passed An Act to Prevent Unlawful Services. It was a direct attempt to place New Hampshire sheriffs outside the law of Indian Stream. It provided a fine of $100 for anyone convicted of serving writs by authority not derived from the government of Indian Stream. The person might be a resident of Indian Stream or of the United States—it made no difference. He might pretend to be an Indian Stream sheriff or other officer, or might presume to act as such. He would be arrested by any genuine official of Indian Stream duly authorized by the constitution to keep the peace, assisted by any man whose help he needed in subduing the usurper of authority. Measuring the reluctance of various citizens to assist, the law provided for them a fine of $10 or three months in jail if they refused.

The law avoided mention of New Hampshire or of the authority of its courts to issue writs. It merely made unlawful the service of such writs by New Hampshire sheriffs in Indian Stream. Study of the wording, which lacks the simplicity of the earlier laws, as though the confusion of the times had been reflected in the thinking of the council, reveals that the intention of the council was to maintain its jurisdiction, and that of its sheriffs and justices, but not to deny the right to reach citizens by lawful process—even New Hampshire process—carried out by Indian Stream officials. The implication is that the New Hampshire courts might work through the officials of Indian Stream. At this time, no Canadian writs had been served in the territory, but the council must have feared the conflicts this could cause. The intention of the council seems to have been in favor of compromise, steadiness in a middle route that would not involve them with authority north or south, while attempting to preserve independence of administration.

This intention would help to explain the appointment and acceptance in August 1835 of Richard I. Blanchard as a New Hampshire deputy sheriff under William White. By then, the June session of the New Hampshire legislature had altered the state's policy, and Blanchard found nothing incongruous about serving as a New Hampshire official and as a councilman of Indian Stream.

The intention of the council and assembly to patch up the shaky foundation of the government appears also in various other laws passed at the same meeting on April 18, 1835. The council realized the nearly impossible situation in which it existed. The laws seem a desperate attempt to legislate away the effects of conflicting factions, to legislate order from growing chaos.

For instance, under An Act to Protect Officers in Their Official Duties, hindering an officer of Indian Stream became as much of an offense as that of unlawfully serving writs. Any person doing so would be fined $100 and jailed until the fine was paid. The hindered official might be of the executive branch, the judicial, the civil, or the military. The council wanted authority to deal with revolt, and might have had in mind New Hampshire proponents such as Luther Parker. The implication is clear.

An Act in Case of Perjury stipulated that anyone who had taken the oath of allegiance and then violated the oath ("acting in contrariety" to the constitution) would have his name stricken from the rolls, would be denied the right to testify in court, and would be fined not more than $25 or less than $1. However, a vote of confidence by two-thirds of the assembly would restore his rights.

An Act to Compel Witnesses to Attend When Summoned was based on an earlier statute that provided for jurors. It allowed travel expense at 4 cents a mile and pay at 30 cents for a half day. On penalty of an unspecified fine, attendance was required "unless disabled by the hand of Providence." Now, the reluctance of a man to testify against a neighbor, friend against friend, was no excuse for temporary escape into the woods.

The original travel allowance for a sheriff of 4 cents a mile in 1832 became 6 cents a mile in 1835. An Act in Amendment of an Act Regulating Sheriff Fees also regulated the sheriff's duties. He was denied a fee for attending court unless his presence had been requested by the court or by the contending parties. Apparently directed against Reuben Sawyer, the act formulated the council's objections to his making a full-time job out of his position, but included the increase of 2 cents a mile as compensation.

According to An Act Authorizing the Council to Deliver Over in Cases, the council had the power to arrest and deliver to the authority demanding him any person convicted of murder, theft, forgery, or any other high crime or misdemeanor who had escaped from any other government to Indian Stream. The council saw the danger of the territory being a refuge to escaped criminals; it realized invasion by outside law officers would result. This was the last recorded act of the government of Indian Stream and was signed by Richard I. Blanchard, Jeremiah Tabor, Burleigh Blood, and William White, all of whom had signed the previous acts.

Alanson Cummings recorded, on April 18, 1835, the names of new members who qualified and were admitted to the assembly "agreeable to the Constitution." Marcus Beacher, of Hereford, had acquired a farm in Indian Stream and was acquainted with Councilman White, another Canadian. Amos Tyler had not appeared before, although the Tyler family had been at Indian Stream for more than ten years. These were the last new members of the assembly. The constitution would not survive another year.

CHAPTER 30

NEW HAMPSHIRE DEFINES ITS CLAIM, 1835

Six weeks of quiet followed the April meeting—a time of waiting while spring came to Indian Stream. The snow drew back into the hills and the birds returned. Green grass sprouted in the clearings as a proof that the cold days of May would pass. The sun at last warmed the earth for planting.

Governor Badger had told John Haynes that he would place the protest against Luther Parker's petition before the legislature in June. Alanson Cummings understood from Haynes that the governor, meantime, would not interfere with them. And indeed no more sheriffs came into the territory. This lull of the spring weeks ended in June with news of the events taking place in Concord.

Governor Badger, on June 8, 1835, spoke to the House of Representatives about the problems at Indian Stream. He reviewed the history of New Hampshire's claim as far back as the survey made by Jeremiah Eames in 1789 and emphasized the need for a definition of state policy. He asked for a joint resolution of the Senate and of the House stating their decision, either to claim possession and to enforce laws, or to abandon the territory pending a boundary settlement. The officers of the state, he explained, were in an impossible position without such a decision to guide them. Governor Badger enclosed with his message the petitions from Luther Parker and from the council, and the notes exchanged between British Minister Vaughn and Secretary of State Forsyth.

On June 12 the documents and the problem reached the House Judiciary Committee, after the Committee on Public Lands had considered them.

At this point, Luther Parker submitted another petition, asking that the territory be given the right to elect a representative in common with a nearby New Hampshire town. This had been a complaint against the state by his opponents, that the state claimed jurisdiction without allowing representation. The Committee on Elections in Concord favored it but withheld final action until the deliberations of the Judiciary Committee could be completed.

The Judiciary Committee excluded from its meetings the representatives of the Eastman Company. It studied the company's claim through the records of the House and Senate, thus neutralizing the pressure that the company planned to apply. The committee shaped an opinion that the northern land belonged to the state. Of the two petitions from Indian Stream, the committee in its final verdict favored Luther Parker's for New Hampshire jurisdiction. It judged the British note and Badger's message in the same light of the state's valid right to the territory. It gave no heed to the sixty-four petitioners against the state.

These deliberations the Judiciary Committee embodied in a report on June 26, 1835. The committee upheld forcefully the claim of the state to Indian Stream and denied to the Eastman Company any title whatever, "either legal or equitable." The resolution proposed by the committee incorporated these two opinions inextricably.

The Eastman Company could muster no real opposition without appearing devoid of ethics or of loyalty to the state. Pearson Cogswell had written to Moody Bedel in May, estimating that their northern land could have been sold for $100,000—if they had been able to get a grant from the state the previous year, as they nearly had. Cogswell was organizing the proprietors for a new attempt that might well succeed and stated: "I have written to our proprietors that they must Attend the Legislature the Coming Session and push it through . . . your age Military Service and influence will have great weight with the Legislature."

The resolution, reported by the committee and readily accepted by the legislature, put an end to Pearson Cogswell's plans and hopes. It put an end to the almost-successful attempts to realize a fortune from an Indian land deed from 1796. Although the Eastman Company continued for over a year to voice its claim, the resolution made both the company and its claim obsolete. Unsubstantiated rumors circulated that the company had immediately sold its title to Boston speculators for $12,000. It may have tried, but Moody Bedel was the only proprietor smart enough to get out in time, or almost in time, and during his life this brought him only a lawsuit with Lewis Loomis and others.

The resolution of June 26, 1835, also wrote, in effect, "Null and Void" across the constitution of Indian Stream. The legislature asserted the state's possession and jurisdiction until the final settlement of the boundary dispute. It went further, by providing Governor Badger with the authority to enforce the resolution. The governor was "requested to render all necessary aid to the Executive officers of the county of Coos in causing the laws of said state to be duly executed within the limits of said territory." In plainer language, this meant calling out the militia.

Danger of collision with Great Britain caused no hesitation. The attitude that prevailed was set forth in the committee's report, which gave a brief history of New Hampshire's activity in the territory, starting with Eames's survey and continuing through the Resolve of 1824, which annexed the territory to Coos County and granted land to the settlers. Such obvious jurisdiction and possession, the committee stated, entitled the state to continue with them until the final boundary was established. The committee put forward this opinion as having been held by Lord Castlereagh when he discussed the subject of boundaries with the American minister, Rush, in 1817. Furthermore, the federal government, through Forsyth, had refused to deal with the problem and had turned it over to New Hampshire. In the opinion of the committee, the legislature should deal with the question by maintaining New Hampshire's honor and dignity, "as well as the rights of those citizens who now claim our protection and the benefit of our laws..."

The New Hampshire legislature followed this recommendation and proceeded to decide on the foreign policy of the United States in relation to Great Britain and Canada at Indian Stream.

On the afternoon of the same day, the legislature passed a resolution that implemented Luther Parker's petition for representation. It grouped Indian Stream with two towns to the south, Clarksville and Stewartstown, as entitled to district representation.

So much for the summer session at Concord. Its sweeping arrangements for Indian Stream at first remained as ineffectual as breezes along the border. Men went about their summer work of haying, laughed at the state's pretensions, or defied the state to enforce its policy. The petition of sixty-four citizens, asking the state to desist, had been disregarded. Defiance was the prevalent mood, although some men said they would wait to see whether the state meant what it said, for a resolution cost little, and if law came, well and good—that's what the territory needed, whether New Hampshire law or Canadian law. But the defiant citizens expressed themselves more effectively through threats to the leading exponent of state intervention, threats soon legalized by a Canadian magistrate. Luther Parker found himself in the perilous position of a man with few friends in hostile country, and he kept alert to defend himself against his neighbors.

CHAPTER 31

LUTHER PARKER ARRESTED, JUNE 1835

A contest began in earnest between Luther Parker and the men seeking intervention by Canada and Great Britain. Danger lay not so much in bodily harm, although that was present. The danger lay in arrest on a trumped-up charge, welcomed by the nearest Canadian magistrate because of Luther's repeated appeals to New Hampshire, and because of his near conflicts with his opponents at Indian Stream. Jail, fines, costs, bail, and long involvement would keep him from his farm, from his mill, and from his store. In this direction lay ruin for his business, and eventual poverty and want for his family. The very complication of which he had warned Secretary McLane in 1832 now threatened him: prosecution by British law. Should he appeal to New Hampshire law, two opposed sheriffs would meet at Indian Stream in an international incident. This had not yet occurred; it awaited a member of the council, Richard I. Blanchard, later that year.

To label the opponents of Luther as Canadians is misleading, for Canada had not yet taken on the nationhood into which it was struggling. Behind the thoughts of men favoring intervention from the north lay the image of Britain, as Emor Applebee was soon to make clear. But before this, according to a Parker family anecdote, a visitation took place that warned Luther of the danger of capture by a posse or of arrest on a Canadian warrant.

After the move from Lake Settlement to the mill property at the mouth of Back Lake Brook, Luther had set up his store in a front room of the house. One day his son, Charles, then seven or eight years old, ran into the living quarters and told his father about a group of men who had lounged into the store in a suspicious manner that indicated no interest in trading. Luther watched them for a moment through a small opening in the door.

He then stepped behind the counter, took up his rifle, and placed it in front of him. His brother Asa joined him with two horse pistols, which he placed on the counter. Luther calmly rolled a ball back and forth in the rifle barrel and eyed the visitors silently until they left.

The names of the men have not come down to us. Later events and testimony show that they had decided to bide their time.

Several men hated Luther to the extent that in December he was labeled by the Canadians as a spy and disturber of the peace, this mainly through testimony of neighbors who had fled to Canada. Alanson Cummings believed that Luther had been sending notes, taken at meetings of the assembly, to Governor Badger. Cummings regarded Badger as an oppressor of the people at Indian Stream and as a man with personal interests in the Eastman Company. Although this last belief was not accurate, Cummings held it as tenaciously as his others. He would have been glad to subdue Luther.

There were other men with similar feelings about Luther. Reuben Sawyer was told by Luther that Reuben should be held and prosecuted for assaulting Deputy Smith. John H. Tyler regarded himself as a British subject, as far as concerned collection of debts at the store of Parmelee and Joy in Canaan, Vermont. He would willingly have joined in eliminating the leader of the New Hampshire men. Emor Applebee and his son had a sense of independence that favored the distant, inoffensive authority of Great Britain, in contrast with the debt laws of New Hampshire.

A list of men opposed to Luther might easily include anyone who thought that ridding the territory of him would solve their troubles with New Hampshire. Clark J. Haynes, far more of an independent than a British sympathizer, a man who at last took up the cause of the state during this period, could not have felt any enthusiasm for Luther's policy of inviting New Hampshire jurisdiction at Indian Stream. Zebulon Flanders, Nathan Judd, William White, Marcus Beacher, Zacheus Clough—the list could include most of the sixty-four men who signed the council's protest to Governor Badger against Luther's request for protection.

For them an opportunity soon arrived. A man named Jonathan C. L. Knight bought land in April 1835 from Moses Thurston, up the river from Luther's mill, toward the Lake Settlement. Almost at once, Knight became embroiled in a dispute with a neighbor, Sampson Thurston, not a retiring type, who assaulted Knight with a butcher knife, or made enough threats for Knight to call it assault and to swear out a complaint before Alexander Rea, the Canadian magistrate in Hereford. Included in the accusation was Luther Parker, who, Knight claimed, supplied firearms to Sampson Thurston.

At about this same time Luther was trying to collect on a bill for sawing boards. Unable to, he moved the boards from the mill yard to the back of the house, to hold until the bill was paid. This again is a Parker family tradition, and no name has come with the story through the years to identify the debtor. Another account describes an altercation in the mill yard between Sampson Thurston and Knight, in the presence of Luther, who made positive statements about the measures that he would take to keep the territory for New Hampshire.

Knight, who had bought his land for $300, seems to have been far from well off, in the tradition of the "yeomen" settling in the territory, and was probably short of cash for board sawing. As to the territorial dispute, his inclinations turned him entirely toward Canada, where he moved after the trouble at Indian Stream. He had little schooling and was unable to write his name. Luther's vehement partisanship in support of New Hampshire outraged him.

Magistrate Rea maintained that Indian Stream was in reality a settlement in the township of Drayton, District of St. Francis, Province of Lower Canada. His authority extended over it, he believed, or should extend there. He issued a warrant on Knight's complaint and addressed the warrant to Reuben Sawyer for execution.

In accepting the warrant, Reuben, an official of Indian Stream in his capacity of sheriff, moved close to a violation of the Act to Prevent Unlawful Services. Like Richard I. Blanchard later did for New Hampshire, he saw no incongruity in his actions. Reuben *was* an official—he did not *pretend* to be one—although he was acting on a Canadian warrant. The distinction was a nice one, no doubt influenced by Reuben's desire to rid the territory of Luther.

Sampson Thurston somehow learned of the warrant for his arrest and that of Luther. He warned Luther, suggesting that Luther come up the River Road along the Connecticut and stay with him. This was the evening of June 28, 1835. Luther took his rifle, or perhaps the horse pistols, which were handier at close quarters in the dark, and started up the road on that rainy night. At a distance from any house, in thick woods, men surrounded him before he could resist. Reuben Sawyer led them. Emor Applebee assisted. There were others, most probably Knight and Emor's son, Benjamin, and perhaps Alanson Cummings. They told Luther he was under arrest in the name of the king.

With the consideration of reasonable men, they took Luther back to his house and allowed him to change his clothes and prepare for the trip to Hereford. They showed no fear of his being rescued by his brother or by friends, yet kept a close watch on him. They crowded into the house. One of them displayed an inordinate interest in Luther's rifle. Violence hovered when Luther told the man repeatedly to put the rifle down. Confiscation of firearms must have been a temptation, especially when they included a good rifle, but was put aside along with the gun.

Luther said goodbye to Alletta and to the children. Alletta went with him to the door. She was six months pregnant, worried, afraid for her husband. He did what he could to comfort her, then allowed himself to be led away. Emor Applebee turned to follow, but first remarked to Alletta with amused vindictiveness that the old British lion was beginning to roar. Alletta had reasons enough to wonder how long her husband would be gone, and later that year she remembered Emor's joke.

Sampson Thurston was not arrested; according to Knight's testimony in December, Thurston "made his escape." There seems to have been no concentrated effort to run him down.

Reuben Sawyer and his men walked with Luther down the road to Fletcher's Mills. They allowed him to stop and ask Kimball Fletcher to carry a message across the river into Clarksville. Luther knew he could count on Miles Hurlburt in that town. Hurlburt would ride to Colebrook for a lawyer. Kimball agreed to go on the errand. Reuben and his posse took Luther on toward Hereford, perhaps sheltering themselves from the rain for part of the night in thick woods. Magistrate Rea arraigned Luther the following afternoon.

Meanwhile, Kimball Fletcher made his preparations for the climb over the muddy cart track into Clarksville. He put a new candle, seven inches long, in his lantern, lit it, and closed the lantern door. It would enable him to see the ruts and stumps in the road before he tripped over them. By opening the door, he could see objects farther ahead of him. He left behind his flintlock rifle. The rain made it useless. Before long he wished that he had it with him, or still better, that he had one of the new percussion cap guns. He crossed the river and climbed the steep hill beyond the bridge. A bear reared up in the flickering light of the candle lantern. Kimball, at twenty-four an experienced hunter, yet found this unnerving, for the bear was a female with cubs. Although she moved aside as he opened the lantern and advanced, she continued to follow behind him for some distance.

His journey and fortitude brought no immediate help to Luther Parker.

Magistrate Rea allowed Luther to remain in Hereford for three days while he waited for bail. On July 1, 1835, Rea committed him to the jail at Sherbrooke, some thirty-five miles farther into the province. A day or two later, Lewis Loomis arrived in Hereford to arrange with Rea for Luther's bail. Rea gave him a note to the magistrates in Sherbrooke. Rea had heard that Mrs. Parker was in a "distressed situation, owing to the imprisonment of her husband."

The jurisdiction of Canada at Indian Stream was important to Alexander Rea. Now for the first time it was officially on the records in action. Rea had made his first move, for personal ambition, for real estate interest, or because of pressure from various former Hereford men now in Indian Stream. Having asserted his authority, he put no obstacles in the way of Luther's release by insisting on a writ of habeas corpus or on other legal delays.

Thus it was that Luther walked out of the Sherbrooke jail beside the champion wrestler of the north country, the customs collector of 1832, a general in the militia, sheriff, and notable citizen of Colebrook. News of Luther's arrest had spread like a forest fire over the border and into New Hampshire. It now took on all the aspects of a violation of the rights of an American citizen. It mobilized the men of New Hampshire behind the resolution of the legislature to maintain law and order in the disputed territory. Governor Badger made up his mind to reply in aggressive terms to the British note of April, now that he had the backing of the legislature. Luther's arrest gave Badger an example of Great Britain's uncompromising policy. He declared that "this indignity cannot be acquiesced in, without derogating from the honor and dignity of the state, as well as causing great injury and inflicting extreme cruelty upon one of her citizens."

On July 13, with a refreshing willingness to inform the federal government and Great Britain of where New Hampshire took its stand, Badger sent to Secretary Forsyth his note asking for Luther's release and included a copy of the resolution by the legislature stating New Hampshire's claim and intention. Badger was not a man to let time slip by waiting for the slow wheels of diplomacy to turn. He did not intend to lose the initiative on the border by hesitating till instructions came through diplomatic channels. He prepared to use the executive power given him by the legislature.

The entire northern part of the state wanted action. A Concord paper expressed the popular view when it printed a letter from a man in Stewartstown describing the arrest of Luther Parker as "open rebellion to the laws of New Hampshire" by the men who arrested him. The writer also stated that the person acting as sheriff in the affair resided at Indian Stream. In this he erred.

Reuben Sawyer had left Indian Stream on July 8, 1835—a date curiously close to the likeliest time of Luther's return from jail. Reuben had gone twenty miles west and north of Hereford to the Canadian town of Barnston, escaping the threats of Luther and other New Hampshire sympathizers in the territory. He left behind crops and property, which he valued at $700. With nobody to protect his property, he did not expect it to remain intact; he was afraid to return unless protected by the British Government.

The diplomatic exchange between Secretary Forsyth and British Minister Vaughn, caused by Badger's note of July 13, resulted in a stalemate. Vaughn quite naturally rejected as unsatisfactory the New Hampshire position set forth by Badger. On July 26, Vaughn asked Forsyth to restrain New Hampshire from forcing its jurisdiction over Indian Stream and thus jeopardizing any future border negotiations.

New Hampshire, however, had already moved to enforce its laws in the territory. On July 20, 1835, Adjutant General Joseph Low ordered Colonel Ira Young to hold in readiness the 24th Regiment in support of Sheriff White. Young was at this time thirty-eight years old, a lawyer from Colebrook, and had been acquainted with Indian Stream since the time when Moody Bedel had lived there in 1822. Young waited for word from Sheriff White.

CHAPTER 32

INVASION THREATENS INDIAN STREAM, JULY 1835

At Indian Stream in midsummer, the white-throated sparrows whistled, sweet but mournful, at daybreak from the tops of the spruces. The cool night air of the north country became warm in the sunshine. Insects hovered over the clearings, where women went to the well, to the spring, or to the brook for water. Flocks of crested cedar birds, wax-sleek, darted from the dead limbs of trees in pursuit of insects in the sunlight. Grass of the swales and meadows grew as high as a man's belt, and continued to grow in the thundershowers that came out of the northwest. Corn and wheat began to mature. Goldfinches with black wings flew across the roads and hid among the weeds of the stump fences. Chickens dusted themselves in dooryards, and hogs wallowed in the sunny muck of barnyards. Vegetation of all kinds flourished, green and heavy.

Little girls made wreaths of daisies and early goldenrod. Boys plucked the leaves from the straight shafts of joe-pye weed to make throwing spears. Their sisters cherished the purple tussocks of the blossoms, and told their brothers not to shoot the spears at the hummingbirds darting over the patches of red fireweed in the burned lands.

Their fathers learned of the ready-order to the militia as they might have taken warning of an invasion. Within three days they had composed and signed a petition to the governor general of Canada for protection from New Hampshire. They dated it July 23, 1835, and began getting signatures under those of the council, headed by Richard I. Blanchard. Sixty-two men wanted help from Canada and signed the petition. The paper noted that already five citizens of the territory had been indicted for insurrection in the May term of the Coos County Court. Signing were many of the men who had taken part for a long time in the affairs of Indian Stream: John Haynes and his four sons, Nathaniel Perkins and his son, Nathan Judd, Jeremiah Tabor and his son Jeremiah, Jr., Elisha P. Tabor, Zebulon Flanders, Burleigh Blood, Abner Hyland, Jr., Richard I. Blanchard, John Perry, Samuel Huggins, Ephraim C. Aldrich, Emor Applebee and his two sons, Benjamin Coon, Alanson Cummings, and Samuel Orsborn. Others—William White and Jonathan C. L. Knight—had arrived quite recently. John H. Tyler, soon to cause the final disintegration of the government, had been in the territory for seven years. Twenty-six of these men had been members of the assembly in 1832.

Opposition to the request for help from Canada can be measured only tentatively, but its result was far more positive than that of the petition. Of the men who had been members of the assembly three years before, ten did not sign the petition. Several who had opposed the assembly or had refused to join it now did not sign. A list can indicate absence, neutrality, or pro-New Hampshire sentiments and does show the rift in the government: Luther Parker (most definitely against the government or outside it), four of the Danforths, David Eaton, Ebenezer and Kimball Fletcher, Asa Parker, Ira Bowen, Nathaniel French, Ebenezer and Silas Gitchell, John McConnell, Elija C. Sawyer, Sampson and Moses Thurston, Phineas and William Willard, and Peter Barnes. (All four mill owners refrained from signing the petition to Canada.) Absence accounts for the lack of action by various men favoring Luther's efforts to hold the territory for New Hampshire. Abial Holt, his former neighbor, had returned with his family to Temple. Absence probably kept David Mitchell and John Mitchell from taking part in the events of the summer and fall of 1835.

A minority these men certainly were. In a deposition made in Canada after his escape when New Hampshire men threatened to take him "dead or alive," Councilman William White estimated that only four or five "heads of families in the settlement" had not signed the petition to Canada. Extending this to ten, the approximate ratio is one to six based on the total of ten favoring New Hampshire and sixty-two favoring Canada. But the "New Hampshire Boys," as they came to be called, were determined, and they spread the news of the petition.

Sheriff White, on July 30, 1835, asked for the militia. Two companies of infantry from the northern towns around Colebrook met at Stewartstown, ready to march north and east into the disputed territory. By that time, Zebulon Flanders had taken the petition to Alexander Rea, the nearest Canadian magistrate, at his farm in Hereford. The date of the petition, July 23,

1835, preceded its delivery to Rea by a few days, during which signatures had been taken. News of its preparation almost certainly triggered Sheriff White's call for troops. The timing shows cause and effect, summarized as follows in three stages: first, Adjutant General Low ordered Colonel Young to hold the 24th Regiment ready to back Sheriff White; second, the council composed the petition to Canada asking for protection; third, Sheriff White asked for troops.

The council faced an invading force. Mediation or bloody, futile opposition appeared to be the choice. No timely protection, or even a reply to the petition, would come from Canada soon enough. Rea had given the petition to John Moore, a member of the Assembly of the Province of Lower Canada. He would in turn give it to the governor of the province—a slow process.

On August 3, 1835, the council sent two men to Sheriff White in Stewartstown, John Haynes and Councilman William White. Rumors had reached Indian Stream that Sheriff White had warrants as well as troops. These warrants could have been for insurrection against the state; they could have been for the debts that dogged men after hard times, youthful follies, or poor judgment, but debts nevertheless, for which they were liable under New Hampshire law.

The two envoys had instructions to tell Sheriff White that the citizens of Indian Stream, still firm in their belief that New Hampshire had no right to govern them, would give in reluctantly to superior force, on condition the militia be withheld. If Sheriff White would call off the troops, the men of Indian Stream would not resist any deputies he sent.

Sheriff White had no more desire for bloodshed than did the council. He agreed to the proposals, provided he had assurances that the men of Indian Stream would not resist his officers. The militia had been ordered to march into the territory in two days. Sheriff White offered to go himself to the settlement and evaluate the temper of the people.

John Haynes and William White accepted the sheriff's offer. They went with him into Clarksville, where the sheriff would spend the night while they crossed the Connecticut and called together the men of Indian Stream.

They met the following day at the house of Ebenezer Fletcher. Thirty-odd men appeared, including Clark J. Haynes, Alanson Cummings, Richard I. Blanchard, and Timothy Haynes. Sheriff White addressed the men, saying that he had left his documents with Colonel Young and so had no written authority to show them, but he assured them that he acted in behalf of New Hampshire, whose governor had determined to hold the terri-

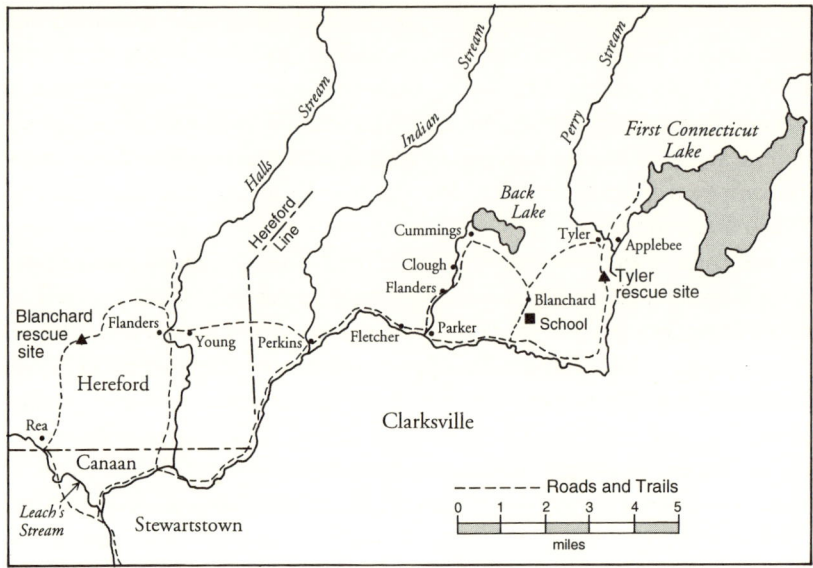

4. By the mid-1830s the Indian Stream territory was laced with passable roads and trails. This map gives a rough indication of where these went; includes approximate home locations of settlers involved in the dramatic events of October 1835; and identifies the two rescue sites. A few sellers had relocated from the pitches shown in map 3.

tory with powder and ball if necessary. Troops would arrive the next day unless the inhabitants acknowledged the jurisdiction of New Hampshire. Sheriff White asked that those men willing to do this range themselves along one side of the room, those opposed to the acknowledgment on the other.

At this point, Alanson Cummings, clerk and justice of the peace for Indian Stream, walked out of the meeting. Clark Haynes, for whom Sheriff White had a warrant, spoke in surrender, agreeing to submit only because Sheriff White and the militia were too powerful for him. Timothy Haynes joined him. Then argument and talk broke out. William Pope said that he would rather leave the settlement than submit to New Hampshire. Others agreed to accept New Hampshire's jurisdiction only because they could not get help from Canada. Eventually the greater number of the men accepted New Hampshire's authority, although often with inner reservations and defiance.

Sheriff White accepted their allegiance to New Hampshire and then went into another room, where he talked to various men about appointing a deputy to act in behalf of the state, to coordinate the work of New Hampshire deputies, and to guarantee the execution of warrants.

This unpleasant job fell to Richard I. Blanchard. Sheriff White appointed him deputy at Indian Stream. His acceptance made him a traitor in the eyes of some of his neighbors, and ranged him alongside Luther Parker and the New Hampshire men. He was thirty-six years old and head of a family. He might easily have stepped aside from the dangers of enforcing New Hampshire's jurisdiction; the attributes of responsibility and bravery should be allowed him. And yet his motives do not come clear.

As a member of the council, did he feel responsible for the good faith of the inhabitants toward New Hampshire? Had he at the last moment been taken with a realization of his American origin, ranged against the possibility of becoming a subject of the British king? Whatever his motives, he became a central figure in the events of the next few weeks.

CHAPTER 33

CANADIAN JURISDICTION?
AUGUST THROUGH OCTOBER 1835

Colonel Ira Young, Captain James Mooney, and the militia stayed at Stewartstown until August 6, 1835, then dispersed to their homes. Five men of Indian Stream wrote to Judge Fletcher of Sherbrooke that they had officially acknowledged the jurisdiction of New Hampshire; because of Sheriff White's forces, they could wait no longer for Canadian assistance. A tense pause ensued and lasted more than a month.

Adeline Haynes in August wrote to her father, Moody Bedel, in Bath, that the State of New Hampshire had enforced its laws at Indian Stream. Consequently, she and "Mr. Haynes" (her husband, Clark J.) did not know how they would get along, for he had a few debts and an old execution against him at Esquire Bell's office. "Mr. Haynes" wished that his father-in-law would assist by coming up, if he felt well enough. They understood he had "prospered in getting some money." Because of work on the new house and barn, "Mr. Haynes" could not come down. "Father Haynes" would tell the particulars of the business.

Evidently John Haynes went south with the letter to see Moody Bedel. By this time John must have been reconciled to Bedel's joining the Eastman Company. Also by this time, Bedel had no interest in that company. On July 11, 1835, he had sold his 12/25 of Indian Stream territory—that is to say, his share of the Eastman Company's land, or hope of land—for $4,000 to Lewis Loomis and two partners. This was the money Clark Haynes had heard about. The rumor exaggerated it.

Lewis Loomis and two other buyers who were with him in the deal had at first been unaware of the damage to the Eastman Company by the legislature's rejection of its claim on June 26, 1835. Perhaps Moody encouraged them in the belief that the claim would be recognized during the next session, as various of the proprietors still hoped. In time, Loomis and his partners decided they had bought a false title, and they sued. Three years after Moody's death, the court found in his favor. Loomis and his partners paid $2,000, not for Moody's title through an Indian land deed, but for his title by actual settlement.

During the month of August 1835, Alexander Rea in Hereford waited for a reply to the Indian Stream petition from the new governor general of Canada, the Earl of Gosford. Rea's interest in Indian Stream dated back at least nine years. In 1826, he had become aware of it through his job as agent for a large landholder in the valley of Hall's Stream. Baron Alexander Grant's claim to seventy-one hundred acres did not extend into the disputed territory, but his agent became interested in the possibilities to the east in the township Canada had laid out and called Drayton. He wrote to Surveyor General Bouchette of Canada that the settlers there should be "quieted in the titles to their lands to a reasonable extent..." and stated that he thought this due them because they had come to settle under the inducement of the twelve hundred acres allowed by the Clarke Proclamation of 1792 for opening new land. He also suggested that Canada build roads into Drayton to raise land values.

A question remains about the motive for Rea's interest. Land speculation for profit seems the logical drive for his continued efforts nine years later to extend Canadian jurisdiction over Indian Stream. Patriotism perhaps entered into his motivation. A friendly sense of obligation toward men settled in Indian Stream from Hereford, a feeling of responsibility aroused by his office of magistrate—these also should be allowed him. New Hampshire men used epithets less tolerant, meddler and schemer.

As soon as he received an answer to the petition (and not from Gosford but from John Moore, who enclosed a letter from the civil secretary of the province), Rea wrote a letter and addressed it jointly to Alanson Cummings, Nathan Judd, William White, and Clark J. Haynes. He asked them to call a meeting for September 26, 1835. This was a Saturday. The meeting appeared important enough to these men for them to hold a second gathering the following day, on Sunday, to make sure all the citizens heard Rea.

The magistrate arrived as he had said he would. He limped to the front of the meeting, for he was slightly lame and used a cane. He read a letter from Secretary Craig to John Moore of the Provincial Assembly. It set forth Lord Gosford's intentions: "every legal protection will be afforded by the Magistry of the District of St. Francis as well to the Inhabitants of Indian Stream as to all others H.M. Subjects within their jurisdiction."

Rea explained this policy and outlined a plan for administration by

Canada. He recommended the appointment of a committee to choose two candidates for magistrates. The men of Indian Stream, accustomed to acting as a political group in their assembly, followed Rea's suggestion and appointed Abner Hyland, Jr., and Samuel Huggins. Rea agreed to forward their names to the Canadian government. He also advised the selection of a committee to draw up a statement listing the acts of jurisdiction by New Hampshire since the date of the petition to Canada. The committee was chosen, but it did not undertake to write the document until later.

Nathaniel Perkins, active in the government since 1832 and now fifty-five years old, stood up to protest. He told Rea that New Hampshire had asserted jurisdiction over the territory and would maintain it. Rea was unimpressed and told Perkins that the state would not be so foolish as to interfere after he had held this meeting and had organized an administration under Canadian authority.

Several days later, Clerk Alanson Cummings took the records of the meetings to Rea, who passed them on to the bench of magistrates at Sherbrooke. The magistrates ordered that the records be "forwarded to Government," as Rea expressed it. No response bolstered the initial organization.

Two weeks went by, after which—by a coincidence too neat for accident—New Hampshire sheriffs arrested a pro-British citizen of Indian Stream, John H. Tyler. The action originated with William Buckminster of Danville, Vermont. He was the proprietor of a tavern and general store in Canaan, just south of Hereford, managed by Josiah Parmelee and Nehemiah Joy. It lay a mile and a half from the international boundary, the Vallentine-Collins Line, which cut across the road to Hereford not far south of Alexander Rea's farm and mill. The line here hindered almost nobody. Men on both sides treated it with debonair disdain or habitual disregard. There were, of course, no fortifications or barriers of any consequence at the customs office.

Except for Luther Parker's store and to some extent Samuel Huggins's place in Lake Settlement, the Parmelee and Joy store was closest to Indian Stream. Men could also trade at Colebrook, a long trip south through Clarksville, or at Stewartstown, across the Connecticut from Canaan. John H. Tyler traded at the store of Parmelee and Joy; he owed money there, which William Buckminster started proceedings to collect. Coincidence or not, Sheriff White and the New Hampshire men welcomed the opportunity to demonstrate their law enforcement at Indian Stream.

Around the middle of October 1835, Deputy Sheriff William Smith of Stewartstown and Deputy Sheriff Milton Harvey of Colebrook arrived at

Fletcher's Mills and walked up the River Road toward Tyler's farm on Perry Stream. They had a warrant for his arrest unless he showed them property they could attach. Because they did not know Tyler, and because they had been warned of resistance—and had sampled it that spring from Reuben Sawyer and Clark Haynes—they stopped to get the assistance of Richard I. Blanchard, the New Hampshire deputy in the territory who had been appointed by Sheriff White.

The three men did not find Tyler at home but located him at another farm where he was working. When Smith asked Tyler to show him property that could be attached and sold to pay his debt, he refused. He told the deputies that he had no choice but to go with them. He would rather walk than be dragged, but he considered himself a British subject, cared nothing for their laws, and wouldn't give bail. Smith, Harvey, and Blanchard led him away.

They had gone about a mile, when nine of his friends and neighbors, having gathered for the purpose, waylaid them and rescued Tyler. The opposition consisted of Alanson Cummings, Emor Applebee, Benjamin Applebee, Levi Applebee, Jonathan Hartwell, Rufus Hartwell, Jonathan Knight, and two others. The clerk of Indian Stream took a prisoner from a member of the council, although his action was directed more toward William Smith and New Hampshire. There seems to have been no violence beyond that suggested by Smith's account that Emor Applebee "interposed" himself between the deputy and his prisoner. Apparently Smith had the ultimate custody of Tyler, for he described him as "my prisoner." The two parties separated.

John H. Tyler at this time was forty-eight years old and had lived in the territory for seven years. His farm, near the corner where the Hill Road came down across Perry Stream, joined the land of Moody Bedel toward Lake Connecticut, recently acquired by Lewis Loomis with the rest of Bedel's claim. Tyler was thus well into the territory, about six or seven miles upstream from the mills of Luther Parker and Ebenezer Fletcher, and only about three miles from Blanchard's house on the slope south of Back Lake.

After his arrest and rescue, Tyler allowed several days to go by. During this time, Alanson Cummings described the events in a letter to Alexander Rea. Cummings wanted help and protection from the retaliatory force, which he believed New Hampshire would send to capture him and the members of the rescue party. No doubt Blanchard would return from New Hampshire, where he had gone with Smith and Harvey, bringing with him more than two deputies, probably troops.

But Blanchard came home alone. Meanwhile, Rea returned from the sessions in Sherbrooke and learned of Tyler's arrest and rescue. Discounting Cummings's letter, he saw no urgency. The men of Indian Stream took no such view; rumors persisted of invasion by New Hampshire militia.

John H. Tyler went to see Rea and made a deposition. He stated under oath that New Hampshire deputies had arrested him unlawfully in Drayton, which was not in New Hampshire but in the Province of Lower Canada. He said that only immediate action would bring them to justice, because threatened invasion by an armed force from New Hampshire would seize all Blanchard's opponents, namely, those men claiming protection from Canada.

Magistrate Rea issued a warrant dated October 21, 1835, for the arrest of Smith, Harvey, and Blanchard. He directed it for execution to Zacheus Clough and Zebulon Flanders.

Tyler took the warrant to Flanders at his house in Hereford. Although Flanders had been an official of Indian Stream as late as that May—sitting on a land judgment committee—and had property in Indian Stream going back to his bridge-building for Jonathan Eastman in 1820, he had regarded himself always as Canadian and at this time maintained a farm in Hereford, where he lived. On March 17, 1835, he had sold the two hundred acres on which he had pitched and started chopping trees in 1820, under the agency of Jonathan Eastman, on Back Lake Brook. Henry Flanders bought it for $100. The title to the land had been secured to Zebulon Flanders by the Resolve of 1824; he could not complain of the state's treatment of him in that action. But because of his connection with the Eastman Company, he had his first difference with Luther Parker in 1829. The location of the land, its fertility, and the security of the title added to its value. A price of $100 indicates that Henry Flanders must have been a relative, perhaps the eighteen-year-old son, taking over the property north of Luther Parker's mill. Zebulon Flanders had returned to Hereford, and there John H. Tyler found him.

Flanders read the warrant, which appeared to be in order, and left his house to go with Tyler to Indian Stream. Because Deputies Smith and Harvey were in New Hampshire, there seemed little likelihood of arresting them. Richard I. Blanchard became their immediate concern, as he doubtless had been all along. At the Indian Stream settlement, they met Zacheus Clough, the other man to whom Rea had addressed the execution of the warrant. Clough could not read but accepted the warrant as genuine and official. This meeting took place about noon, perhaps on the road to Fletcher's Mills. Beyond the mills, Flanders and Tyler parted, Flanders going along the road north of the Parker mill and past his former house. Tyler walked up the River Road toward his farm at Perry Stream.

Zacheus Clough had been in the territory since 1825, when he cleared two acres of land on Back Lake Brook near the lot later farmed by Timothy Haynes. He had not completed his pitch and instead had gone into a sawmill venture with moderate success, paying off a mortgage held by Elija Sawyer by sawing one hundred and twenty-five thousand feet of boards. Although a member of the assembly in 1832, he had never been active in the government. Of late he had sided with the Canadians in the settlement.

The young man toward whose house Zebulon Flanders was walking, Alanson Cummings, had lived for a number of years near Back Lake. In May 1835, he bought land at the outlet, the same "mill lot" owned by his father, Archelaus, before the move to Canaan. Through a number of deals involving Marcus Beacher, Elija Sawyer, William Patton, and Ira Bowen, through several deeds sprinkled liberally with "wherefore" and "aforesaid," Alanson managed to straighten out the title. His care in the legality of his documents was in marked contrast with his boldness in rescuing a neighbor from New Hampshire's sheriffs. He bought the property for $110. Because he had no money (presumably), he gave promissory notes payable over a period of five years.

His behavior in other ways was at odds with that expected from a son of "Squire" or "Judge" Cummings, a New Hampshire man born and raised, who returned from Vermont to his hometown, Temple, before he died. Other members of his family found no attraction in the prospect of the Canadian intervention that Alanson sought. His sister was married to one of his opponents, Kimball Fletcher. His younger brother, Archelaus, Jr., was married to Mary Fletcher, and in Canaan followed the standard life of a young farmer, with leanings toward business, which he finally took up in Colebrook. Alanson appears erratic by comparison.

On the October day when Zebulon Flanders planned to spend the night at his house, Alanson still held the office of clerk of the territory. Now, however, since Rea's meeting he was an official not of the former independent government of Indian Stream but of the administration sponsored by Canada. Alanson had stopped keeping records of deeds in September, when Nathan Judd presented an old deed giving him title to land from William Hyland southwest of John Haynes's lot (except twenty acres reserved for spruce timber from which to saw boards). About the same time, Alanson recorded a deed by which his father bought the land of James Abbot on Alder Cove at Lake Connecticut; more correctly, he bought Abbot's claim to a certain area, for the bounds cut across Samuel Huggins's land north to the "great ridge," along that to a corner near Huggins's west clearing, and down to the outlet of the lake across land of Peter Barnes. Thus Alanson, near the end of his tenure as clerk, recorded the last evidence of disputes over faulty, conflicting surveys and property rights. By this document Archelaus claimed land of Barnes who, five years before, claimed more than half of Archelaus's "betterments."

So ended the records in the leather-bound account book, which contained also the constitution and legislation of independent Indian Stream. The pages of deeds, the time and work of copying begun by John Haynes and continued by John A. Mitchell, were not wasted. Disputes about land continued for years. The book would be taken into court and consulted by judges, among them a son and a grandson of Ephraim C. Aldrich.

Alanson Cummings, in his house that evening of October 21, 1835, doubtless saw the records of deeds as a valuable reference in establishing property rights under the Canadian administration in which he would be active. He must have dreamed of a bright future for the territory, even perhaps looking ahead to the settling of the forested ridges that lay between his house on the little lake and Canada. A more immediate matter was the next day's demonstration of Canadian authority: the arrest of Richard I. Blanchard.

During the evening, Zacheus Clough joined Zebulon Flanders at Alanson's house. Nearby a road led south of the lake past Blanchard's farm. Waiting for daylight, they gathered around the fireplace, where the big log smouldered through the chill night. They slept.

CHAPTER 34

CANADIANS ARREST A NEW HAMPSHIRE SHERIFF, OCTOBER 1835

On the morning of October 22, 1835, Zacheus Clough and Zebulon Flanders walked over the ridge south of Back Lake, from Cummings's house a distance of two or three miles, to Blanchard's farm. The road wound through spruces and hardwoods. In the thickets of young beech trees, pale brown leaves clung and rustled in the morning breeze. The maples and the great yellow birches were almost bare. In places where springs seeped from icy, flat ledges of slate, the cart track became muddy. The slippery clay forced Clough and Flanders to dig in their boot heels, going downhill, and to kick hard with the edges of their leather soles, going uphill. The road led them to the slope that opened across the Connecticut valley toward Clarksville.

White frost lay on the withered corn in Blanchard's clearing. Beyond, in the lowlands, tamaracks had lost their summer disguise as evergreens and now stood yellow against the green spruces. Their twigs would soon be as bare as those of the yellow birches. Snow would whisper on the dead leaves that covered the ground, till it silenced itself in its own blanket. Under the gray sky, the distant forest seen from Blanchard's clearing had a misty appearance as the innumerable twigs etched a haze against the far ridges.

John H. Tyler joined Clough and Flanders. In all likelihood, he met them at the junction of the road up from the Center Schoolhouse, having walked over the hill from his house near Perry Stream. They had only one musket among them and probably more fear than they admitted to each other at this last moment. They could not know how much of a fight Blanchard would make. He might use the gun that every settler kept handy in his house.

Zacheus Clough assumed the leadership as they went up to the house. Richard I. Blanchard opened the door. Clough told him they had a warrant for his arrest. Blanchard demanded to know by what authority. By the king's. Blanchard asked Clough to read the warrant. Clough took out the paper, attempted to read it, and could not. Irritated and flustered, Clough gave inadequate thought to Blanchard's request to read the warrant himself, and handed it over. Flanders saw the danger—how easy it would be to turn, slam and bar the door, and drop the warrant into the stove or fireplace. Flanders took the paper from Blanchard.

They allowed him two hours to arrange his farm work, to prepare for an absence, and to say goodbye to his wife, Sally, and the children. Blanchard may have dawdled and made excuses, argued, threatened. Sally may have refused to feed Clough, Flanders, and Tyler.

The Canadians neglected to watch the fourteen-year-old son, David. He slipped away—quite likely engaged in the morning chore of cleaning out the cow barn, he jammed the fork in the manure pile and escaped to the woods, going for help from the neighbors.

Whatever happened, Clough, Flanders, and Tyler had lost the advantage of early and speedy surprise. In those two hours, the men of the settlement began to gather—both factions. With Blanchard in custody at last, Clough, Flanders, and Tyler had gone scarcely half a mile when they learned that Clark Haynes had galloped off to New Hampshire for men to rescue Blanchard. To counteract this, they asked Alanson Cummings, Emor Applebee, and his son, Benjamin, to help guard Blanchard during the journey to Hereford and Magistrate Rea. Half a mile after these reinforcements joined them, they met James Washburn and Jerry Aldrich, the twenty-two-year-old son of Ephraim. Ordering these men to come with them, they walked down the River Road another mile and a half to Fletcher's Mills, where Aldrich and Washburn ran away.

Some time before this, according to a tradition of the Parker family, the men passed Luther's mill at the mouth of Back Lake Brook. Luther and Asa had left to arouse the New Hampshire men, but Alletta Parker came to the door and saw Blanchard in the custody of Canadians and Canadian sympathizers, as her husband had been earlier that year. By this time Luther's case had been dismissed.

Blanchard, seeing Alletta, called out, "It's my turn now, Mrs. Parker."

"I'm sorry, Mr. Blanchard. I hope you'll not be gone long."

Leaving behind Parker's mill, and then Fletcher's Mills and the bridge to Clarksville, the party walked steadily and quietly to Indian Stream, where they crossed on the bridge and turned to the road laid out by Canada over the hill behind Nathaniel Perkins's farm. This route avoided the main road to Canaan. They climbed through the open pasture, past ledges, and through the spruces at the top. Beyond, an equally steep slope dropped to the valley of Hall's Stream. There they came into undisputed Canadian territory. They stopped at the farm of a Canadian named Young, whose son was a peace officer of Hereford. Bernard Young, after asking to see the warrant, agreed to provide dinner and to accompany them on the remainder of the walk over the next ridge to Rea's house on Leach's Stream.

While they were at dinner, Ephraim C. Aldrich rode up with two men from Clarksville, Miles Hurlburt and Joseph Pope Wiswell, and young David Blanchard. The Clarksville men were the first in New Hampshire to be alerted by Clark Haynes. At Fletcher's Mills they had learned that Blanchard and his captors had gone on down the road toward Canaan and Hereford. They rode in pursuit, taking the same route over the ridge after they crossed Indian Stream. Near the crest, at the last farm before going down into Hereford, they were told that the Canadians had passed.

The New Hampshire men hesitated, discussing the risk of taking arms into Canada. At last they sent the guns back with Joseph Wiswell, father of Joseph Pope Wiswell and a justice of the peace in Clarksville. The senior Wiswell had been visited earlier in the morning by both Clark Haynes and Luther Parker on their way to Stewartstown, where Captain Mooney of the militia lived.

Wiswell rode back with the guns, accompanied by two or three other men. They met Emor Applebee and demanded that he surrender, because he had been involved in the abduction of Blanchard. Applebee raised his musket and warned them not to come any nearer; he wouldn't be taken alive. Wiswell and his men did not press their authority against his determination and his musket.

Meanwhile, the remainder of the New Hampshire men had caught up with the Canadians at Bernard Young's house. Ephraim Aldrich and Miles Hurlburt obtained permission to talk to Blanchard. They suggested that he try to escape while they held off his captors. Because of the number of guards, estimated by Hurlburt at a dozen, the plan seemed too desperate and was abandoned.

The New Hampshire men contented themselves with watching the house and deciding their next move, arguing about various ways of getting help or of intercepting the Canadians by ambush farther along toward Rea's, for they knew that was the destination of Blanchard's captors. The men who came from south of Indian Stream understood the background of the border dispute. One of them, John Harriman, lived in Stewartstown, four miles from Fletcher's Mills, where he took his logs and grain. Out of curiosity he had attended one of Rea's meetings in September, and he held a low opinion of Rea's reputation. Others, also familiar with the contending factions at Indian Stream, proposed delay and compromise. There was a short talk with Flanders and Clough. Flanders said that he and Clough had no authority to arrange any compromise.

The New Hampshire men gave up temporarily and turned south to reach the road that led from Indian Stream to Canaan. The men on foot had to run to keep up with those on horses. Along the road to Canaan, they met reinforcements led by Ephraim Mahurin of Columbia. With him were several men, among them Hiram Fletcher (a lawyer of Colebrook and son of Ebenezer), the deputy Milton Harvey, and Horatio Tuttle, a blacksmith. Mahurin and Fletcher had learned of Blanchard's capture from Clark Haynes. Strongly opposed to Canadian jurisdiction, angered by British refusal to recognize New Hampshire claims, concerned about their friends at Indian Stream, they were ready to use force in rescuing Blanchard. They rallied other men and started north at once, moving fast up the road through Stewartstown, on horseback, and carrying arms. Mahurin had a double-barreled shotgun, Fletcher a rifle. The deputy, Milton Harvey, although acting under no authority but his own, carried a horse pistol. Horatio Tuttle had a musket with bayonet.

The two groups of men exchanged news. Mahurin described the gathering of men at Canaan. Aldrich pointed out the route that the Canadians would follow. Mahurin took charge and led the mounted men toward Canaan.

Back in Hereford, Flanders and Clough, assisted by Bernard Young and a neighbor, Prouty, guarded Blanchard as they crossed the valley of the meandering Hall's Stream. They waited at Flanders's house while Clough asked another neighbor, Marcus Beacher, to join them. Beacher, a new member of the Indian Stream Assembly since April, still owned his farm there but had returned to his other farm in Hereford. Clough was taking no chances of being outnumbered, although he had fewer men now than he had at Young's, seven or eight.

Continuing along the road into a tributary valley, they followed a wooded ravine up the slope of the western ridge. Again Clough stopped and recruited the aid of another man at a farm on their way; he told Pascal G.

Blood that he needed help because New Hampshire men would probably try to rescue Blanchard. Blood agreed to join the guards shortly.

This ridge they called Hereford Hill. One of the last before the great flatlands of Canada, it separated Hall's Stream and Leach's Stream, another tributary of the Connecticut. Leach's Stream entered the Connecticut to the west of the village of Canaan, in somewhat the same way that Hall's, Indian, and Perry ran from the north. It had never been a serious contender for boundary distinction because it ran to the west of the disputed territory and did not extend into the true highlands of treaty notoriety. The road over Hereford Hill rose in a steep, sharp climb, into spruces again, through pasture lands rocky and rough, useful only for grazing cattle and sheep. Beyond the summit, the road dropped quickly west into the valley of Leach's Stream near Rea's farm and mill. There it joined the road south across the line into Canaan.

The men guarding Blanchard walked past Pascal Blood's house, expecting Blood to catch up with them momentarily. They had gone about two hundred yards beyond the next house, belonging to Moses Perley, when suddenly a horse and rider galloped toward them and rushed by. Flanders recognized James Minor Hilliard, the hunter and woodsman who also practiced the trade of carpenter when he could not hunt or trap. Hilliard reined in behind them. Ahead, eight or ten armed men waited. To Flanders they appeared to be led by the former commander of the fort at Stewartstown during the War of 1812, Ephraim Mahurin. He also recognized Joseph Pope Wiswell, Thomas Piper, and Horatio Tuttle. Milton Harvey, the deputy sheriff, was with them, as well as Thomas Blodget, a farmer of Stewartstown, Samuel Weeks, Jr., of Colebrook, and Miles Hurlburt, all New Hampshire men and obviously determined to rescue Blanchard. They had evidently taken a shortcut up from Canaan by cart tracks and logging roads. They showed no hesitation about being armed and on Canadian soil.

Bernard Young, the Hereford peace officer, was a little ahead of the other Canadians. The blacksmith, Horatio Tuttle, called out to him, "Young, you poor mean scoundrel, I am sorry to see you here."

"Not sorrier than I am to see you, Mr. Tuttle."

Tuttle's reply was to level his musket and bayonet at Young and order him to stand or be blown through. As Young's companions came up behind him and stopped before Tuttle and the other men who leveled their guns, Young saw Ephraim Mahurin dismount near Blanchard. Mahurin kept his shotgun ready and ordered Blanchard to mount his horse. Flanders and Prouty objected, and an altercation began. Young spoke to a New Hampshire man near him whom he recognized, Thomas Piper, a farmer from Stewartstown who appeared reluctant to enter into the proceedings. Young told him that he had not been obliged to come. Piper said he had been obliged and otherwise would have been liable to a $50 fine. Young pointed out that the others could not compel him to assist them beyond Stewartstown Bridge, the limit of New Hampshire. Beyond lay Vermont and Canada. Piper did not reply.

Miles Hurlburt, watching, saw some of the Canadians easing away toward the woods, to escape or take cover, he thought. He heard Tuttle command them to stop: "Stand or God damn you I'll blow you through!" Mahurin was trying to persuade Blanchard's guards to release him. Prouty kept his arm locked in Blanchard's.

Mahurin's description of the event, framed the following year, deals with controlled actions and forceful attitudes. He had learned "by express" (meaning Clark Haynes or Luther or Asa Parker), in Colebrook, of Blanchard's being taken "to Sherbrooke." Without giving details of his motives or of events leading to his arrival on Hereford Hill ahead of "twelve or more persons" who had Blanchard in custody, and making no mention of the shotgun, he gave his version of the encounter, with emphasis on the causes. He stated that

on meeting them, one of our company, I think, commanded them to stop, and used some derisive language, which was promptly disapproved by Mr. Hilliard and myself, and we informed the party who had Blanchard in custody, that we wished to have no difficulty with them, that it evidently arose from the circumstance that the boundary line was not fully settled between the two governments, and that as the state of New Hampshire had for a long time claimed and exercised jurisdiction over the tract, and the claims of actual jurisdiction by the Province being very recent, and as we believed, originating in the aforesaid Rea, we felt it our duty to retake Blanchard, and to protect the officers of said settlement from arrest by officers from the Province, and that we should take him at all hazards, but wished to do it without any trouble or hard words with them.

Flanders described the encounter two months later:

Among the party we advanced until we came up with them, when they commanded us to stand and surrender every damned one of us. I asked, "by what authority, gentlemen?" "This is our authority," brandishing their weapons; "we will take you prisoners, because we are able;" after some noise and conversation they agreed to let all go but John Tyler, Clough, Blanchard, and myself, particularizing us by name: we none of us were willing to surrender, and said we would not, and they threatening to "blow us through" and commanding us to fall in. After some consultation among themselves they agreed to let all go, provided we would give up Blanchard, our prisoner; I said we would not, and told Prouty to keep fast hold of the prisoner, and that they should not have him unless by force of arms. Ephraim Mahurin thereupon dismounted, and walking around to where Prouty stood, cocked a double barreled gun and leveled it at his breast, upon which I called out to Prouty to stand back and let go the prisoner, as that was force enough.

Prouty, according to Hurlburt, kept his hold till Blanchard put his foot in the stirrup of the saddle on Mahurin's horse.

Marcus Beacher watched and commented defiantly. Alanson Cummings and John Tyler stayed clear of the argument.

Among the New Hampshire men, Tuttle and Blodget continued to demand the surrender of Clough and others, while Mahurin confronted Blanchard's guards. Bernard Young told Clough not to go by mere telling, but to make them use force. Pascal Blood exchanged words with Mahurin and with Blodget, telling Blodget to fire if he chose, but "that he or his party should not take Clough off with them."

James Minor Hilliard, seeing Blanchard mounted on Mahurin's horse advised letting the others go. The New Hampshire men surrounded Blanchard. Mahurin walked beside the horse, and they turned back toward Canaan.

Mahurin later deplored the abusive language of Blood and Beacher, commenting that "we told them they might say what they thought fit, as we should not be led into a quarrel with them but should let King William and General Jackson decide the matter."

CHAPTER 35

BLOODSHED IN HEREFORD, OCTOBER 1835

The Canadians and the men from Indian Stream watched Blanchard and his rescuers disappear, and listened to their cheering. All except Prouty were eventually of one mind; he started back home while they continued on west to Rea's to tell him of the armed intervention by New Hampshire men. They had gone but a few rods when five or six men on foot came out of a little piece of woods—New Hampshire men, some of whom they recognized but did not later identify—reinforcements or another party trying to prevent them from taking Blanchard to Rea. The New Hampshire men paused, then turned back into the woods. The Canadians walked down into the valley of Leach's Stream. There Magistrate Rea lived in his farmhouse, not far from his mill and blacksmith shop. The buildings were on the road leading over a small hill toward the line and Canaan.

Rea at once wanted depositions, but the complications of taking the statements of the eight or ten men who crowded into the room, and the lateness of the hour (midafternoon) led Rea to summarize the events of the rescue, to which all the witnesses could agree, regardless of their individual versions. By five o'clock the men were leaving. Several of them were miles from home; Tyler, Alanson Cummings, and the Applebees faced a good twelve or fifteen miles of walking. Some of the men took the easy route south to Canaan rather than climb back over Hereford Hill. They seem to have been unaware of the crowd of New Hampshire men and Vermonters gathered at the store of Parmelee and Joy.

Rea's work as magistrate was almost done, but he never completed the papers that day, for there was more to be added. He became aware of a commotion, of voices on the road below his house. A man returned to the house and told him the New Hampshire "fellows" were coming. Rea scarcely believed this, thinking they would not dare violate Canadian territory again. From the window he saw others, who had been making statements, halted in the road before two mounted men. Although he later estimated the distance at fifty rods—eight hundred and twenty-five feet—he formed the decision somehow that he should go out and keep the peace. He left behind his cane ("contrary to my usual custom of wearing a stick"), so that nobody would think he might use it for a weapon. His lameness, cause of the New Hampshire men's epithet, "Old Pumplefoot," did not prevent him from walking out quickly with Bernard Young and Zacheus Clough. According to the son of Zebulon Flanders, who stood nearby, Rea said to them, "When I tell you, hitch upon them."

The two men causing the commotion, as Rea learned, were Ephraim C. Aldrich and Miles Hurlburt. To their recollection, made in sworn testimony almost ten months later in August 1836, they had stopped to talk with a man who lived on the road beyond Hall's Stream. They did not detain the man, or anybody else, and were talking peaceably. Statements contradicting this, they said, were false in every particular, especially those of Rea. Aldrich and Hurlburt deposed that they saw Rea coming toward them as fast as he could, hallooing and bellowing, more like an enraged madman (Hurlburt recalled) than any reasonable being. Rea commanded them off the king's highway.

A version entirely different came from Rea. He thought that Hurlburt was drunk.

John Tyler, whose debt to William Buckminster had touched off the sequence of events, again was the indirect cause of this second, more impromptu invasion of Canadian territory. When Tyler's friends and neighbors had rescued him from Deputy William Smith a week or so before, they had not settled Tyler's case. Smith returned to Colebrook and reported to Sheriff White. He was advised by White to offer a reward of $5 for Tyler. This Smith did, and the offer was still in effect when Mahurin and his companions returned with Blanchard to Canaan and the tavern-store of Parmelee and Joy.

Smith had not been with the men rescuing Blanchard; being unarmed, he had stayed at Canaan, loaning his horse to an armed man. Now one of the rescue party told him that he could have taken Tyler, if he had gone with them. Talk turned to the reward and to the legality of taking Tyler on Canadian soil. This talk grew into a general enthusiasm for going over the line and taking Tyler prisoner, to show the Canadians another thing or two. The rum sold at the store entered into this enthusiasm.

Late afternoon dispersed various responsible citizens. The crowd dwindled from the hundred-odd, many of them armed, to a group of less than half that number. Earlier, Ephraim Mahurin had paused only fifteen minutes before starting back on his twenty-mile ride to his home in Columbia. Richard I. Blanchard did not linger. Luther Parker had ridden north with Hilliard and others after spreading the news of Blanchard's capture. He had not joined the rescuers. He loaned Aldrich his pistols and Asa his horse for their excursion to intercept Blanchard's captors from a direction other than that of Mahurin and Hilliard. He seems to have refrained from any part in the later episode of the day.

Hiram Fletcher, the lawyer from Colebrook, was taking an early supper at the tavern when Joseph Wiswell, the Clarksville justice of the peace, came to him. Wiswell had not yet left to visit Archelaus Cummings at his house three-quarters of a mile from the store. He told Fletcher that some men were going after John H. Tyler and wanted an "advertisement" of the $5 reward; Deputy Smith did not have one of the papers with him. Would Fletcher make out one for Smith to sign? The Colebrook attorney replied that he had missed one meal that day and didn't intend to miss another, but he outlined briefly what the paper should state. Wiswell undertook to write out, accordingly, the causes and terms for the reward. Smith signed the document and passed it on to Captain Mooney of the New Hampshire militia.

Mooney was at the store on his own responsibility. As he had told Clark Haynes early that morning at his house in Stewartstown, Colonel Young was away, and he could not act without orders. But when Haynes described the "mob from Canada" that had taken Blanchard, Mooney saw the crisis as serious enough to risk personal action. After Haynes left to continue spreading the alarm, Mooney picked up some men and arms in a baggage wagon and rode to Canaan.

The piece of paper that Deputy Smith gave Mooney satisfied most of the men they had the right to go and take Tyler. Hilliard advised against it, but the project had gone beyond moderation. Raised glasses and shouts endorsed a full-scale raid to capture Tyler, and also Rea, Clough, and Flanders.

There were rumors of additional cash awards and free rum. Josiah Parmelee and Archelaus Cummings, Jr., later denied these, pointing out that the tailor from Canaan, A. J. McKinnon, who had spread such stories and had made a deposition to that effect for Canadian investigators, possessed a notoriously bad reputation in dealing with the truth. All the same, whether offered for the capture of the Canadians or not, rum flowed down various throats.

Ephraim Aldrich and Miles Hurlburt did not wait for the organization of a force of men to cross into Canada. They rode ahead. Not far over the line, they encountered some of Blanchard's captors and, eventually, Alexander Rea.

From Rea's house the men in the road were clearly visible. John Tyler came out of the house with Rea but hesitated after a short distance when he saw Aldrich and Hurlburt "drawn up" in the road. He soon climbed over a fence and made off, but heard Aldrich shout, "Shoot him down, Goddamn him!"

Alanson Cummings "was standing at some distance from the scene," and his testimony can be discounted, though not his prudence. As he watched the action, he saw "Aldrich lift up his sword and make a blow at somebody, and saw Hurlburt present and fire his pistol." He saw a number of men appear beyond, "to the number of sixty or seventy all armed, and some of them fired their guns as they came up; a little while afterwards I heard them call out 'bring on the baggage waggon.' I then went away and saw nothing more of them."

Pascal Blood was one of the first to leave Rea's house after the depositions had been taken. He met Aldrich and Hurlburt on the road. Although he noticed they were armed with a sword and a horseman's pistol, he rode up to them and shook hands (he stated in his testimony) and thought he might persuade them to return to Canaan with him.

Marcus Beacher rode from Rea's yard with Pascal Blood. He stated later that Aldrich was armed with a sword and pistols, and Hurlburt with a horseman's pistol and a pocket pistol. They exchanged a few words, "we asking them what they meant by stopping us," Beacher stated, "they saying they should let us know."

Zebulon Flanders recalled that Aldrich and Hurlburt were drawn up on horseback, with a sword and pistols, and "belts of white leather across their breasts." Nobody else took notice of these belts. Flanders asked Aldrich what he meant. Aldrich replied most definitely, according to Flanders's deposition: "Damn you we will let you know what it means!"

Flanders thus described his exchange with Aldrich, who had signed the appeal to Canada:

I told him he was going too fast, when he replied, "Flanders, have I not always used you well?" to which I said, that I knew nothing to the contrary, and had I not used him well likewise. He said, yes, I had, until I had stolen one of their citizens, meaning Blanchard. I told him he lied; I had not stole one of their citizens. What made me angry and speak to him in this manner was, that a short time before he had been a staunch Canadian.

At this point, Rea, Young, Clough, and the Applebees came up, Rea shouting and hallooing (in the New Hampshire men's view), or (in Rea's view) with "the intention of doing my duty as Magistrate to keep the peace."

Bernard Young had gone out of Rea's house at the warning that "they are coming" and had seen Aldrich and Hurlburt fifty rods away. Rea joined him, asking, Young recalled: "You are not afraid to go down, are you?" They started down the road.

Rea's actions, when he confronted Aldrich and Hurlburt, led the New Hampshire men to believe they were in danger of being taken prisoner. Rea ordered Young to seize the bridle of a horse . . .

Flanders recalled:

By this time [after his exchange with Aldrich] Mr. Rea, with the other persons who had been making their depositions, came up, not one of them with arms of any kind. Mr. Rea went up to Hurlburt and asked him what he meant by stopping people on the King's highway. Hurlburt said he would do what he had a mind to. Mr. Rea desired him to take himself off to the other side of the line, they did not want anything of him there. He said he'd be damned if he would go for him, and that he would go when he had a mind. "What's that you say?" said Mr. Rea, walking up to him, when Hurlburt said, "advance one step further and I'll blow you through." Mr. Rea then stood still; Hurlburt presenting his pistol to Mr. Rea, who told Mr. Young, a peace officer, to take charge of that man, and take him prisoner.

Young understood Rea to tell him to seize the bridle of Aldrich's horse, but Aldrich had warned Rea to stay away from Hurlburt, "or he'll do you an injury." They exchanged words Young could not hear, words Rea stated had to do with his reasonable request that Aldrich, "if you have any influence with this drunken fellow, take him and yourself peaceably away over the line: we want nothing of you here, and we cannot allow the peaceable inhabitants to be stopped in this manner."

Afterward, neither Rea nor Young recalled noticing Aldrich's sword . . .

Time moved faster than the varied accounts would indicate. Pascal Blood rode on toward the line, passing two horsemen trotting fast northward. He did not notice the mounted men in the mill yard and behind the blacksmith shop, who later appeared to those facing Aldrich and Hurlburt.

Elisha A. Terril had joined Aldrich and Hurlburt, who sent him back for reinforcements.

Bernard Young stepped forward and seized the bridle of Aldrich's horse.

Zebulon Flanders heard someone—he thought it was Hurlburt—shout, "Goddamn you let go my horse!"

Aldrich drew his sword and struck Young with it on the neck, nearly driving him to the ground.

Rea grasped Aldrich's sword arm, then the horse's bridle.

Flanders heard the words, "Damn him shoot him down."

Aldrich struck Rea on the head with his sword, cutting through the straw hat he wore. Aldrich then wheeled his horse.

Hurlburt fired the horseman's pistol from twelve or fifteen feet.

Young: "I heard the report of a pistol and received its contents."

Flanders: "I saw Young fall and get up again."

Rea: "From the exertions Young made after the carbine was fired, I did not suppose that he had been wounded."

Beacher: "Upon this the persons who were with Mr. Rea being unarmed, picked up stones, with which they succeeded in driving Aldrich and Hurlburt to the distance of four or five rods."

Hurlburt: "[Two of the stones] hit me with great force, when I discharged the pistol at the assailants . . . did not aim at anyone in particular, did not think of hitting anyone, but to frighten them."

Aldrich: (Describing a large stone thrown by Rea) "[weighing] as I should judge eight or ten pounds, which hit me on the head near my right eye and broke the bone at the corner of my eye."

Young: "I then saw Hurlburt making off in the direction of the line, shouting out 'Shoot them, damn them come on.' I then saw a number of armed men coming out of Mr. Rea's Mill yard, upon which the persons who had accompanied Mr. Rea, left the ground and ran in different directions; previous, however, to the persons coming out of the mill yard, after Mr. Rea had been struck with the sword, and the pistol had been fired which took effect on me, the persons with Mr. Rea took up stones and drove them off. As I was making toward Mr. Rea's house, I heard the report of three or four guns. I stopped a moment to examine the extent of the wound which I had received, and found that the ball had entered my right thigh and passed through, injuring one of my testicles. Looking up, I saw Mr. Rea making through one of his fields toward the bushes."

Rea: "The persons who had been stopped, as well as myself, then took up stones and pelted Aldrich and Hurlburt, who made off on their horses, but on observing an armed party of five or six men coming out of the millyard at the back of the blacksmith's shop, where they had been in ambush, they wheeled around and returned with them. The party who came from the mill-yard at this time fired three shots from muskets with bayonets on them which did not take effect. One of the balls struck the knoll where I was standing, which ball I have now in my possession. At this moment I perceived another party coming round a point of hill below the mill, consisting of ten or twelve armed men, with a baggage waggon in their rear. This party fired two shots at us, which did not take effect, as they had not come within range at that time.

"On perceiving this last party I observed to the persons with me, that they had better provide for their own safety by flight as we had no arms and could not resist such odds. From the threats I had heard made use of, and the brutal state of intoxication in which I supposed many of them to be in, I had every reason to expect that they were determined to have me, dead or alive. I consequently, with a view to divert the attention of this mob from my family and dwelling, passed through some bars that were down in the fence of my pasture field, and stopped to put up two of the bars to prevent horsemen from overtaking me as they otherwise would, and whilst putting up the bars, the said Ephraim C. Aldrich snapped two loaded pistols at me, which missing fire he threw at my head. I then made my escape into the bushes, but Aldrich having got off his horse pursued me on foot with drawn sabre, followed by four or five others, and owing to my lameness I stumbled several times, and having fallen over a large log, Aldrich overtook me as I had fallen on my face, and grasped my neckhandkerchief and made a plunge at me with his sabre, but facing around in sufficient time to seize it, and in the struggle to divert it from my person, it was forced into the ground about two feet where I managed to detain it until his followers came up, he in the mean time kicking and trampling on me and swearing that he would have my heart's blood."

According to Pascal Blood, who had left the scene earlier:

When I turned around the corner of the road at the top of the hill the road was full of armed men, to the number of from sixty to one hundred, some with guns and some with pistols. I saw Captain Mooney among them. They had a waggon with two horses among them, driven by one Jessee Corbit. Among the company I recognized Doctor Enoch Terrill, Robert Terrill, Stephen and Moses Hodge, one Dalton, and Jeremiah Kelly. I then went on to Canaan, in the state of Vermont, to the house of Mr. Cummings, and whilst I was there Aldrich and Corbit passed with Mr. Rea in the baggage waggon, and Aldrich, swinging his sword, cried out as he passed, "We have got the old captain, damn him, with his head bound up." About a week after this I went up to the blacksmith's shop, on Mr. Rea's farm, and there met with Mr. Josiah Grout, who, in the course of the conversation, told me that a pistol had been lost, the one that Aldrich had snapped, and then thrown at Mr. Rea, as it did not go off. Grant [Grout] and I went up, and where I was told that Mr. Rea had gone over the bars of the fence, and where Aldrich had fired at him, I found, after a slight search, the pistol with the percussion cap, snapped and broken, but the charge was still in the pistol. I gave the pistol to Mr. Grout, and I now believe that it is in the possession of Mr. Rea, as he told me so.

CHAPTER 36

CANADIAN MAGISTRATE A PRISONER IN VERMONT, OCTOBER 1835

In Canaan, Hiram Fletcher had finished his supper and had gone out behind the tavern and stable to shoot at a mark with Minor Hilliard. When he learned that the baggage wagon, which drew up at the store with its shouting escort of riders, contained not John Tyler but Alexander Rea, he began to have doubts about his association with his fellow New Hampshire men and former neighbors at Indian Stream. He had heard shots toward Canada but took them to be men discharging their guns so they wouldn't be carrying them loaded when that was not necessary: to prevent accidents, he said in his deposition. The men who had rescued Blanchard had done this earlier.

Fletcher did not wave his rifle and yell triumphantly, as Rea claimed. He might have yelled, "Hurrah for Jackson!" He did not yell, "Here is old Rea, we have got the damned old rascal!" He was nearsighted and could not see as far as the road and wagon clearly enough to identify Rea, and he was at the moment about to get his horse from the stable.

Rea's captors asked Fletcher for a sure way to hold him to answer for his attempts to place Indian Stream under Canadian jurisdiction. Fletcher thought Rea had acted like a "judicial monster," not like one of His Majesty's justices, in the arrest of Luther Parker and Richard Blanchard, but he put aside personal opinion in giving advice to the New Hampshire men: dress Rea's wounds, wash him up, and send him home. They had no right to capture him anywhere, even in New Hampshire, much less seize him in Canada—though Rea may have resisted them and pelted them with stones.

That they had a live magistrate to return to his home might be traced to faulty percussion caps in the pistol that Luther Parker had loaned Aldrich;

to Aldrich's inaccurate jab with the saber; to Hurlburt's unsteady hand and aim; and to Rea's tenacity in holding the saber sheathed in the ground until the other New Hampshire men came up.

Witnesses on both sides agreed about the action that took place in the bushes. Dr. Terril of Clarksville, armed with a carbine and two pistols, arrived first at the scene of the struggle between Rea and Aldrich. Asa Parker, Joseph Pope Wiswell (later to have supper with his father and Archelaus Cummings), and a man named Small followed Terril. Soon after came running Captain James Mooney, Jeremiah Aldrich (Ephraim's son), and six or eight others recognized by Marcus Beacher, who was watching from the road.

Miles Hurlburt dismounted and followed them into the woods. He found Dr. Terril protesting with Aldrich over his kicking Rea when he was down. Aldrich wanted Rea to release the sword. Rea would not, unless promised his personal safety. The man named Small, carrying a musket with bayonet, guaranteed Rea his life, and he pointed out to Aldrich that Rea had surrendered. After further words and kicks, Aldrich agreed. Rea released his grip on the sword. Small helped Rea up. Aldrich took him by the other arm. Dr. Terril led the way back into the field, Asa Parker and Joseph Pope Wiswell bringing up the rear with bayonets and threats. They half carried Rea, his face and shoulder bloody from the cut on his head. They called for Mooney to bring up the baggage wagon and placed Rea on the seat beside Jesse Corbit, who drove the two horses. Aldrich climbed up beside him with his sword; Terril and Wiswell climbed in back.

Marcus Beacher, still watching from the road, heard them shout, "Hurrah for Jackson, we have got the damned old he one!" James Mooney rode up to Beacher and asked him where Clough and Flanders had gone. Beacher replied (he stated in December): "I don't know, the last I saw of them, they were on the run, and your blood hounds after them." Mooney and his men rode back toward Vermont. Flanders and Clough had escaped. Marcus Beacher returned to Rea's house, where Bernard Young lay wounded.

At the store of Parmelee and Joy in Canaan, Aldrich unloaded Rea from the wagon and marched him through the men gathered there—not all of them sober, by any means—and into the big room with its counters of goods, hardware, and groceries. At the rear of the store, Aldrich announced to Nehemiah Joy that the time had come for rum. Two witnesses thought it had been promised. The capture of Tyler might have been an agreed-to cause for celebration in rum; the capture of a wounded Canadian magistrate was another matter altogether. The sobering thought of consequences put a stop to the rum, which Parmelee and Joy had allowed to flow. It particularly stopped any to Aldrich. Joy told him he'd had enough.

With Wiswell and Tuttle, Aldrich wanted to take Rea to Colebrook and Lancaster. Aldrich considered Rea to be in his custody. Rea protested the illegality and the lack of a warrant, and he claimed the right to protection under Vermont law, represented by Herman Nichols, a young magistrate. Rea appealed to Nichols for protection. As Aldrich and his companions tried to drag him to the door, Rea grabbed at the counter and at a man standing there, while Nichols protested to Aldrich. Rea refused to move, declaring they would have to use force to make him go.

Josiah Parmelee had seen enough. He interfered, along with Nichols, and took Rea into another room, where some of the more serious citizens of Canaan had gathered: Justice Ingham and his son, Archelaus Cummings, Sr., and Dr. Charles Heaton and his son. The tailor, A. J. McKinnon, followed to help bind up Rea's wound. This was a cut in the left side of his scalp, about an inch and a half long and down to the bone.

Aldrich continued to demand his "prisoner." McKinnon heard Aldrich say that he was taking Rea to Lancaster—and, by God, would be there by morning. Parmelee again interfered. He demanded to see Aldrich's warrant, and finally ordered him out, according to Rea. "Walk out, sir," said Parmelee, "I want your room, not your company." He finally made Aldrich leave, still protesting.

Talk in the room turned to possible further action by the "mob," which might require dangerous resistance to its armed men by the law-abiding citizens of Canaan. But the mob dispersed itself. Rea was given refreshment about eight o'clock. Sometime later, in the cold October night, he went home with a Hereford man named Dean, accompanied by McKinnon. There he met Zebulon Flanders and several other men of Hereford who had been unsuccessfully pursued by New Hampshire men. He found his family safe, but greatly alarmed. Bernard Young lay in bed waiting for Dr. Heaton. Rea sat up with him that night.

Young stayed in bed for fifteen days at Rea's house, and then spent two weeks in bed at his own house, in great pain. His wound continued to inconvenience him; his health remained poor. As late as Christmas he was unable to do much work to support his family. He could not pay the doctors. He owed $19.75 to Dr. Charles Heaton of Canaan for service in surgery and fourteen visits. He owed to Dr. Henry Watson, surgeon of Sherbrooke, for two visits, £5.

Rea ascribed the cause of the "outrage on the twenty-second day of October" to his having issued warrants against Luther Parker and Richard Blanchard. In this oversimplification, he was basically right. Bernard Young hit upon the more general reason: "I know of no cause for the people of New Hampshire mal-treating Mr. Rea, but have heard it assigned as a reason that he exercised jurisdiction over the inhabitants of the Indian Stream Settlement in the township of Drayton, which the inhabitants of New Hampshire contend he has no right to do, but that they have it under their own jurisdiction."

Not to mention rum.

CHAPTER 37

THE OCCUPATION OF INDIAN STREAM, NOVEMBER 1835

In the two weeks that followed Blanchard's rescue and Rea's abduction, officials of New Hampshire and Canada waited and watched. Governor Badger received various accounts of the disturbance. Although the news about the incident brought evidence of an explosive situation, yet it clearly demonstrated that New Hampshire men would resist any encroachment by Canada. North of the border, Rea made an immediate communication to authorities in Sherbrooke about the outrage; they alerted the two deputies to the provincial assembly, Moore and Guy. There seems to have been a delay or falling off of urgency as the news was sent farther from the border. The deputies notified Lord Gosford, whose eventual move was to appoint an investigating commission.

The members of the Canadian faction at Indian Stream prepared to defend themselves. They later claimed to have been encouraged in this by the Canadian magistrate, Rea, and assured of protection. There is no record of the threats that passed between them and the men favoring New Hampshire, but the inhabitants lived in dread from day to day during these tense, unhappy weeks. Families faced winter in the constant knowledge that over the ridge or upstream along the river lived a man who in his heart wanted their men dead. In the woods various armed prowlers were not all hunters of game. Yet they did not shoot at each other from behind trees. The ingrained New England tradition took over again after the abrupt explosion of October 22. Respect for the individual and for order again kept an uneasy peace.

Rumors of "fortification" reached Concord, linked with the names of the Applebees and their house at the junction of Perry Stream and the Connecticut. On November 7, 1835, Governor Badger sent Adjutant General

Low north to investigate the reports of rebellion along the border. He also gave Low the authority to use the militia if Low thought the situation required it.

Governor Badger was then serving his second year in office. He had the reputation of never swerving from a course of action once he had entered upon it, yet because of his good sense, he was not generally considered obstinate. In June and July he had made up his mind that Indian Stream should become—or, as he viewed it, should remain—New Hampshire territory. A Democrat and a Jackson man, he wanted a firm policy in the north, based on complete rejection of British claims. And the legislature had backed this policy with sufficient authority for him to carry it out. He was fifty-six years old, descended from an old family in Gilmanton, wealthy, and experienced in New Hampshire politics and law. He cherished a sincere feeling for the "honor and dignity of the state" and saw nothing wrong about taking a firm stand against Great Britain, regardless of federal policy. He seems to have cared nothing for British might; the probable wrath of Lord Palmerston failed to impress him. Two weeks after New Hampshire citizens had invaded British territory and wounded a magistrate and deputy, he authorized Low to use troops in territory claimed by Great Britain.

General Low went north with this authority at his discretion. On his arrival at Lancaster, he consulted with Sheriff White. He learned at once that the excitement caused by Blanchard's arrest and rescue was far greater than he considered safe for the peace of the border. In the next day or two he talked with Colonel Ira Young, with Captain Mooney, with Lewis Loomis (now General Loomis), with Luther Parker, and with other men of Indian Stream. He came to the conclusion that New Hampshire faced an insurrection in the vicinity of Indian Stream, aided and abetted by various Canadians and Canadian authorities, who added to the danger by their determination to punish the New Hampshire men "concerned in the late difficulties."

Before he left Lancaster for Indian Stream with Sheriff White on the morning of November 11, he wrote to Governor Badger of his decision to detach and order into service a militia force sufficient to maintain jurisdiction and to help the sheriff execute the laws of the state.

On November 13, 1835, General Low ordered Colonel Young to provide men. As he had in August, Young ordered a detachment of the 6th Company, 24th Regiment, to rendezvous at Stewartstown under Captain James Mooney and Ensign Amos Drew. They marched at once to Indian Stream. By evening, Mooney and Drew, with sixteen privates and two sergeants, had taken up quarters at the house and mill of Luther Parker. Captain Mooney set guards at the roads near Fletcher's Mills. He then prepared to march farther upstream to the Applebees' fortified house. Already snow had fallen in the settlement. Winds blew cold down the valley, where the guards paced, and stars glowed in chill winter brilliance.

Marcus Beacher, accompanied by William Whitman of Eaton, Canada, encountered three of the guards. Beacher recognized Robert Terril and William Butler of Stewartstown. Ordered to stand, Beacher, unaware that he faced troops on duty, took note of the guns, swords, and pistols. He remembered the treatment of Rea. Both he and Whitman heeded the order to stand or be blown through.

They considered themselves on legitimate business in the territory. Beacher wanted to get some "goods and chattels," which he had left at his farm there. Whitman was a neighbor of William White, the former member of the council who had recently fled to Canada when threatened by the men of New Hampshire. Beacher and Whitman were going to help Mrs. White move to Eaton to join her husband.

The guards took them to Luther Parker's house, where Captain Mooney followed Colonel Young's orders to detain persons attempting to enter or leave the territory. Mooney suspected Beacher and Whitman of going to warn the Applebees. He, of course, knew that Beacher had been in the party conducting Blanchard to Rea. He had no intention of freeing the Canadians and losing the advantage of surprise in his planned daybreak attack on the fort.

While Beacher and Whitman were held prisoners, armed men tramped in and out through the candle-lit rooms, napped in corners, or gathered about bivouac fires outside. At three o'clock in the morning, Captain Mooney ordered his men to fall in.

Up the River Road with the men of the 6th Company marched Richard I. Blanchard and General Lewis Loomis. Blanchard, as deputy sheriff, had with him warrants for the arrest of the Applebees. For light to guide them over the ice of puddles and frozen ruts, the men had candle lanterns and the glow from the sky reflected on the snow. At last, about daylight, they walked over a rise of ground. Ahead of them lay the bridge across Perry Stream near its junction with the Connecticut. The stream dropped here from its slow course through the meadows west of the Applebee house, and sluiced over its rocky bed toward the rapids of the larger river.

The Applebee house stood on the far side near an outcropping of ledge. The windows and doors were barricaded against musket shot. Emor Applebee, forty-five years old, lived with his family in the two-story house.

He had cleared more than twenty acres, some of it cultivated for corn and hay. The state had allowed him one hundred and fifty acres of his claim in 1824, not recognizing the remaining unsurveyed fifty acres. His aversion to authority, especially that of New Hampshire as represented by its sheriffs, had given him a reputation for outlaw behavior that persisted (at present unsubstantiated) in rumors of smuggling cattle to Canada. His son, Benjamin, left a record of his thoughts and hopes when he turned state's evidence (so to speak) against Canada. Benjamin stated under oath that he never would have thought of resisting officers of New Hampshire, "had I not been advised so to do, and assured I should be protected in so doing by the government of Canada, by Alexander Rea of Hereford, Lower Canada."

Captain Mooney halted and deployed his men. A plank of the bridge had been torn up. The Applebees intended to make a stand there at the property line; Emor and Benjamin advanced with muskets to warn off Mooney and his men. Richard I. Blanchard announced that he had warrants for them. In the altercation that followed, the Applebees threatened to shoot anyone who approached.

This defiance of a sheriff deputized by White made Captain Mooney advance and take charge. He stated his orders to support Blanchard or any New Hampshire sheriff. He gave the Applebees his simple intentions: to capture them, dead or alive. Emor ordered Mooney off his land in the name of the king. By that time, Captain Mooney's men had surrounded the house. Emor tried to send a "messenger." Captain Mooney's men drove him back.

Into this temporary stalemate, General Loomis moved as a more neutral representative of New Hampshire, not a local opponent of the Applebees, as was Blanchard. He advised the Applebees to surrender. They could not escape. He would take them to law officers before whom they could state their case; if they could establish the "rectitude of their intentions," that they would not resist New Hampshire jurisdiction and authority, they would be permitted to return home. The Applebees had no real choice. They laid down their arms, which Captain Mooney ordered his men to secure. A search revealed spare muskets in the house. The Applebee women objected strenuously to this invasion of their home.

At that moment, reinforcements arrived for the Applebees, but too late. Of the several men who appeared, only one was armed. The group took in the situation quickly and disappeared into the woods.

Captain Mooney and his men, with General Loomis in charge of Emor and Benjamin Applebee, marched back to Luther Parker's house.

A detail from the 6th Company drew the charges of the captured guns.

The Applebees had loaded them with one-ounce balls and pistol bullets, similar to buckshot, and with powder enough to spray the countryside. One gun had seventeen pistol bullets in it. A rifle had a load of seven larger bullets. The spare guns held charges made of an ounce ball and seven to twelve pistol bullets. All guns were turned over to Sheriff White for evidence before the Grand Jury of Coos County.

From Luther Parker's house, General Loomis took his prisoners to Lancaster. Adjutant General Low sat down to write to Governor Badger. The Applebees had both told substantially the same story about their Canadian backing, to which Benjamin took oath in his deposition almost a year later. They had acted under the direction of a Canadian justice of the peace. (In his letter to Badger, Low refrained from naming Rea.) This magistrate had told them to order from their farm any New Hampshire authorities who approached them; if further pressed, they were to defend themselves with firearms; if outnumbered and faced with capture, they were to retreat to Hereford for protection.

During that day, November 14, 1835, various men from Indian Stream came to Luther Parker's house and assured General Low that they had supported New Hampshire's jurisdiction in the past, but despaired of protection and law enforcement by the state. Hence they had joined the Canadian faction, forming a group of sixty out of seventy-five legal voters, in an appeal to Canada for protection under the laws of the Crown. General Low wrote to Governor Badger that the citizens, once in doubt and uncertainty, were reassured by "the measures your Excellency has adopted in relation to this troubled section." The citizens expressed satisfaction because "they are to be delivered from that state of anarchy which has so long existed." General Low mentioned Deacon Nathaniel Perkins as a man who came forward in support of New Hampshire. The well-disposed citizens of the settlement, General Low concluded, now were assured of their protection by New Hampshire, and the rebellious of prompt subjugation.

Viewing the occupation from a wider perspective, Low pointed out that because the border troubles had occurred "in a great measure by the interference of a foreign power, the National Government will, doubtless, indemnify the state for the expense that has, or may be, necessarily incurred in maintaining our jurisdiction." In this Low showed optimism unjustified by events. The national government waited until 1849 and 1852 to reimburse New Hampshire.

General Low enclosed with his letter from Indian Stream his general orders to Colonel Ira Young the previous day, and an order commending

Colonel Young and various citizens for "their late patriotic services." He clarified this by an identifying phrase: "and more especially for rescuing one of our executive officers from the lawless imprisonment of a foreign power." Three days later, having taken thought about this praise for unauthorized vigilante action and invasion of a foreign country, he issued another order to Colonel Young, this one from Lancaster, somewhat removed from the excitement of the border. "Understanding that Deputy Sheriff Blanchard may have been rescued from the Canadian Authorities after he had been forced without the limits of the United States and as the Government disavow wholly any interference with the affairs of the British Province, I wish it distinctly understood that the Order of November 14th, 1835, having reference to the rescue of an executive officer, is to apply only so far as it respects the jurisdiction and rights of the State of New Hampshire."

When the (Concord) *New Hampshire Patriot* printed Low's communications to Governor Badger on November 23, its editor discreetly omitted the enthusiastic phrase about Blanchard's rescue, nor did he include the later order.

Alletta Parker watched the armed men of the militia, with their muskets, bayonets, pistols, and swords, moving about her house. She may have inwardly hated the tramping of snow and mud over her floors, but she was happy that Luther's cause had military support. Emor and Benjamin Applebee were no longer central figures in defiance of New Hampshire, no longer dangerous opponents of her husband. She remembered Emor's comment when he had been in the group that arrested Luther the previous June, that the old British lion was beginning to roar. Now she said to Emor, "Well, Mr. Applebee, the old eagle is beginning to scream."

Both Marcus Beacher and Alletta Parker witnessed the departure of the Applebees for Lancaster in the charge of General Loomis and a detachment of the 6th Company. Beacher noted they were to take the route through Clarksville and Colebrook; this would place them, once they crossed the bridge at Fletcher's Mills, south of the disputed territory.

Meanwhile, at Perry Stream, about half an hour after the militia left, Jonathan C. L. Knight approached the Applebee house. He found a door and window smashed, quilts and blankets strewn on the floor, a chest of drawers open, clothes lying about, and a section of the floor torn up. Mrs. Applebee had a bruised hand. She showed him a comb broken from her hair. Other "females" complained to him of ill-treatment, but if they talked of their resistance, of their attempts to escape for help, he failed to mention this to the Canadian investigating commission the next month. He might also have mentioned, but did not, a certain L. Applebee who had signed the petition to Canada, and he might have described how the Applebee family was prepared to face the first month of winter without Emor and Benjamin, but he did not. Jonathan C. L. Knight was an uneasy visitor. An armed party of New Hampshire men had tried to arrest him, but he managed to escape. The same party had taken prisoner Amasa Huggins and Timothy Huggins. Knight made rapid preparations to leave the territory.

The two other Canadians, Beacher and Whitman, remained under guard at Luther Parker's house until after the Applebees had been marched away. Colonel Young then ordered Captain Mooney to release them.

The two men set out to complete their errand, and a day later encountered again the restrictions imposed by New Hampshire's occupation of the territory. About four-thirty on the afternoon of Sunday, November 15, Beacher was driving in a sled drawn by two horses past Luther Parker's house. With him rode Whitman, Mrs. Ann White, going to join her husband in Eaton, and Polly Judd. They had packed in the sled some household goods and a trunk, on which sat Mrs. White and Polly.

A man armed with a musket and bayonet stopped them. Captain Mooney came out of the house and asked to see what Beacher had in the sled. Mrs. White refused to get off the trunk. Captain Mooney told her she would have to go back, for his orders from General Low were strict: nobody who was in debt could be allowed to take his goods from the settlement until his debts were paid. Mrs. White and Polly Judd got off the trunk. Captain Mooney opened it and saw that it contained clothing and goods of no interest to a sheriff with a writ of attachment. Mooney examined the load on the sled, then allowed Beacher to drive on.

The sled runners moved as the horses leaned into the traces. Beacher drove more slowly past Fletcher's Mills, for the hill was steep and the bank of the river fell away to the left. Ice had formed on the stones of the swift water. It had crept out from the snowy shores and into the pools. Winter freeze-up had arrived. Below the mills, the road leveled for the drive to the bridge over Indian Stream. Beacher probably crossed the stream and continued down the valley by the easy route, dropping off Polly at Nathan Judd's house before he turned up into the sanctuary of Hereford along Hall's Stream. The route over the ridge behind Nathaniel Perkins's farm was steep for a team with a loaded sled.

The husband of Mrs. White was not the only man who left the territory after having actively favored Canada. Certain men left with greater haste and secrecy than William White. Warrants for rebellion were out, backed by Captain Mooney and his troops. Jonathan Knight, after his escape from arrest and his visit to the Applebees, knew the danger of resistance and headed for Canada. Eventually he settled in Barford, having left behind property he valued at $500. William Pope, who had attended the meeting in August with Sheriff White at Fletcher's, seems to have gauged the trend of events accurately and in plenty of time to move ahead of them, probably as soon as his crops were in. John H. Tyler and Alanson Cummings went to Compton, some twenty miles northwest of Hereford. Cummings died there the following July at the age of thirty-three.

Benjamin Applebee served a sentence—or as he expressed it, was "detained"—in the Lancaster jail for six months and three days for resisting a deputy sheriff of Coos County. Emor's sentence or detention extended beyond August 1836, when he was still in jail. Records of the trials were burned in a fire at the Lancaster Courthouse in November 1886. Emor returned to the territory at an unknown time after serving a sentence of a year. He died there on March 27, 1842, aged fifty-two, and was buried in the cemetery above the Center Schoolhouse, four months before Daniel Webster and Lord Ashburton signed the treaty that settled the boundary north of his old home.

After the capture of the Applebees, winter gripped the valley of the upper Connecticut, and all of New England. It was the beginning of a winter long remembered for its bitter cold. News came inland that along the coast harbors froze over from Nova Scotia to New York. Stories circulated of good skating from Boston to Cape Cod, and of starving families, such as one in the hills north of New York, weakened by lack of food and fuel, frozen to death in the numbing cold.

On November 16, 1835, Colonel Young provided for a more permanent garrison to guard the territory, in place of the detachment ordered out on November 13. He called for drawing by lot from nine companies of militia a force more than twice as large, consisting of forty-two privates, one drummer, one fifer, and four sergeants. Ensign Drew and Captain Mooney were to continue in command. The detachment that had taken the Applebee house was discharged by November 25. The new troops improvised shelter around the Parker house. They escaped the increasing cold in tents, sheds, barracks, and in the house itself. With the continued snow and cold, the danger vanished of invasion by Canadian troops or of retaliation by the "rebels" of the territory. The New Hampshire troops prepared to serve their three months' duty in quiet patrolling of roads. Captain Mooney, quartered in the house, made himself agreeable to the Parkers. He liked to read quietly during his spare time, while with his foot he rocked the cradle of the baby, Amanda Malvina, born in September. He also kept his notes, books on expenses, orders, and writing equipment in the house. The duty at Indian Stream would for him be relatively comfortable; for the men it would be cold but without bloodshed. He commanded a force adequate to hold the territory if Canada should attempt limited occupation or support of the rebels.

Instead, Lord Gosford appointed a three-man commission to investigate aggression and invasion. On December 29, 1835, Captain Mooney's guard turned them back near Fletcher's Mills, an act that the commissioners were careful to describe in their report written three days later to Lord Gosford: "in our progress through the Indian Stream Settlement, in the prosecution of our enquiries, we were stopped in the highway, near the house of one Fletcher . . . by a military guard, composing a part of the force above mentioned, who, at the point of the bayonet, commanded us to stand, and would not permit us to pass, although made aware of the authority under which we were acting."

For their part, the commissioners gave the guard no satisfaction about their business or intentions. They lingered a while, then returned down the river toward the bridge over Indian Stream, and from there to Canaan and Hereford.

The guard, under the command of Ensign Drew, also turned back Captain Hayne of the Royal Staff Corps. He had been engaged by the commissioners to survey the area, including the roads near Rea's farm, the Vallentine-Collins Line as it crossed the district, and the new Forty-fifth Parallel established by Dr. Tiarks in the survey of 1818.

Hampered by the "extremely unfavorable weather" of the latter half of December and by the disturbed condition of the neighborhood, Hayne could not complete his diagrams and plans to his satisfaction. He found no indications of Dr. Tiarks's survey, but he did locate the cedar post of Vallentine and Collins at the southeast angle of Hereford, marking the end of the province's southern boundary. A line traced east and west in the field by the post was plainly visible. Two of Hayne's civilian helpers refused to go with him beyond Hall's Stream to this post. Only one man would accompany him across Indian Stream, such was "the excitement and alarm which the presence of the New Hampshire troops have occasioned."

Surveying up the Connecticut with his solitary helper, Captain Hayne came within a few chains of Luther Parker's house and the barracks. Ensign Drew advanced and demanded his business and by whose authority he surveyed the area. Captain Hayne refused to reply, although he knew who Drew was, until Drew identified himself and *his* authority, as derived from the State of New Hampshire.

Captain Hayne returned downstream, still convinced that Great Britain's claim to the territory was valid, and that the king of the Netherlands had made a proper award. But he understood that the disputed border was "peculiarly detrimental to the interests of Government, and particularly so to the poor settlers who have established themselves on or near the frontier."

In the further tightening of security, Nathan Judd found himself arrested for rebellion against New Hampshire. Many of the inhabitants had sworn allegiance to the state soon after the occupation and the capture of the Applebees. Judd had refused to receive amnesty in this manner. Late on the evening of Christmas Day, he had visitors at his home near the mouth of Indian Stream. Deputy Sheriff Richard I. Blanchard came with a warrant for his arrest. Accompanying him were Captain Mooney, Luther Parker, and Ephraim C. Aldrich. Luther Parker had been appointed justice of the peace by Governor Badger, but this probably did not give him sufficient authority to issue such a warrant, especially as he was a resident of the disputed territory. They took Judd to Luther Parker's house that night. The next day, Blanchard and Parker, along with Joseph Morrill of the 6th Company, having arrested Abner Hyland, Jr., on the same charge of rebellion against New Hampshire, brought both men before Justice Drew of Stewartstown. Justice Drew set bail at $200 each, to ensure their appearance at the May term of the court in Lancaster and their "good behavior in the meantime."

In these cases, as with those of the Applebees, court records are missing, presumably because of the same courthouse fire in 1886. Three days after his arrest, Judd gave his deposition on the incident to Short, Pomroy, and McKenzie, the Canadian commissioners who came to Indian Stream to take it. Judd's only comment about a reason for his arrest was that he had "declined submitting to the jurisdiction of the State of New Hampshire." A year and one month later, at fifty-one, Nathan Judd died and was buried in the cemetery at the edge of the meadows along the winding Indian Stream.

New Year arrived with deep snow and continuing cold. North, in Canada at Lennoxville, the commissioners spent New Year's Day composing a report to Lord Gosford. About a month later, the governor general wrote to the British chargé d'affaires in Washington, Charles Bankhead, outlining the repeated attempts at jurisdiction by New Hampshire, the military occupation, and the "outrage" at Hereford. He enclosed the report of the commissioners, with attached depositions by Rea, Young, and the other men involved in the events of October 22. Lord Gosford refrained from offering any suggestions

> as to the specific redress, that ought to be demanded on the present occasion; and I the more readily abstain from this, under the persuasion that it requires nothing but a knowledge of the facts to induce the Government of the United States to adopt measures which will at once prove satisfactory to His Majesty's Government, and prevent the repetition of occurrences, tending to disturb the harmony and good understanding which now exists with so much advantage to both nations. I have the honor, etc., Gosford.

Charles Bankhead sent a copy to John Forsyth, secretary of state. Bankhead pointed out the "extreme embarrassment which must arise to the two Governments from the military occupation by the State of New Hampshire of the territory in question." He interpreted Lord Gosford's reactions in stronger terms than his excellency had put them himself, in referring to the military occupation: "It is a proceeding, which if persevered in, will oblige His Majesty's Governor of Lower Canada to take measures to repel; but which his Excellency would be very loath to have recourse to, if it could possibly be avoided." Bankhead went on to say that he confidently hoped the president would obtain full and prompt redress for the invasion and would use the power of the federal government to prevent further disturbances to the harmony and understanding so happily existing between Great Britain and the United States.

By February 1, 1836, a peaceful winter appeared certain at Indian Stream. General Low reported to a representative of the *New Hampshire Patriot* the successful, quiet occupation of the northern border. He had kept in close communication with the guard and had spent much of his time in the area.

In the final accounting, General Low considered himself on duty at the governor's order of November 7, 1835, until February 18, 1836. His expenses included baggage transportation, Concord to Indian Stream and return, two hundred miles each way, at $2 per hundred miles "for each 100 of baggage as per regulations, making $80" (i.e., a thousand pounds of baggage). He listed pay of $383.70, and subsistence of $247.60 at twelve rations a day; so he appears to have had with him a clerk and two servants. He drew the rations at Indian Stream and Concord. The total was $713.30 for three months and twelve days of service.

On February 1, Low was in Concord, considering the approach of the day when the service of the men at Indian Stream expired. He wrote to Colonel Young in Colebrook, and included orders providing for a reduced detachment. But in his letter he explained that the troops might not be necessary, if "it shall be thought safe for the Inhabitants at Indian Stream and for the interests of the State to Dispense with a Military force then this Order now given will be countermanded." He asked for information from Young about the need for a force at Indian Stream, possibly through the May term of the Coos Court. He advised Young to get the opinion of General Loomis. Low foresaw an increasing possibility of international complications, which had not impressed him in November, and noted, "I do not wish to take an undue share of responsibility on these *War Measures*." His concern drew his pen under the words he had already capitalized.

On February 8, 1836, he sent Young an order for quarters, rations, and straw for the new detachment, "expense not to exceed the present contract." Four days later, he sent Young an order discontinuing the troops, because "the condition of affairs are now such at Indian Stream the services of a Guard may be dispensed with." He did, however, give Young authority ("clothe you with Power enough") to use his discretion in the future, "to the amount of your whole command." Low repeated to Young the policy of New Hampshire: "It is the desire of the Governor as well as the desire of this department that our citizens at Indian Stream be fully protected in the exercise of their civil rights."

Captain Mooney ordered his men to strike tents and pack sleds. The men marched away from Luther Parker's house and mill on Back Lake Brook, to the strains, doubtless, of the fife and drum.

This exodus took place at the same time the British chargé d'affaires notified the secretary of state that it might require force to repel military occupation. On February 18, 1836, there was no longer any military occupation.

On February 21, Bankhead also sent a report to Lord Palmerston, the secretary for foreign affairs, in London. He outlined the acts of violence, the intransigence of New Hampshire, and its occupation of the territory with troops, and concluded with the statement that he would communicate Mr. Forsyth's reply to Lord Gosford. The three weeks' voyage of the ship bearing the dispatch across the Atlantic had no real delaying effect on ensuing diplomacy. Lord Palmerston received Bankhead's report on March 17, 1836. He took no definite action until July 1837.

Palmerston followed a policy of moderation and patience completely at odds with his later stand after the burning of the *Caroline*, when Canadians sent in flames over Niagara Falls the American steamer that had been supplying Mackenzie's mock government on Navy Island. His policy on the

Hereford incident was at variance also with his noted aggressive imperialism, but there was little territory to be gained, unless by an arrangement of the entire border dispute from New Brunswick westward. Palmerston foresaw no advantage in demanding punishment of the New Hampshire men who had invaded Canada, when such a demand seemed a diplomatic blind alley. As the unlikely mediator in Jackson's quarrel with France over American claims, which had brought the two nations to the brink of war, Palmerston found himself in danger of upsetting his relations with his ally, France, if he broke up his own friendly relations with the United States.

Although earlier, in December 1835, the colonial secretary, Lord Glenelg, had given Lord Gosford authority to use force in stopping "violation of British territory," Gosford never interpreted this as extending to an attempt to drive out New Hampshire troops. On December 16, 1835, Ralph Metcalf, New Hampshire's secretary of state, had written to Forsyth at Governor Badger's request, asking for federal troops. Both Senator Isaac Hill and Levi Woodbury entered the Washington discussions. By January 1836, Hill learned that "the Executive" had declined to interfere unless Canada moved to take forcibly any territory of the United States. Hill wrote to General Low that an understanding existed between the two governments to leave jurisdiction as it had been until the boundary was settled, and that Bankhead had privately written to Gosford suggesting he follow this policy.

No official announcement came from either government, and consequently there was unrest in the territory. The February removal of the militia set in motion again the conflicts of the two factions. By March, New Hampshire men agitated for the return of the militia. Kimball Fletcher was going to resign as postmaster. Richard Blanchard wanted to give up the office of deputy sheriff. They were afraid of being "carried into Canada," on charges of holding offices in territory claimed by Great Britain. Men of the Canadian group, who had fled, began returning to the settlement. Only Luther Parker and Ephraim Aldrich were daring enough to continue opposing them actively.

The rumor circulated that New Hampshire had given up jurisdiction. Colonel Ira Young wrote to Low about the fears of the citizens, but thought the danger exaggerated. A meeting of men from Indian Stream, Stewartstown, and Clarksville appealed to Low for reassurances of New Hampshire's jurisdiction and readiness to stop Canada. When this arrived from Low, and they learned that Young had the power to act, they met again and publicly commended Captain Mooney and his troops for the winter occupation, and the action of the state government. Blanchard and Fletcher did not resign, but the citizens of the territory were far from relaxed. Canada had issued indictments against all those involved in the October raid. The Canadian faction was undefeated and obstreperous.

These dangers and uncertainties brought Parker, sometime in the spring of 1836, to a momentous, if reluctant, decision. In May he drove a team and covered wagon from his home to the bridge at Fletcher's Mills leading to the road through Clarksville. He there began a long journey to Wisconsin. Alletta and the children had gone on ahead by canal boat, steamer, lake schooner, and wagon to join her brother. They left behind a season of cold and of crop failure; frosts every month caused poverty and short rations in the settlement.

And the boundary dispute remained as unresolved as the consequences of the fracas at Hereford. The new governor, Isaac Hill, inherited the task of replying to Gosford's charges, which Badger had received from Forsyth before his term expired. Governor Hill felt as strongly about New Hampshire's rights as had Badger.

CHAPTER 38

SOLUTIONS, MAY 1836 THROUGH JUNE 1850

The migration of the Parker family represented for Luther a bitter disappointment; to a lesser extent it represented hope. The Parkers were returning to the log cabin days of ten years before. Luther left behind his house and mill, certain tools and equipment, lumber, and land. He gave up his position as justice of the peace, which might have led to more influence in the territory and even in the state, should his ambition have turned him to politics. These things he abandoned. But there were compensations. He left behind also his enemies. He gained land—fertile, according to Alletta's brother, Alvin French, and beyond dispute in the United States of America. There he would not find himself a British subject, or prisoner.

The exact reasons behind his decision to move are unknown. Although the jurisdiction of New Hampshire had been enforced temporarily, it was far from as complete as the governor liked to pretend, or really believed. The men who defied New Hampshire came out boldly again when the militia left. The assumption is fair that they never forgave Luther for his share in bringing New Hampshire law into the territory, and that they took measures to show it, such as boycotting his mill and store, if nothing more violent.

For Luther, abandoning the territory he had worked to save for New Hampshire must have seemed like a betrayal of himself and of those who had helped him, Blanchard, Mahurin, Hurlburt, Clark Haynes, Aldrich, Mooney, and others. The only hint of the desperation that prompted him lies in the tradition that he spoke bitterly of the past as he climbed aboard his wagon to head west: "Ten years of my life gone for nothing!"

Luther finally settled on 320 acres of land at the outlet of Little Muskego

Lake, south half of section 9, town 5, range 20 west. Here were no disputes over boundaries and survey lines, for the area had been surveyed by the federal government. But land speculators still preyed on the settlers. Two years after Luther had brought his family to the log cabin he built, the settlers banded together and entrusted him with bidding in their claims, no bidding against each other, no speculators to be tolerated. Luther later became active in the politics of the county. He sponsored its division and the separation of Milwaukee County in a contest that ended with success on April 7, 1846.

This second frontier life in a log cabin, the farm work, and hard labor in the woods bore down on Luther. He no longer had Asa to help, for Asa settled fifteen miles southwest of Milwaukee. The country was new and raw. In August 1838, the girl baby who had been rocked by Captain Mooney died of a fever, not quite three years old. Again in August, eleven years later, Alletta caught typhoid and died.

Luther married again at the age of fifty. In 1852, he returned to Indian Stream, which had become the town of Pittsburg. He "discharged certain obligations there," visited his friends, and returned to Wisconsin. The trip had been in part an attempt to restore his health. He died in June 1853 and was buried at Durham Hill Cemetery, with the epitaph:

> What thou art, I was.
> What I am, thou soon will be.

Alletta's epitaph was: "Those who knew her best loved her most."

In 1836, the year Luther left Indian Stream, the situation of the boundary and the antagonistic attitude of many of his neighbors remained unchanged. Although in June of that year Governor Isaac Hill assured the legislature that the territory was completely under the jurisdiction of New Hampshire, many of the men of Indian Stream would have disagreed. The view from Indian Stream and from the capitol at Concord coincided scarcely at all. Except for the show of force by the militia, which had gone, nothing had changed the boundary dispute. Therefore, the simpler—and to the inhabitants, more immediately pressing—question of land titles remained, as did the varied sentiments of the men.

The New Hampshire legislature, to which Governor Hill presented the British complaints, passed them to the Committee on Military Affairs. The committee reported three resolutions that would deal with the problem. The legislature passed them after slight alterations. The most important reiterated New Hampshire's policy in the north. The state was to "continue the possession of the Indian Stream Territory and maintain jurisdiction of this state over the same, until the question of the boundaries now in dispute between the United States and Great Britain affecting the limits of said Territory shall be finally settled." The second resolution required the governor to appoint an investigating commission. The third provided for the publication of one thousand copies of the commission's report. This was June 16, 1836.

In late July, the commission began its northern investigation. One of the members, John P. Hale, was a graduate of Bowdoin College, class of 1827, and a future United States senator who would denounce slavery as well as floggings and spirit rations in the navy. Hale joined General Low and General Young in Colebrook. General Low was a member of the commission. Young—the Colonel Ira Young of the occupation—was acting as adviser on local matters. The third commissioner, Ralph Metcalf, did not appear in the scene that John P. Hale described when he wrote to his wife, Lucy, in Dover. She had wept at their parting, and upon his arrival in Colebrook he wrote her a cheerful letter about the beautiful valley and the neat village with its handsome white-painted meetinghouse, complete with steeple and lightning rod. He found the parlor of the public house, in which he was writing, surprisingly comfortable. There was a handsome carpet upon the floor, a brass fire set, flag-bottomed chairs (now more commonly known as rush-bottomed chairs) "precisely like those in our front room," crickets covered and stuffed for footstools; why, the room was as well furnished as any at either of the two taverns in Dover!

John P. Hale discreetly said very little about his mission when he wrote to Lucy. He told her that he would be busy for a week taking evidence, but he did not mention that it would be from men involved in the border trouble of the previous fall. He quickly turned to comments about the luxuriant hay of the meadows, about the mountains on either side of the river, and about the sheep and cattle, which the people raised and drove to market, in Boston mostly, although some went to Quebec. The farmers also produced wool, pork, butter, cheese, and wheat, but counted little on raising corn because of the early frosts.

About two weeks later, John Hale was ready to set out for Indian Stream. He wrote to Lucy that he would leave Colebrook on August 8. With General Low, General Young, and Ephraim H. Mahurin as surveyor, he would explore the source of the Connecticut River, traveling in the woods for a week. They had hired three men to carry packs, including a St. Francis

Indian. One of these men was—although Hale perhaps did not realize it when he wrote to Lucy, for he did not mention the man's name—James Minor Hilliard, the hunter, and the horseman who first accosted the Canadian guards of Blanchard. So the commissioners had with them two active participants in the case they were investigating.

The chief purpose of the trip lay not so much in seeking the source of the Connecticut as in relocating the survey lines that Jeremiah Eames had run forty-seven years before. The commission wanted evidence of the long validity of New Hampshire's claim, as a legitimate reason for its forcible jurisdiction in the territory. They followed the Connecticut through the settlement, past Fletcher's Mills, past Luther Parker's former house and mill, up the River Road and to the end of that cart track at Burleigh Blood's farm on the lake. They pressed on into the forest toward the northeast corner of the state marked by Eames in 1789. There in the highlands they found the birch tree still standing.

James Minor Hilliard, taking notice of the lay of the land, proposed that the brooks nearby, which had long been assumed to run into the St. Lawrence, actually ran into the Magalloway and the State of Maine. Therefore, the northeast corner should be six or eight miles farther north. Hilliard was most confident of this from his hunts in the area. The party separated into two groups and explored the ridges north of Third Lake. Then they followed the Eames line west, using his journal.

When the commissioners finally assembled their report, it included depositions from Mahurin and Hilliard, who testified about the old boundary line as well as about the rescue of Blanchard. Also in it were depositions from Hurlburt, Aldrich, Mooney, Blanchard, Hiram Fletcher, Samuel Danforth, Nathaniel Perkins, the deputy sheriffs Smith and Harvey, and others who were not so closely involved with recent events. This testimony often dealt with subjects not directly related to Gosford's charges, but having a bearing on New Hampshire's jurisdiction through sheriffs' writs as far back as 1817, or by implicating Rea as an agitator of the disaffected in the territory. In their summary, the commissioners described the arrest of Tyler on a legitimate writ. They classed the arrest of Blanchard as actually abduction by an armed body of men, on the "absurd charge of having assisted in serving a writ duly issued by the competent authority of the county of Coos."

On the subject of the encounter with Rea by Hurlburt and Aldrich, the testimony admitted that the two men had misunderstood their right to retake Tyler but emphasized that they had been attacked by Rea. The commissioners stated it thus: "No sooner were these individuals over the line than they were set upon in a furious, boisterous, and outrageous manner by the individual before referred to." This was Rea, the cause of all the trouble.

The tone of the report remained the same through its treatment of various subjects: justified right in the rescue of Blanchard, because of Rea's usurpation of authority in the territory; mistaken innocence in the attempt to retake Tyler; self-defense in the wounding of Rea and Young; careful disregard of Rea's capture and abduction to Canaan; disregard of the military occupation, mentioned only in Mooney's testimony; and accumulation of evidence on previous, early New Hampshire jurisdiction and surveys.

In conclusion the commissioners stated: "the inhabitants have been assured that the protecting energies of the state are extended to all within her borders while the lawless and the vicious have been made to feel that their remote situation affords no sanctuary for crime."

The commission made its report to the November session of the legislature. Governor Hill sent the report and the depositions to Secretary Forsyth in Washington. The governor wrote his own opinion: "I flatter myself that the evidence these papers exhibit will not only satisfy the president that the aggression complained of originated with the subjects of his Britannic Majesty's province, but that the claim made by the British authorities of right to that territory is without foundation or any possible construction of the Treaty of 1783; and that as the executive head of this state, I am bound to insist that the General Government owes it to New Hampshire, that she shall be protected in the quiet and peaceable possession of that entire tract."

Secretary Forsyth sent the report and depositions, with Hill's letter, to the new British minister, Henry S. Fox, on January 12, 1837. If Forsyth thought the governor's letter to be diplomatically difficult, he made no excuses, and no mention of the intentions of the "General Government" in dealing with the governor's request for protection in possession of the area. Fox regarded this stepping aside from the boundary dispute as an entirely proper position on the part of Forsyth; the dispute was soluble only through negotiations of the British government and the federal government, and the latter must "negotiate such minor arrangements with the several State Governments interested in the matter." This solution was still five years away.

Fox sent the documents to London and Lord Palmerston. The secretary for foreign affairs received them on the anniversary of the birth of the first president of the United States, February 22, a reminder that the former colonies could be a continuing nuisance. He again delayed a final reply or final action.

Events ticked on relentlessly. Van Buren took the presidency in March 1837. King William died and was succeeded by his eighteen-year-old niece, Victoria. Explosive complications in governing Canada were rapidly leading to the abortive but internationally dangerous rebellions in the fall of that year, Papineau's in Lower Canada, and Mackenzie's in Upper Canada. The British lack of understanding, which preceded Lord Durham's reform recommendation for Canada, was typified in Fox's attitude toward the inhabitants of Indian Stream. By contrast, his summary of the border problem was acute.

He had written to Palmerston referring to the documents of Gosford and Hill:

I apprehend that the inferences, which must unavoidably be drawn from the above conflicting charges and allegations, are these:—that the territory on the disputed line of frontier has become the asylum of vagabonds and outlaws from both sides, who profess allegiance to one country or the other, or to either, according as it may suit their own lawless purposes; and that no regular or peaceful jurisdiction can, in the present unsettled state of the boundary question, be exercised by either country, within the disputed territory, while the magistrates and subordinate agents of authority, from both sides of the line, mutually warn off each other . . . and I am afraid, moreover, that the same, or rather a gradually worse state of things will continue to prevail, until the long pending question of the boundary line between Great Britain and the United States shall be satisfactorily settled.

Palmerston finally wrote to Fox on July 22, 1837, officially ending the Hereford incident. He dismissed the charges, evidence, and countercharges by reiterating the British position that the territory was part of Canada. He instructed Fox to "declare in a friendly but firm manner, that Her Majesty's Government will feel it their duty to use all means in their power to protect from aggression the Subjects of Her Majesty, and the territories of Her Majesty's crown; that force will be repelled by force; and that the responsibility of all the evils which may ensue from such collisions must rest on the heads of those who become the aggressors."

At Indian Stream, the "rebels" must have been disappointed at this growl from the British lion, for they were unrepentant. Governor Hill had spoken of safe jurisdiction; the commissioners wrote of the protecting energies of the state. Many men of Indian Stream laughed at the pretensions of the state. Others cursed. Kimball Fletcher took his own measures to ensure his own security and authority. He had been appointed postmaster on December 12, 1836, and found that officials of the United States, as well as those of New Hampshire, were not beyond the attention of various men who had defied the state's jurisdiction. He slept prepared for a raid, his rifle on the wall, a smoothbore loaded with buckshot in the corner by the bed, and a double-barreled pistol under his pillow.

James Mooney, no longer captain of the 6th Company, felt the necessity of warning the adjutant general and at the same time of expressing his anger at the "rebellious fellows" in the territory. On May 26, 1838, he wrote to General Low, describing their attitude toward militia duty. The men spouted "like a whale" in derision because no fines were collected from them for their nonappearance at training. Indian Stream had been attached to, or "assessed to," the 6th Company in September 1836, after Mooney had completed his command. Warned to appear for inspection on the first Tuesday in May 1837, at Stewartstown, the men of Indian Stream had made a controversial showing.

Mooney described it to Low: "Those that were friendly to the state appeared or made excuses. But those that were in rebellion at first are so now. They sware they will not train or pay a fine, that the State of New Hampshire might undertake to collect fines in that place if they dare do it, etc."

During the fall training, the men had not changed their defiant attitude. By the spring training of 1838, Captain Drew—the former lieutenant or ensign—told Mooney that Colonel Moore agreed to disassess Indian Stream from the 6th Company. If New Hampshire wanted the men there to do military duty, declared Colonel Moore, it might go there and organize a company; he didn't intend to. Former Captain Mooney heartily disapproved of this soft attitude toward the "rebellious fellows." The implication is very strong that had he and Colonel Young been in command and vested with the authority to use the militia, which they held in 1835 and 1836, they might well have occupied the territory again to stop such nonsense.

Fortunately for American-British relations, they were not in authority. Colonel Moore's decision was wiser than he knew. Troops and arrests in Indian Stream settlement at this time, added to other border incidents west and east, the burning of the steamer *Caroline*, the murder of Durfee, and the arrest of McLeod, plus the impending "war" in Aroostook, could have been the breaking point of diplomacy. Lord Palmerston was running more true to form: belligerent and threatening, he refused an apology and maintained his demands, although his position appeared untenable in the American view and in that of some of his countrymen. If an outbreak had occurred at Indian Stream in 1839 when Maine troops camped along the Aroostook and Congress voted troops and men in the event of war, Winfield Scott might not have been able to negotiate a truce with New

Brunswick. The uneasy peace at Indian Stream worked to the advantage of diplomacy.

The turning point in the sixty-year boundary dispute came before it exploded into war, when in faraway London the ministry of Lord Melbourne fell in 1841, taking with it Lord Palmerston. The new ministry under Sir Robert Peel, the Earl of Aberdeen, valued peace and negotiation. For the United States, the Whig victory of 1840 had resulted in the appointment of Daniel Webster as secretary of state to President Harrison.

Both Webster and the British plenipotentiary, Lord Ashburton, knew that the border incidents and claims were not worth another war. Webster had long been familiar with the problem and was fitted to make an enduring settlement. Lord Ashburton's American visits, American business interests, and American wife placed him on terms of tolerance in the negotiations. He was also of the opinion that the lands under dispute had no value and should not deter settlement. Both Webster and Ashburton were determined on agreement. They signed a treaty on August 9, 1842.

There had been wrangling among the agents. Mitchell's map rose from the archives to haunt the last negotiations of the dispute it had started. The State of Maine was unhappy, New Brunswick was unhappy, and French Canada protested in behalf of the two thousand French-Canadians turned over to the United States in the Madawaska valley.

Webster thought the treaty entirely satisfactory to the United States. He estimated that he had secured more than half the disputed territory and four-fifths of the value. Lord Ashburton had achieved his corridor between the boundary and the St. Lawrence, and he cared not a snap for the territory given up.

New Hampshire could not complain at all. The line followed through the area of the old Eames survey, from the highlands at the end of the Maine boundary to the head of Hall's Stream, and down to the Vallentine-Collins Line separating Vermont, New York, and Canada. The exact location of the boundary in the ill-defined highlands, through swamps and thick forest at the sources of Indian Stream and Hall's Stream, was not so simple. In the process, legends were born about the liquor capacity of the American crews and about their success in moving the line to the northward. The final territory included that which Mahurin and Hilliard described in 1836 as draining into the Magalloway. The rabbit-ear shape of the state's northern silhouette became permanent. For a short distance of about two miles, from Hall's Stream to the Connecticut, the Vallentine-Collins Line became the boundary between Vermont and New Hampshire.

Men at Indian Stream, before the signing of the treaty, had triumphantly, or with resignation and surrender to the inevitable, petitioned the New Hampshire legislature to be organized into the town of Pittsburg. The House and Senate agreed, although the boundary, in December 1840, had two years to wait. In June 1850 the legislature took up the problem of land claims, referring to a survey of state lands made the previous year by Richard Blanchard's son, David, now twenty-nine years old. The legislature granted to each actual settler on the public lands in Pittsburg, who had entered on the same since 1824, the lands in his possession, not exceeding the amount of one hundred acres.

The End

AFTERWORD

Jere R. Daniell

🌿 The ending of Daniel Doan's manuscript left an important part of his story untold. He wrote but a single sentence on what for Indian Stream inhabitants was the logical conclusion of their effort to establish effective authority at Indian Stream—the successful petition for incorporation as the town of Pittsburg. Incorporation meant that settlers, most of whom had come from New Hampshire or Vermont, could function legally within a familiar framework of government. By the time the Webster-Ashburton Treaty became law, Pittsburg residents had held town meetings, elected town officers, raised town taxes, and chosen men to serve in New Hampshire's state government.

Just when the petition movement got started is not clear, but it could have been as early as 1838. By then conditions at Indian Stream were far different from what they had been in 1835, the year of confrontation. Luther Parker, a major source of controversy, had gone to Wisconsin. Canadian officials were under instructions to avoid conflict as long as territory inhabitants accepted the hypothetical line halfway between Indian and Hall's Streams as the temporary boundary. Moreover, dissolving the council and assembly had reduced conflict east of the line. Indian Stream residents continued to govern through the neighborhood school and highway districts, which antedated the constitution and thus were unaffected by its demise. They may also have continued the informal practice of meeting annually at the schoolhouse south of Back Lake. Finally, relations with New Hampshire's state and Coos County officials had improved. The militia never returned, there were no additional arrests for nonpayment of personal debt, and without support from Canada few settlers remained willing to defy state authority.

Whenever discussion about petitioning New Hampshire for incorporation began, the idea quickly became popular. Nathaniel Perkins, Richard Blanchard, Clark Haynes, Abner Hyland and other district leaders gave their approval. The state legislator from Clarksville, a member of the clan of Youngs clustered south and west of Indian Stream, brought news from Concord that gave the petition movement an unexpected boost: New Hampshire would probably abolish the imprisonment for debt law. Attempts to enforce that law had been a major source of alienation from the state and its officials.

The advocates of incorporation drew up a formal petition (which has not survived) sometime during the summer or fall of 1840. On Tuesday, December 1, according to the legislative journal, "Mr. Young of Clarksville presented the petition of the inhabitants of the territory of Indian Stream, praying to be organized into a town by the name of Pittsburg." The Committee on Towns and Parishes prepared a bill for incorporation, which quickly passed in both the House and Senate, was signed by the governor, and on December 10 became law. Clark Haynes, David Rowell, and Richard Blanchard, or "any two of them," were empowered to call the first town meeting. It was five years and two months earlier that Blanchard had been rescued in Hereford.

The first legal town meeting took place March 9, 1841. After electing town officials the assembled men voted that the highway and school districts should "remain bound as they have been heretofore." The men next elected Nathaniel Perkins as their New Hampshire legislative representative and cast their votes for the state governor. All in all it was a most orderly and satisfying gathering.

Towns in New England are frequently labeled "Little Republics." The Indian Stream Republic was now the town of Pittsburg, New Hampshire. Pittsburg remains an incorporated town today with approximately one thousand inhabitants.

Readers who have enjoyed Daniel Doan's historical narrative may want to visit the Indian Stream territory. Physical remains from the days of the republic abound. The old schoolhouse, now a private residence, stands at the intersection of Route 3 and Hill Road. The main village in the town is near Ebenezer Fletcher's mill site—visitors can hear the rushing water of the

Connecticut just as Fletcher did by circling around back of the town hall. The Pittsburg Historical Society building, across from the town hall, contains numerous household relics from the mid-nineteenth century.

Perhaps most fascinating are the cemeteries. Three should be explored. Burleigh Blood and his family are in a small burial ground just off Route 3 near the outlet of First Connecticut Lake; the site also includes a grouping of modern hand-molded grave markers for descendants of one Haynes family branch. At the opposite side of the old republic, on a dead-end road just west of where Route 3 crosses Indian Stream, is a well-maintained modern burial ground with many nineteenth-century stones for various members of the Judd, Young, Haynes, and Blanchard families. The centerpiece of this cemetery is the Tabor family monument, an imposing obelisk inscribed on one side "Parker Tabor, 1809–1851" and "Jeremiah Tabor, 1782–1843." Two miles up the road is the Tabor farm. Bring your camera.

Still richer in monuments of the early settlers at Indian Stream is the "Hollow" cemetery, located just up Hill Road past the old schoolhouse. There lie generations of the Barnes, Blanchard, Perry, and Haynes families. My favorite headstone, handsome and remarkably well preserved, memorializes John Haynes, who was eighty-five years and five months old when he died in 1854. He had witnessed more at Indian Stream than any other single individual. Daniel Doan has provided his own memorial to Haynes and other community builders in one of New England's most remote frontiers.

BIBLIOGRAPHY

UNPUBLISHED PAPERS, DOCUMENTS, DEEDS, ETC.

Bath. Town records, microfilm. New Hampshire State Library, Concord, New Hampshire.
Bedel (Moody) Papers. Assorted papers, letters, commissions, bills, and documents directly related to Moody Bedel, stored in a maroon box. Referred to in my notes as the "Moody Bedel Papers." New Hampshire Historical Society, Concord, N.H.
Bedel Papers. Assorted papers and letters of the family stored in a maroon box. Referred to in my notes as the "Bedel Papers." New Hampshire Historical Society, Concord, N.H.
Coos County Register of Deeds. Vol. 1, 1860. Courthouse, Lancaster, N.H.
Davis, Mrs. W. Raymond (of Farmington, Maine). "History of the Coos Trail in Maine and New Hampshire." (Typed, bound manuscript at New Hampshire Historical Society.)
Hale (John P.) Papers. Letters and documents sorted and stored in file boxes by year. New Hampshire Historical Society, Concord, N.H.
History of Lisbon. A manuscript in the office of the Town Clerk, Lisbon, N.H., by Guy S. Rix (circa 1910).
Indian Stream Papers. A scrapbook collection of deeds, accounts, petitions, letters. Referred to in my notes as "Indian Stream Papers Scrapbook." New Hampshire Historical Society, Concord, N.H.
Indian Stream Papers. Assorted papers stored in a maroon box, eleven inches by twelve inches by four inches. Referred to in my notes as "Indian Stream Papers, Maroon Box." New Hampshire Historical Society, Concord, N.H.
Indian Stream Records Book C (or Indian Stream Journal). A leather-bound account book containing records of the constitutional meeting, the constitution, legislation passed, and deeds recorded. New Hampshire Historical Society, Concord, N.H.

Kimball, Mrs. T. Wendell. "The New Hampshire End of the Coos Trail." (Typed manuscript bound with the "History of the Coos Trail in Maine and New Hampshire," by Mrs. W. Raymond Davis, supra.)

Philip's Grant Papers (or Indian Stream Proprietors' Records). Vol. 2. A scrapbook containing deeds, depositions, petitions, and letters dealing with the proprietors of Philip's Grant, i.e., the "Eastman Company" of my usage, in their exploration and "development" of the northern lands deeded them by the Indian chief Philip. Referred to in my notes as "Philip's Grant Papers Scrapbook." New Hampshire Historical Society, Concord, N.H.

Philip's Grant. Records of proprietors, 1797–1834. Vol. 1, including minutes of meetings; a brown, leather book. In my notes and text, I usually refer to the Proprietors of Philip's Grant as the "Eastman Company"; this is a record of the minutes of the "Eastman Company." New Hampshire Historical Society, Concord, N.H.

Post-occupation papers on Indian Stream. These are in two scrapbooks titled Historical Collections (Vol. III, 1875–76, pp. 176–210) and Manuscripts (Vol. 1, pp. 137–179), containing the same material, copies and originals of letters and documents, 1835–1836, dealing mainly with the events following the occupation of Indian Stream, as seen from Washington, Concord, and Indian Stream. I refer to them in my notes as "Post-occupation Papers." New Hampshire Antiquarian Society, Hopkinton, N.H.

Proprietors' Records of Deeds of a Tract of Land called Bedel's and Others' Grant. This is a microfilm of copies of early records of the town of Pittsburg, N.H. It includes deeds of the Bedel Proprietors, records of their meetings, early tax lists of the settlement, constitutional meetings, meetings under the constitution, and tax inventories terminating in 1834. In my notes and text I usually refer to the Proprietors of Bedel's and Others' Grant as the "Bedel Company." So this microfilm is a record of the "Bedel Company" and of the independent government. I call it the "Pittsburg Microfilm." New Hampshire State Library, Concord, N.H.

EXPLANATORY NOTE ON PUBLISHED MATERIAL

The following bibliography includes not only reference works pertinent to the New Hampshire border, but also standard histories to which I have had recourse. These latter might seem too basic, except that I am not a student or scholar of history who has all simple information at his fingertips. I had thought to include *Rabble in Arms* by Kenneth Roberts, for his portrayal of Colonel Timothy Bedel; I have refrained because of its being too far afield. Still farther afield was my pursuit of Fort Wentworth, from its connection with the Eames family. This confirmed the research of Roberts for *Northwest Passage*, as I suspected it would. (Major Rogers did not build a fort in 1755 at the mouth of the Upper Ammonoosuc, contrary to the statements of two markers near the highway in Northumberland.) These excursions afield, topographically and by way of documents or books, might go on indefinitely. The

Bibliography

diary of Ensign Drew may exist somewhere, but I found it not, nor any other undiscovered source. Fortunately there was a wealth of unused material.

I wish I could say that I have left no stone unturned. I have left several, because at last I realized that I must call a halt to research and get to the writing, which was the main object; no complete treatment being available, this seemed worthwhile, if at the sacrifice of learning more and more about less and less. For the future investigator of details, I would like to suggest Mr. Brown's definitive work, *The Struggle for the Indian Stream Territory*, in which he was the first to describe the two land companies; his references and research are most complete, particularly into state legislature records. And for the active antiquarian who might like to discover the abandoned homesites now deep in the woods at Pittsburg, I would suggest maps, compass, possibly scuba for Lake Francis, and Perley Fearon's book, *Pittsburg Puckerbrush*, if the investigator can find a copy. Mr. Fearon printed only a few on a mimeographing machine, which is a pity, for it has the flavor of the north country.

PUBLISHED SOURCES

Adams, James Truslow, Editor in Chief. *Dictionary of American History.* New York: Charles Scribner's Sons, 1940.

Aldrich, Edgar. "Our Northern Boundary. The Provisional Government of Indian Stream, 1832–1835," *Proceedings of the New Hampshire Historical Society.* Vol. II, pp. 366–397.

Aldrich, Edgar. "The Affair of the Cedars and the Service of Colonel Timothy Bedel in the War of the Revolution," *Proceedings of the New Hampshire Historical Society*, Vol. III, 1895–1899, pp. 194–231.

Andrews, E. Benjamin. *History of the United States.* 2 vols. New York: Charles Scribner's Sons, 1894.

Audet, Francis J. "La République d'Indian Stream," *des Mémoires de la Société Royale du Canada*, deuxième série 1906–1907, tome XII, Section 1. (English Translation Copy in New Hampshire Historical Society Library.)

Bacon, Edwin N. *The Connecticut River and the Valley of the Connecticut.* New York: G. P. Putnam's Sons, 1906.

Beard, Charles A. and Mary R. *A Basic History of the United States.* Garden City, New York: Garden City Books, Doubleday and Company, 1944.

Belknap, Jeremy. *History of New Hampshire,* ed. John Farmer. Dover, 1831.

Bittinger, The Reverend John Quincy. *History of Haverhill, N.H.* Haverhill, 1888.

Blood, Henry Ames. *The History of Temple, N.H.* Boston: Rand and Avery, 1860.

Brown, Roger Hamilton. *The Struggle for the Indian Stream Territory.* Cleveland: Western Reserve University Press, 1955.

Burt, Alfred LeRoy. *A Short History of Canada for Americans.* Minneapolis: University of Minnesota Press, 1942.

Chandler, Charles Henry, and Sarah Fisk Lee. *The History of New Ipswich, New Hampshire 1735–1914 with Genealogical Records of the Principal Families.* Fitchburg, Mass.: Sentinel Printing Co., 1914.

Charlton, Edwin A. *New Hampshire As It Is.* Claremont: Tracy and Company, 1856.
Child, Hamilton. *Gazetteer of Grafton County, N.H., 1709–1886.* Syracuse: The Syracuse Journal Company, 1886.
Coles, Harry L. *The War of 1812.* Chicago: University of Chicago Press, 1965.
Crawford, Lucy. *History of the White Mountains,* ed. Stearns Morse. Hanover: Dartmouth Publications, MCMLXVI.
Cummings, Albert Oren. *Cummings Genealogy, Isaac Cummings 1601–1677 of Ipswich in 1638 and some of his descendants.* Montpelier, 1904.
Dwight, Timothy. *Travels in New England and New York,* Vol. II, Vol. IV. New Haven, 1821, 1822.
Fearon, Perley E. *Pittsburg Puckerbrush.* Canaan: Perley E. Fearon, 1965.
Fletcher, Ebenezer. "The Narrative of Ebenezer Fletcher, a Soldier of the Revolution" (Written by Himself). Introduction and notes by Charles I. Bushnell. New York: privately printed, 1866. (This is a cousin of the Ebenezer Fletcher of Indian Stream.)
Fletcher, Edward H. *Fletcher Family History, The Descendants of Robert Fletcher of Concord, Massachusetts.* Boston: Rand, Avery & Co., 1881.
Fogg, Alonzo J. *The Statistics and Gazetteer of New Hampshire.* Concord: D. L. Gurnsey, 1874.
Gardiner, Samuel R. *A Student's History of England,* Vol. III. London: Longmans, Green, and Co., 1897.
Harper's Encyclopedia of United States History. New York: Harper and Bro., 1901–1902.
Historical Notes of Bath, New Hampshire. Littleton: Bicentennial Committee on History, 1965.
"An Historical Sketch of the Northern Boundary of New Hampshire," *Collections of the New Hampshire Historical Society,* Vol. II, 1827, pp. 267–290.
History of Coos County. Syracuse: W. A. Fergusson and Co., 1888.
History of New Ipswich from its First Grant in MDCCXXXVI to the Present Time. Boston: Gould and Lincoln, 1852.
Hodgson, Alice Doan. *Thanks to the Past, The Story of Orford, New Hampshire.* Orford: Historical Fact Publications, 1965.
Hutchinson, Bruce. *The Struggle for the Border.* New York: Longmans, Green, and Co., 1955.
James, Marquis. *Andrew Jackson, Portrait of a President.* New York: Bobbs Merrill, 1937.
Lisbon's Ten Score Years, a bicentennial pamphlet, Lisbon, 1963.
Madison, James. *The Federalist,* No. X ("Special Interests and the Union").
Marshall, Gertrude Weeks. *The Indian Stream Republic and the Indian Stream War, an Authentic Bit of New Hampshire History.* Groveton, 1935.
McClintock, John N. *History of New Hampshire.* Boston: B. B. Russell, 1888.
Merrill, Eliphalet and Phineas, *Gazetteer of the State of New Hampshire.* Exeter: C. Norris and Co., 1817.
Miller, W. H. *History and Genealogies.* Richmond, Kentucky, 1907.
Morison, Samuel Eliot., *The Oxford History of the American People.* New York: Oxford University Press, 1965.

Bibliography

The New Hampshire Patriot, newspaper published in Concord by Isaac Hill, (years of reference: 1835–1836).

"North American Boundary B., Proceedings and Correspondence," Section X, Vol. XXXIX, "Aggression and Violation of Territory of Lower Canada by Citizens of New Hampshire, 1836," *Parliamentary Papers 1837–1838*, London, 1838.

Parkman, Francis. "A Vacation Trip," *Francis Parkman, Representative Selections,* with introduction, bibliography, and notes, ed. Wilbur L. Schramm. New York: American Book Co., 1938, pp. 49–65.

Paullin, Charles O. *Atlas of the Historical Geography of the United States,* ed. John K. Wright. Washington, D.C., and New York: Carnegie Institution, and the American Geographical Society, 1932.

Phippsburg—Fair to the Wind. Lewiston: Phippsburg Historical Society, Twin City Printery, 1965.

Potter, C. E. *The Military History of the State of New Hampshire.* Concord: McFarland & Jenks, 1866.

Powers, The Reverend Grant. *Historical Sketches of the Discovery, Settlement, and Progress of Events in the Coos Country and Vicinity 1754–1785.* Haverhill: J. F. C. Hayes, 1841.

Reid, R. L. "The Indian Stream Territory, an episode of the North-East boundary dispute," *Proceedings and Transactions of the Royal Society of Canada,* 3d Ser., Sec. 2, Vol. 34 (1940), pp. 143–171.

Report of the Adjutant General of the State of New Hampshire for the year ending June 1, 1868, part 2, pp. 269–287. Manchester: John B. Clarke, State Printer, 1868.

Report of the Commissioners to Indian Stream, November 1836 (published per the legislative resolve of June 16, 1836).

Report, "Committee on Military Affairs to whom was referred Senate on Bill No. 25 entitled a bill for the settlement of the claims of New Hampshire against the United States, 10 August 1846" (library of New Hampshire Historical Society pamphlet).

Runnels, The Reverend M. T. *History of Sanbornton, New Hampshire,* Vol. 1. Boston: Alfred Mudge and Son, 1882.

Sanderson, The Reverend Henry H. *History of Charlestown.* Claremont: Claremont Mfg. Co., 1876.

"Secret Journals of the Acts and Proceedings of Congress," Vol. II, *Foreign Affairs, 1775–1781.* Boston: Thomas B. Wait, 1820.

Showerman, Grant. "The Indian Stream Republic and Luther Parker," *Collections of the New Hampshire Historical Society,* Vol. XI (1915).

Silver, Helenette. *A History of New Hampshire Game and Furbearers.* Concord: Evans Printing Co., Inc., 1957.

Somers, The Reverend A. N. *History of Lancaster, N.H.* Concord: Rumford Press, 1899.

Speare, Mrs. Guy E. *More New Hampshire Folk Tales.* Brattleboro: Stephen Daye Press, 1936.

Stackpole, Everett S. *History of New Hampshire.* New York: American Historical Society, 1916.

Sutherland, The Reverend David. "Address Delivered to the Inhabitants of Bath on the Evening of January 23, 1854" (historical appendix by The Reverend Thomas Boutelle). (Pamphlet in the library of the New Hampshire Historical Society.)

Van Landt, Franklin K. *Boundaries of the United States and the Several States.* Geological Survey Bulletin 1212. Washington, D.C.: United States Government Printing Office, 1966.

Walling and Hitchcock. *Atlas of the State of New Hampshire.* New York: Comstock and Cline, 1877.

Willey, Benjamin G. *Incidents in White Mountain History.* Boston: Nathaniel Noyes, 1856.

SUPPLEMENTARY BIBLIOGRAPHY

Jere R. Daniell

Daniel Doan Papers, Special Collections, Dartmouth College. Most quotations in the introduction are from correspondence in the folder labeled "Letters on Indian Stream Project" in Box #1 of the papers.

Journal of the Senate and House of New Hampshire, November Session, 1840 (Concord, 1841).
Laws of the State of New Hampshire, November Session, 1840 (Concord, 1840).
MacDougall, Ruth Doan. "My Old Man of the Mountain," *Appalachia,* no. 199 (Dec. 15, 1994), pp. 10–16.
Town Record Book, Town Office, Pittsburg, N.H.

UNIVERSITY PRESS OF NEW ENGLAND
publishes books under its own imprint and is the publisher for Brandeis University Press, Dartmouth College, Middlebury College Press, University of New Hampshire, Tufts University, Wesleyan University Press, and Salzburg Seminar.

LIBRARY OF CONGRESS CATALOGING-IN-PUBLICATION DATA
Doan, Daniel, 1914–
    Indian Stream Republic : settling a New England frontier, 1785–1842 / Daniel Doan ; edited by Ruth Doan MacDougall, with an introduction and afterword by Jere R. Daniell.
      p. cm. — (Library of New England)
    Includes bibliographical references (p.   ).
    ISBN 0-87451-767-2 (cloth: alk. paper). — ISBN 0-87451-768-0 (pbk.: alk. paper)
    1. Indian Stream Republic—History.   2. Northeast boundary of the United States.   3. Pittsburg (N.H.)—History.   I. Daniell, Jere R.   II. Title.   III. Series.
F42.C7D63   1997
974.2'1—dc20
                                                96–9836